CACTUS PEAR FOR MY BELOVED

Samah Sabawi is an author, playwright and poet, and a recipient of multiple awards both nationally and internationally. Her theatre credits include the critically acclaimed and award-winning plays *Tales of a City by the Sea* and *THEM*. In 2020 Samah received the prestigious Green Room Award for Best Writing in the independent theatre category, and was shortlisted for both the NSW and Victorian Premier's Literary Awards. With Stephen Orlov, Samah edited the anthology *Double Exposure: Plays of the Jewish and Palestinian Diasporas*, winner of the Patrick O'Neill Award, and she co-authored *I Remember My Name: Poetry by Samah Sabawi, Ramzy Baroud and Jehan Bseiso*, edited by Vacy Vlazna, winner of the Palestine Book Award.

ALSO BY SAMAH SABAWI

Plays
Tales of a City by the Sea
THEM

Poetry
I Remember My Name: Poetry by Samah Sabawi,
Ramzy Baroud and Jehan Bseiso
(edited by Vacy Vlazna)

Anthologies
Double Exposure: Plays of the Jewish and Palestinian Diasporas
(co-edited with Stephen Orlov)

SAMAH SABAWI

CACTUS PEAR FOR MY BELOVED

A FAMILY STORY FROM GAZA

PENGUIN BOOKS

UK | USA | Canada| Ireland | Australia
India | New Zealand | South Africa | China

Penguin Books is part of the Penguin Random House group of companies
whose addresses can be found at global.penguinrandomhouse.com

Penguin
Random House
Australia

First published by Penguin Books, 2024

Cover illustration courtesy Shutterstock
Cover design by Christabella Designs © Penguin Random House Australia Pty Ltd
Typeset in Adobe Garamond Pro by Midland Typesetters, Australia

Printed and bound in Australia by Griffin Press, an accredited
ISO AS/NZS 14001 Environmental Management Systems printer

A catalogue record for this
book is available from the
NATIONAL
LIBRARY National Library of Australia
OF AUSTRALIA

ISBN 978 1 76134 497 8

penguin.com.au

MIX
Paper | Supporting
responsible forestry
FSC
www.fsc.org   FSC® C018684

*We at Penguin Random House Australia acknowledge that Aboriginal and Torres Strait
Islander peoples are the Traditional Custodians and the first storytellers of the lands on which we
live and work. We honour Aboriginal and Torres Strait Islander peoples' continuous connection
to Country, waters, skies and communities. We celebrate Aboriginal and Torres Strait Islander
stories, traditions and living cultures; and we pay our respects to Elders past and present.*

These words are written on the stolen land of the Boonwurrung Wadawurrung and Wurundjeri peoples of the Kulin nations. I thank them for the privilege of living on their soil and dreaming beneath their sky. I acknowledge their custodianship of this land, their elders past and present, and acknowledge all Indigenous peoples around the globe whose lands and cultures have been ravished by colonisation.

For our children

These are your stories — born of truth,
sprinkled with wonder, aged with time

My parents in the garden, 1967. I am in my mama's belly.

All the rivers run through me
I'm torn into banks, grooves and deltas
The birds carry me in their crops
The roots in the forest consume me
My bones settle in the bellies of whales
My spirit flutters in darkness
Who else but you can gather my pieces
And return to me my features
Who else but you
My beloved

Abdul Karim Sabawi

CONTENTS

PROLOGUE

BABA

QUEENSLAND, AUSTRALIA, 2018

I park my father's old Camry in the last remaining disabled spot outside the Logan Shopping Centre. I switch off the tired engine and it squeals with gratitude before it slumps into silence.

'Baba!'

I nudge him.

He does not respond. He sits in the passenger seat, still like a mountain, ancient like eternity, fragile like a poem. His dark, round face a rugged terrain of countless tear tracks and glorious laugh lines. His brown eyes hold a thousand and one stories in a glance. His lips move to the rhythm of a verse that he whispers like a sacred prayer. He's somewhere else. He is always somewhere else. And it is this constant state of absence that makes his presence more splendid.

I know better than to rush him. I wait.

Heat replaces the cool air inside the car. My skin burns under the relentless rays of a blazing Australian sun, beaming through the windscreen.

'They don't call it the Sunshine State for nothing!' I mumble, as I slather on another layer of sunscreen.

Only seconds have passed, but already the air grows thick and humid. Sweat beads fill the grooves on Baba's cheeks. His red golf T-shirt clings to his belly, damp with perspiration.

'It is hot in here, Baba!' I say, as I dust off the dandruff sprinkled on his shoulders and adjust his black sun cap. '*Yallah* Habibi,' I beg.

He turns his head, exasperated. It takes a few seconds for his eyes to focus, as if he is dragging himself away from a distant world. But he gets here, and when he does, and in true Baba fashion, he snaps into character.

'First,' he declares with a theatrical voice, 'fetch me my trusty steed.' He points out the window to the line of shopping carts nearby. 'Pick a solid one that I can charge into the battlefield with!'

'A shopping trolley?'

'Yes.'

'But Baba,' I wipe the melted make-up off my face. 'Your walker is a much better steed. The physiotherapist said you should . . .' he rolls his eyes, but I push on, '. . . you should always use your walker. It gives you the support you need. I'll get it for you. It's in the boot.'

'Well, it can stay there,' he insists. 'A walker? Do you want my friends to think I'm an old man?' He fakes outrage with a mischievous smile, and it is in that instant that I see *him*. I see him. The wounded fighter who drank the sorrow of loss and bled his pain into captivating verses. The wanderer who traversed every corner of the world searching for a home. The hungry Palestinian refugee who swallowed the Arabian desert and landed on Australia's shores. I see him – poet, revolutionary, entrepreneur, Aussie sheep farmer and now, aged pensioner. Him! I see all of him. My *baba*. And my heart, like my make-up, melts.

I capitulate. In my fifties, I've become much more under-standing of the need to hide the appearance of old age, even at the expense of comfort. Vanity, like poetry, runs in the family.

I fetch the trolley and help him out of the car. First he leans on me, then shifts his weight onto the trolley. It takes him a few minutes to adjust his balance, slowly stretching one leg, then the other, before shuffling his sandal-clad feet across the hot asphalt, jaws clenched and back lifted as straight as he can possibly manage.

Halfway to the entrance, a soft whimper escapes his lips. He quickly wipes the pain from his face and forces a smile as he glances sideways, embarrassed I may have heard his moan. I pretend I did not.

'Baba, you were right,' I say. 'This trolley makes you look at least twenty years younger.'

He grins.

We make our way into the shopping mall. I am blown away by his popularity.

A hipster Caucasian with a beautifully groomed beard standing outside the barber shop smiles and waves. 'Lovely day, George!'

Soon after, a vivacious blonde in her sixties, wearing full make-up and freshly arranged hair, winks at him.

'George,' she says with a husky voice, 'I took your advice and sprinkled sumac on my fish.' She places her hand on his shoulder and whispers loud enough for me to hear, 'Why don't you come over to my house tonight? I can show you how well I can do it.'

OH MY GOD! I scream in my head. Is she flirting with my father?

I hide my shock. Baba does not hide his joy.

'Sure,' he laughs wholeheartedly, adding with a great deal of dramatic flair, and in his most charming, heavy accent, 'but you must promise you will not take advantage of me. I am a married man!'

The woman giggles pleasurably as she sashays away, leaving the scent of her floral perfume behind.

A few steps later, a young Māori woman wearing the mall's security uniform is delighted to see him. 'Good morning, George!' My father returns the greeting with equal enthusiasm.

We arrive at his favourite cafe. A couple in their seventies wearing a healthy Queensland glow and matching white shirts, shorts and runners, bounce to their feet.

'George! Right on time, as always. We held your table for you.'

Their smiles light up their suntanned faces. They move the chairs out of the path of his trolley and hand over the table in what appears to be a daily ritual, before they wave goodbye.

My father looks sheepishly at my bemused expression as he lowers himself slowly onto the seat.

'You see? I am the most important person here,' he brags. 'Everyone knows me!'

'Clearly,' I shoot back, 'they don't have a clue.'

I feel unsettled, resentful – even angry. There goes my baba, exiled to the edge of the earth, leaning on his shopping trolley every day through this small-town mall, pretending to be someone else. Pretending to be George. George! A non-Arab, non-Muslim immigrant, who makes up for his heavy accent with a good sense of humour and a great deal of charm.

A voice of reason struggles to make its way through the cracks of my mind's anger. 'Why can't you let him be? Why must you blame him?' George fits in places Abdul Karim cannot.

I draw a deep breath, hold it for a few seconds, then I exhale. I know that what I am about to ask once uttered, will be irrevocable.

My father will latch onto it, and not let go. But right now I am more convinced than ever of the urgency of my request, as I see fragments of our history slipping through the trembling fingers of this old man who calls himself George, and falling, scattered like dust particles, all over the shiny tiles of this nondescript shopping mall.

Baba orders a cappuccino and I order a blueberry muffin. We sit across the table from one another. I begin to pitch my idea.

'You want to write my story?'

'I want you to be my research subject for . . .' before I finish my sentence and say PhD, he reaches for my muffin and takes a big bite. I am distracted. I want to protest. I want to say, 'Don't eat sugar – you are diabetic!' But it is too late. He has swallowed the piece whole. 'Pick your battles, Samah,' I say to myself.

I watch as he draws a long sip from his cappuccino to wash down the sugary treat. 'I will consider your proposal,' he says, nodding. 'After all, you are a writer – and mine is the best story you will ever write.'

'Well, Baba,' I tease, 'I'm sure I could come up with better stories if I wanted to.'

'Nonsense.' He laughs and reaches for the rest of my muffin. I surrender.

'Why didn't you ask me sooner? I am too old to enjoy being famous now.'

'You've had enough fame. *Khalas*. Everyone knows you back home.'

'Yes, but here they only know George.'

A long silence passes between us before he speaks again. This time he is stoic. 'You want to reconstruct my life with your words?' His eyes pierce through me as if weighing up my worth both as daughter and as writer. I smile confidently.

'That is a lot of faith you are asking for. You want me to open my old wounds and let you pick at them?'

'I will be gentle, Baba – and it will be therapeutic for you. We will spend a lot of time together. This will be fun.'

'You want to bribe me with your attention?'

'You get my attention anyway, so what's the harm if I were to get something in return?'

He laughs, and mulls over the proposal. When he takes too long to respond I confront him with my words of truth.

'Baba, you ate my muffin. You owe me.'

He laughs and tries to sit up straight in the chair, but an expression of pain shoots across his face. Irritation takes hold of him. His mood shifts.

'I'm not an old, open book with falling-out pages and faded ink that needs to be reprinted.'

'Of course, you are not.'

'I'm not an abandoned, derelict building that needs to be restored.'

'I know, Baba. I promise. I will look after your – really, our – stories.'

'I have to approve your transcript.'

'That goes without saying.'

'Writers, they always make promises before they begin writing. Once they put words to paper the words grow into worlds, and the worlds open possibilities where temptations lurk, and hidden secrets beg to be revealed.'

'I promise to do no harm to you, or others. I will weave fictional characters in places where real people choose not to be named. I will be truthful to the historic events and to your own personal story. I . . .'

I begin to tell my father about the ethics course we had to do before starting our research, about what it means for him to be my research subject – his rights, my responsibilities. I explain how I will use standpoint theory and oral testimony to explore trauma, but he holds up his hands to stop me.

'You know, one never needs to work so hard to convince a story-teller to tell his story.' He reaches for my hands and wraps them in his. 'I want to do this. The question I struggle with right now is which stories will I tell you, and what stories will you write?'

'What was it like to grow up in Gaza? Why did you leave? I want to write about your journey into exile.'

'My journey into exile?' He laughs out loud. 'Ha! Exile is not a journey. A journey begins somewhere and progresses towards something. Exile refuses to take me anywhere but exile itself.'

I have the urge to record every word he utters. 'Baba?' I pull out my phone. 'Is it okay to record our conversations from now on?'

He nods.

'If you were writing your life, Baba, where would your story begin?'

'I will tell you where it does not begin. It does not begin with my birth, just as it will not end when I die. Stories are powerful and meaningful only when woven together. My story is part of a tapestry of stories, it is not mine alone. If you pull it out of that tapestry it will unravel and will lose its meaning. Do you understand?'

'I do, Baba. I do!'

1

KHADIJA

GAZA, PALESTINE, c. 1940

Before Baba was born, Khadija climbed up the sycamore tree and refused to come down. Hair uncombed, face unwashed, clothes stained, sharp splinters shooting through soft hands and bare feet, Khadija sought refuge inside the thick green foliage and wept.

Down below, her husband, *Sheikh* Hussein, limped in circles around the majestic trunk.

'Khadija, be sensible. Come down,' he ordered.

'Khadija, get down from that tree now!' he commanded.

'Khadija, come. I am your husband. I am grieving, just like you,' he pleaded.

'Khadija, I need you,' he sobbed.

Khadija did not come down.

Days passed. The *sheikh* resigned himself to the familiar helplessness of a cripple, and the stinging solitude of grief.

News of Khadija's madness spread. Relatives and neighbours from near and far came in waves. Some, driven by a genuine desire to help; others, seduced by a morbid curiosity to stare grief in the eye. Grief, unapologetic and unwavering, stared back. Their hearts were shattered by Khadija's gut-wrenching howls. Their clothes were drenched from her falling tears.

The wind echoed Khadija's sorrows across the fields, swooping over the hills and valleys of Palestine. A restless night breeze carried her name, and whispered it into her mother's ears:

'Khaaadiiijaaa . . .' 'Khaaadiiijaaa . . .' 'Khaaadiiijaaa . . .' the wind hissed and breathed.

Khadija's mother tossed and turned in her sleep, but the relentless whispers of the wind refused to give her reprieve. 'Khaaadiiijaaa . . .' 'Khaaadiiijaaa . . .' 'Khaaadiiijaaa . . .' the wind whooshed and hissed and hissed and whooshed until Aziza finally woke, startled, her hand on her heart and her daughter's name on her lips.

'Khadija!' Aziza shouted her daughter's name into the night, waking up her husband, Ibrahim, from his deep slumber.

'Oh Aziza, why are you screaming your daughter's name in the middle of the night?'

'Something is wrong.' Aziza got up. 'Khadija needs me,' she said, as she ran outside.

Ibrahim, used to the accuracy of his wife's intuitions, asked no more questions of her. What was the point? He knew his wife would be well on her way to her daughter's rescue.

Aziza threw her veil over her head and prayed for God's mercy as she ran with urgent steps into the barn.

'I am coming, my daughter. I am coming, *ya binty*!'

She repeated her prayers to God for strength and patience as she mounted her donkey and rode all the way along the Mediterranean shore from the town of Salama near Jaffa in the north of Palestine, to the Tuffah district of Gaza, eighty kilometres to the south.

When Aziza finally arrived west of Mohatta Street in Tuffah, Gaza, she was greeted by a welcoming committee of excited, bare-footed and scantily dressed children who formed a circle around her, and competed to tell their version of the story of how Khadija, the wife of their respected *sheikh*, had climbed up a tree and had refused to come down.

Aziza listened for a few moments before she impatiently shooed the children away and entered the *sheikh*'s home.

In the front yard, under the sycamore tree, Aziza lifted the hem of her dress and waded into her daughter's puddle of tears. She opened her arms wide and looked up at the branch where Khadija crouched. She drew a deep breath to subdue her chaotic, drumming heart before she spoke softly.

'Khadija, my beloved *binty habibty*, come down.'

Khadija did not move. She did not make a sound. Aziza tried again and again and again.

'Come down, my child. Come down, piece of my flesh and fragment of my soul . . . My arms will carry your pain. My heart will share your sorrow. My eyes will cry your tears . . . Come down, my beloved. *Ya binty ya habibty*, come down! *Mishan allah*, come down.'

There was a slight movement on the branch above as Khadija parted the leaves and looked down at her mother.

When Khadija finally spoke for the first time in weeks, this is all she said.

'I am not your daughter. I am a cat. I swallowed all my children.'

2

MOFTIYA

GAZA, PALESTINE, c. 1918

You could say the story began earlier, more than twenty years before Khadija climbed up the sycamore tree.

On a cold winter night, in a small, mud-brick room in the Tuffah district, Moftiya crouched on all fours, nails dug into the threadbare mat and body fluids leaking from eyes, nose, mouth and gushing in lumps from the space between her legs. Behind her squatted a cheerful midwife, Om-Baker, who seemed unfazed by the mess of amniotic fluids, blood and faeces that poured out of Moftiya and splattered all over the hem of her *thawb*. Birthing is messy business and Om-Baker had seen it all before, though she would later muse that she had never witnessed a birth like Moftiya's: 'That woman is made of steel. She did not scream. Not even once.'

Om-Baker's hands rubbed the small of Moftiya's arched back gently, as she cheered and directed her.

'Only a few more inches . . . push . . . push . . . push . . . Yes, I see the head! Yes, push!'

Moftiya squinched her face and pushed all the air out of her lungs, and with that, she also pushed out the baby that had colonised her womb. The midwife greeted the newborn with a cry of joy, prayers and astonishment – for out of Moftiya's very dark, scrawny flesh had slipped a seemingly healthy, plump, white baby boy with blue eyes and blond hair.

Om-Baker swiftly cut the cord, and as she handed the baby over to his mother she couldn't help but say, '*Mashallah Alhamdulillah*, thank God the baby has his father's looks.'

Moftiya knew what the midwife meant. The world had been spared another ugly creature, like her. She also knew that she would be hearing similar sentiments from her neighbours. She didn't respond to Om-Baker's cruel comment, but did that which Moftiya did so well. She focused on survival. She focused on suppressing the onslaught of feelings that washed over her, all at once – pain, joy, pride, relief, fear, hunger and anxiety. She had too many feelings that she needed to control. And she had to be in control. Moftiya never lost control. So, she said nothing. Her face was set like stone, revealing nothing. Not even a smile for her newborn baby.

'What name will you give him?' Om-Baker asked, as she placed the baby on Moftiya's breast.

'Hussein,' was all that Moftiya said.

Hussein's mouth latched on to Moftiya's breast for two whole years, suckling to the rhythm of English boots stomping the grounds of the Holy Land. The war had ended and British soldiers were canvassing their empire's latest conquest: Palestine. The jewel in their empire's crown.

Moftiya hated armies and wars. She never understood why grown men took to their guns to settle disputes, and she had very little patience for political speak. She was a practical woman, more concerned with finding daily bread and, from time to time, extracting secret doses of happiness away from the hardships of life. And her life was full of hardships.

The odds were stacked against Moftiya from the moment she was born a girl with very dark skin, in a world that values boys and where beauty is measured by the fairness of a woman's skin. If that wasn't enough, Moftiya was born into a very poor family that either neglected or could not afford to care for her. In her toddler years, she was afflicted with an eye infection that caused her eyelids to be fused closed as green pus formed in and around her eyes. The infection went untreated for so long, Moftiya eventually lost one eye to it.

When Moftiya got her period and became eligible for marriage by the standards of the time, no one came to ask for her hand. Who would want to marry a one-eyed, poor, bony and very dark young woman?

Years passed, and she gave up on ever finding a suitor. She learned to depend on herself. She learned to thicken her skin in the face of the cruelty of others who mocked and belittled her for her bad looks and bad fortunes. She became formidable. She allowed nothing to get to her, and if her feelings were ever hurt, no one ever knew. She was tough as nails – a quality she held on to, even when the unimaginable happened and a tall, handsome man with a small patch of land came to ask for her hand. That man was Ahmed.

Ahmed was the most handsome man in Tuffah. It was said he melted hearts with a passing glance. He had fair skin, sculptured cheeks, wide, green eyes, thick, hazel hair, muscles that bulged out of his shirt and a physical form that made the girls of Tuffah blush with desire whenever he passed. Everyone knew that Ahmed could

have had any woman of his choosing, so of course Ahmed searched
for the most beautiful woman he could find. He found Nijma, the
most beautiful woman in all of Palestine.

It was said that jaws dropped and eyes widened every time
Nijma walked into a room. It was said that her skin was white as
milk and soft as butter, her eyes blue as the sea, and her lips perfectly rounded and voluptuously full. It was said her hips swayed
with so much elegance, they commanded the earth beneath her
feet to move to their rhythm. It was said her smile was seductive,
her walk provocative and that her scent ignited a feverish madness
in the hearts of all men. Those who saw her could not take their eyes
off her. Those who did not, risked their lives for a passing glance.

All of this proved to be a terrible curse for Ahmed. The constant
attention his wife received tortured and drove him to the edge of
madness. He fought with her every time she stepped outside their
home. He fought with anyone who looked in her direction, be it
on purpose or by accident. He fought with his neighbours and his
friends. He even fought with the gentle breeze that dared touch
Nijma's fair skin. Ahmed became a man possessed with an all-
consuming jealousy that plunged him into the throes of doubt and
rage and destroyed his relationship not only with his wife, but with
everyone he knew. The marriage was pure agony. It could not – and
it did not – last.

Nijma walked away, and Ahmed swore an oath to Allah never
to marry a beautiful woman again. To prove his commitment to
this sacred oath, he instantly set out to find the ugliest girl in the
district. Everyone knew who that girl was: Moftiya.

Ahmed found peace of mind with Moftiya, and Moftiya found
a roof over her head and a child in her belly. It was a good arrange-
ment while it lasted, but it hardly lasted long. Just as Moftiya gave

birth to their son Hussein, a boy born in the image of his father, Ahmed's life ended, his blood utterly wasted at the altar of British colonialism.

Ahmed had foolishly believed that if he, and others, fought alongside the British against the Ottomans, His Majesty King George VI would reward this show of solidarity with freedom and independence. Free Palestine. That did not happen. Soon after Ahmed was martyred in the Battle of Beersheba, and before his blood, and the blood of his lost fellow countrymen dried up, Britain had made a promise to establish a homeland for the Jewish people on the land of Palestine. No hope of freedom nor independence was on the horizon for the indigenous Arab population.

Suddenly Moftiya found herself to be a widow with a young son to raise. She wasted no time grieving the life she almost had. She was grateful that although Ahmed left no savings, he had at least given her the ownership of his small patch of land in Tuffah. With shelter sorted, all Moftiya needed was to find food.

She found work grinding grains for a wealthy family who lived in the Christian quarter, far from Tuffah and from her neighbours' judgemental eyes. Servants were looked down upon, and she had a son to think about. She wanted Hussein to grow with his head held high, never to feel that he was less than anyone else.

Moftiya snuck out of her home every morning before the dawn prayer, in her only hand-stitched long dress, with her white veil loosely draped over her head, concealing both her thick black hair and her one damaged eye. She took her son with her, scooping him up gently into her arms and cooing him to stay quiet as they made their way discreetly out of the district and into the green vegetable fields, the banana plantations and orange groves that encircled their world in Tuffah.

At work, Moftiya watched over her son with her one good, loving eye as she rotated the hand mill to grind the grain into soft flour. The circular motion of the basalt gave her time to reflect on her misfortunes and losses. It also gave her time to dream. She was raising a son, and soon he would be walking and talking and, before too long, he would be taking care of her. Someone would finally love her and take care of her.

But her dreams began to shatter as she watched her son crawl, and crawl, and crawl . . . right through his toddler years. Moftiya was once again staring her cruel fate in the eye. Her son's legs were too weak to lift the weight of his body. Something was terribly wrong.

Devastated, she began a manic search for cause and cure. She wanted to save him in the way she was not saved as a child when she lost her eye to her parents' inaction. What if her attention and tenacious persistence to cure her son were to save his legs and enable him to walk? What if she could right the wrongs she had suffered through caring for him? What if they didn't have to be *that* family, the one with the one-eyed mother and handicapped son?

Moftiya's days fell into a routine. Mornings at work, afternoons pacing hospital corridors and evenings bowing, kneeling and prostrating on prayer mats in mosques and holy shrines. Doctors prescribed colorful pills that came in small bottles, and holy men prescribed blessings stuffed inside velvety pouches and tied with ribbons.

By nightfall, exhausted, Moftiya would lie down on her mattress, Hussein in her arms, her one brown eye gazing into his two perfect blue eyes, her left hand wrapped around his small body and her right hand placed on his forehead. It is in this position that she always opened her heart to the seventh sky: 'My beloved Allah,' she would implore, 'I have no one but you. You alone know my burden. You alone know my suffering. You gifted me this boy – this beautiful, fair-skinned, blue-eyed boy. But you gave him broken legs. Why? Why would you give a poor, one-eyed widow a helpless, crippled son? Please, God of mercy, God of compassion, God of all things – don't abandon us!'

Moftiya ended her nightly ritual with a healing *rukiah*, reciting three times the almighty verse, *'And when I am ill, it is Allah who cures me.'* She would then blow air into her open palms, where she had gathered all the blessings from her prayers, and rub them all over Hussein's body.

3

SHEIKH HUSSEIN

GAZA, PALESTINE, c. 1918–1933

As Hussein grew older, he began to understand the severity of his condition. He became aware that something was terribly wrong with him. He learned to wobble beside his mother, heaving his weight on a wooden stick, dragging his feet along like dead weight. Men mostly ignored him, women looked at him with pity and children pointed at him and called him the three-legged boy. He retreated inwards, entertaining himself with his rich imagination and endless curiosity. His able mind worked hard, too hard, as if it needed to compensate for his disabled body.

During the never-ending waiting hours at hospital, the young boy invented a game. He was five years old when the idea of this game first came to him. It began when he asked a nurse who passed by the waiting room what the sign on the wall said. The nurse answered as she rushed by, 'Wash your hands, darling. It says, "wash your hands".'

Hussein stared at the sign, marvelling at how a drawing of lines, dots and curves could say so much. A few minutes later another nurse passed by, and Hussein asked what another sign said – then another, and another. There were signs all around him. '*Waiting Room*', '*Keep quiet!*', '*Reception*', '*Maternity Ward*', '*Children's Clinic*', '*Stop*', '*Main Entrance*', '*Ring the bell*', '*Emergency*', and so on, and on and on.

Hussein played his game with devotion. He considered the signs, memorised the shapes of the words, sounded the words out and compared them with each other, looking for common threads. He deconstructed and reconstructed the parts of each word until he made sense of all its parts. He played this game for months, using signs, flyers and anything that had writing on it. He continued playing for a whole year, until one day, much to his mother's surprise and to the astonishment of everyone who knew him, Hussein was reading. And not just reading signs – he was reading everything, even reading the newspaper. A true miracle, especially given that most people in Tuffah at the time were still illiterate.

Moftiya's pride was bittersweet. What was she going to do with a boy who could read but not walk? Her brain could not imagine the usefulness of reading, when the only world she was accustomed to was one that relied solely on physical labour. But she had come to accept that no number of bottled pills, velvety pouches, spiritual healing, Sufi whirling, chanting, humming or praying was going to give her son's legs the strength needed to carry the weight of his body. She had accepted that destiny is stubborn, and fate inescapable. So really, what else was she to do but to support Hussein on his new path, and to help him source as many books for free that she could get her hands on?

Reading unlocked the door for Hussein into a world of infinite possibilities. His young mind was constantly churning, thinking, memorising, learning new ideas and abandoning old convictions.

He navigated this path on his own, without teachers or tutors but with hunger, courage and curiosity. Until the day came when the crippled boy from Tuffah freed himself from the confines of his disabilities and redefined his place in the world. Not as a crippled boy, but as a learned reader and a useful member of his community.

A different kind of routine began to emerge. Every morning, neighbours, who had long ignored the one-eyed widow with the crippled son, started to come in droves. They came to hear Hussein read the daily newspaper. They came to ask Hussein to write letters for loved ones. They came to ask him to read letters or legal correspondences they had received. In the evening, parents brought their sons and asked if he could teach them to read and write. Hussein was only ten years old when he opened a home school, a *kottab*, for boys and for men of all ages. It was his war on illiteracy and his deep knowledge, seemingly in everything else, that earned him the highly respected title of '*Sheikh*' at an unusually young age.

Later, when he turned eighteen *Sheikh* Hussein applied to the British Mandate government of Palestine for a licence to officially run his school. An education liaison officer was dispatched to inspect the *kottab*. The officer was impressed by the *sheikh*'s education, his book collection, his curiosity and breadth of knowledge. He overlooked his young age and issued him a teaching licence on the spot. The *sheikh* named his school *Madrasat Sorour Al-Atfal*, the Children's School of Joy. The school did not run on the same schedule of government schools; it took into account the needs of families who worked in the fields and who needed their children with them during the sowing and reaping seasons. The *sheikh* put together a flexible schedule that ensured no student was left behind.

The school earned just enough money to enable Moftiya, finally, to stop working. No mother could have been prouder! She used the

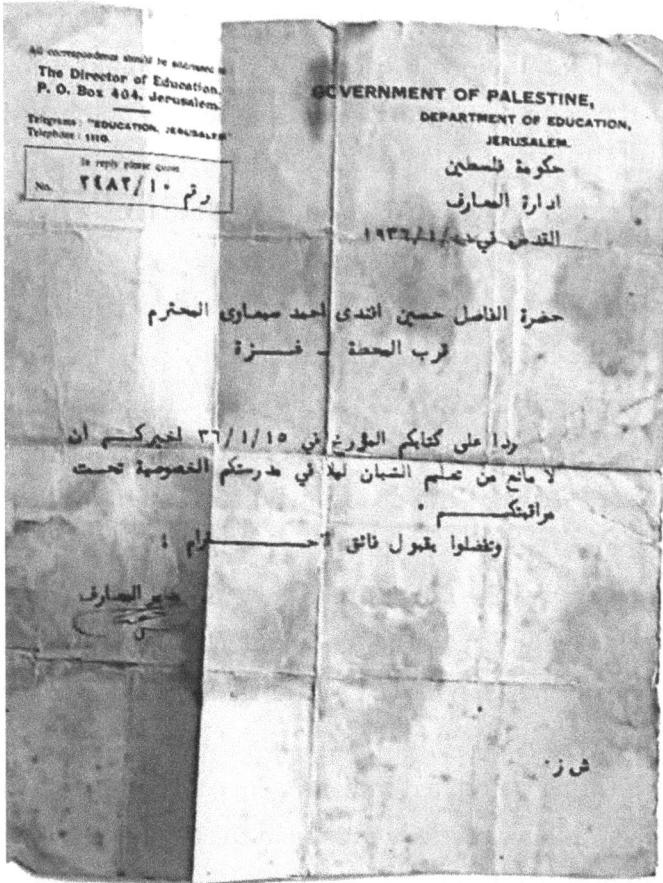

The licence granted to *Sheikh* Hussein for his *kottab*.

last money she received as wages to buy herself a few chickens she could raise.

🌵

It became a constant. Every evening, after the *Maghrib* prayer, the men of Tuffah would trickle into the *sheikh*'s home – the affluent and the poor, the educated and the illiterate, the young and the old – and sit around him in a circle. The evenings always began with the *sheikh* reading the day's newspaper. Heated discussions would inevitably follow. Most of the time the men enjoyed the input of the young, learned *sheikh*, like the time the British army shot and killed Palestinian protestors in Jerusalem and he spoke about the British policy of riot control in India, drawing similarities between the two anti-colonial struggles.

The *sheikh* followed news from India with dedicated passion. He was struck by the rise of Gandhi, and by the creative ways in which Gandhi utilised acts of non-violent civil disobedience to challenge the ruthless colonisation of his country. But the men of Tuffah were not always impressed by India's example.

One night the enthusiastic *sheikh* read an article about Gandhi's protests of the British Government's monopoly on salt-making. The men looked at each other and smiled, as if to say, 'There he goes again with his Gandhi and his India.' But the *sheikh*, unfazed, pressed on. He explained how the British Government had passed a law in 1882 that prohibited Indians from collecting or selling salt.

'Can you believe that?' he examined the faces of the men. 'Salt. A very vital mineral that India produces is denied to the Indian people by the colonial powers and, as if that's not enough, the Indian people are required by the British Authority to pay taxes,' he paused for emphasis, '*for their own salt.*' There was no reaction. He tried again. 'You see, Gandhi wanted to take a symbolic stand against this injustice. He marched 400 kilometres to the sea to make his own salt.'

The men were quiet, unmoved. The *sheikh* stared at their faces as they sat in silence, some sipping on their tea, some puffing on their cigarettes, some doing both at the same time. Finally, Abu-Sa'adah, a close neighbour in his thirties, broke the silence with the clicking of his tongue, 'Tsk,' before he said with a dismissive wave of his hand, 'Our dear *sheikh*. What do you think one man can possibly do?'

The men nodded and shrugged. The *sheikh* swallowed his irritation.

Abu-Awny chimed in with a very low voice, 'And, how much salt can one man make?' Abu-Awny's house was next door to the *sheikh*'s, and they shared an open fruit and vegetable garden in between. It was for that reason that Abu-Awny always spoke in varying degrees of whispers, afraid if he raised his voice his wife Fatima would hear him and summon him back to the house to help with the endless chores.

Salem, a neighbour from across the road who had a distinctly deep and grating voice, weighed in. 'Britain is a great power. These protests will not defeat an empire. The *Engleese* will eat the protestors alive – and they will not even need to add salt.'

The men laughed. The *sheikh*'s face grew hard, holding back his mounting frustration. He looked around the room and there, amongst all the smiles and laughter, was one other face hard like his own. Not laughing, but thinking – deeply thinking. That face belonged to Ibrahim, the train driver from Salama, who often visited whenever his work allowed it. The *sheikh* examined Ibrahim's face and wondered if the rumours were true. He had heard that Ibrahim had joined the underground resistance. Perhaps, the *sheikh* thought, Ibrahim's work at Palestine Railways gave him the means and the cover to facilitate the transporting of fighters and weapons across Palestine. If only he could have had a moment with Ibrahim alone.

Ibrahim noticed the *sheikh*'s gaze settled upon him, so he threw him a lifeline. He asked a question that he knew would steer the discussion back onto the right track.

'How many people followed Gandhi's lead?' asked Ibrahim.

'Five million!' the *sheikh* answered happily and appreciatively. 'Five million have joined Gandhi's protest and have defied the British Government!'

The men were finally impressed. But only because the *sheikh* was too clever to reveal the rest of the story. He chose not to tell them that Gandhi was taken to prison. Such details would have defeated the spirit of an already defeatist crowd. The *sheikh* really wanted to advocate for the idea of non-violence as means to confront tyranny. This was something close to his heart, so close it was lodged inside his rib cage, nourished by his innate desire to believe that intellectual strategic tactics could be more effective than physical strength. Simply put, the doctrine of non-violence for the young *sheikh* was personal: he was handicapped, and had no physical strength. Intellectual power was all he had.

When the *sheikh* turned fourteen – when his voice deepened, when a bulge grew out of his neck, when hair appeared on his face and all over his body, when his armpits began to smell, when his nights became achingly pleasant and his mornings became awkwardly embarrassing, when his mother moved out of his room – that's when he knew. He had anticipated it. He had read about it. And now he was finally ready.

'I need a wife. Will you help me find one?'

The *sheikh*'s words came as a surprise. The men in his nightly circle were stunned, and looked at each other with unease. The crippled *sheikh* wants to get married? How? A few awkward moments passed before Abu-Sa'adah, the most forward of his friends, broke the silence.

'Ahem,' he cleared his throat. 'Our dear *sheikh*, what are you going to do with a wife? Teach her how to read a newspaper?'

A wave of guarded subdued laughter rolled from one side of the room to the other. The men did not want to ridicule the *sheikh*, but they couldn't keep their amusement quiet. Who would allow his daughter to marry a cripple?

'If she would like to,' the *sheikh* responded, smiling, 'I will teach her how to read a newspaper.'

'What we are trying to say,' Abu-Awny chose his words carefully, 'is that women need . . . physical . . . er . . .'

Abu-Sa'adah, ever the joker, winked and gestured crudely to his pants. The men could not hold back their laughter.

Sheikh Hussein sitting on his mat, in front of his blackboard,
in his one-room bedroom and classroom, c. 1959.

'I know,' the *sheikh* insisted. 'Believe me, I'm good. It works. I am certain I can satisfy *the physical* needs of a woman.'

The men cheered and applauded.

'Do you have any preferences?' Ibrahim, who had been quiet through the entire affair, asked.

'All I want is someone with a good heart and a strong, able body! I want nothing more.'

The *sheikh* was under no illusion – he knew it would be hard to find a woman who would accept marrying a man with disabilities. But he believed his other half was out there. He just needed to start the search. He asked everyone who came to visit him that week to spread the word. And that was how Khadija came into his life.

4

KHADIJA

SALAMA TO GAZA, PALESTINE, c. 1920–1947

Khadija grew up in Salama, a village on the central coastal plain east of Jaffa, famous for its bananas and citrus groves. Khadija was raised, with her brothers Hafez and Marwan, by her mother Aziza and her stepfather Ibrahim. Their home stood on the outer edge of town, where newly paved roads reached out and touched the lush, green surrounding fields.

Khadija was not like other girls. Her mind was simple, her features plain and unremarkable, and her body tall, wide and strong. She didn't capture the attention of the women who frequented social gatherings in search of brides for their sons and brothers. Aziza tried to recruit matchmakers to find her daughter a husband, but one after the other, the matchmakers shook their heads and clicked their tongues. 'Tsk. She looks too big, too strong, too unpretty,' they would say disparagingly. 'She has no feminine features, no wealth, no *hasab* or *nasab*.'

Dismayed, Aziza often wondered what a worse fate would be for her daughter – that she might never get married or have a child

of her own, or that she might marry someone who will find it hard
to tolerate her simple mind and her less-than-average looks?

When Ibrahim came home from a trip to Gaza and told Aziza
there was a wise, handicapped *sheikh* in Tuffah seeking a bride, a
light bulb switched on inside her head and hope dug its trenches
deep inside her heart.

'Did the *sheikh* say what his requirements are?' Aziza asked,
breathless with anticipation.

Ibrahim took great pleasure watching Aziza's chest rise and
fall. He took his time. He spoke slowly, relishing every moment,
delivering the news in drips, balancing pause and suspense. 'Let me
try to remember.' Pause. 'The *sheikh* . . .' Drip. 'What did the *sheikh*
say?' Suspense. 'I know . . .' Pause.

'Oh, for God's sake,' Aziza exploded, throwing a cushion at
him. 'Just say it!'

Laughing, Ibrahim answered at last. 'The *sheikh* said all he
wants is a woman with a good heart and a strong body – that
nothing else matters.'

Aziza threw her arms around Ibrahim and kissed him. He was
in heaven. He held her, hoping for the kiss to last, hoping it would
lead to wonderful things, but Aziza only had one thing on her
mind – her daughter's destiny. She pushed her husband away and
got to work.

She dressed up her daughter swiftly, powdered her cheeks, drew
red lipstick on her lips and stuffed tissues inside her to pad her
flat chest, before she finally whisked her off to Tuffah to meet the
sheikh.

And that's how it was.

Khadija found happiness and love in the *sheikh*'s home. He
relieved her of the burden of thinking and making decisions, and

she took care of all the physical work required to keep the house and the school running. At night they took care of each other, and relieved each other of all the day's stresses. Her physical attributes complemented his intelligence. They fit together, and perfectly completed one another.

Before long, Khadija became pregnant. The couple felt they held the whole world in the palm of their hands, until after nine months of joyous anticipation – after one hundred and thirty thousand movements in the womb, after two thousand one hundred and sixty kicks, after one hundred and eighty nights of heartburn, one hundred and thirty contractions, twelve hours of labour – and after the midwife shouted at Khadija to push, push and push dozens of times, after one long, guttural howl, the baby was born. Silent. Still. Cold.

The midwife wrapped the lifeless infant in a cloth and took him away. His parents never got to hold him. A piece of their hearts was torn out of their chests and quickly buried in a cemetery far from their reach. Khadija's breast milk wasted away. Every drop, every leak that dampened her dress, reminded her of the child she would never hold.

But hope always manages to spring from the pit of despair. One morning, Khadija woke and the world was smiling again. New life was growing inside of her. Another nine months of anticipation, yet more countless baby movements and kicks, more heartburns, more contractions and more 'Push, push, Khadija, push!' until another boy came out of her. A crying, warm, frightened baby – a live baby. They named him Ahmed, after his late grandfather.

Khadija and the *sheikh* cherished every breath he took, every movement, every smile and every tear. They even cheered when Ahmed passed gas, and fussed over the colour of his poo.

Khadija learned how to bathe him, nurse him, change his soiled cloths. And at night, she and the *sheikh* watched over him and breathed in his scent until the three of them drifted into sleep.

Khadija revelled in how she finally became part of the neighbourhood's mother circle. She had her own stories to tell of sleepless nights, teething aches, sore nipples and colic.

Ahmed was only nine months old when he was struck by a mysterious illness that quickly claimed his life. Once again Khadija and the *sheikh* were left with gutted hearts and an empty baby basket.

It took longer for Khadija to recover this time. She moved around the house in silence. She cleaned and cooked without any emotions, avoiding eye contact – especially with the *sheikh*. She was worried that the only thing they would see in one another's eyes would be their shared grief, a deep ocean that swallowed them both into the darkness of inconsolable sorrow.

The *sheikh* kept himself busy with his students and his new business idea. He had saved enough money to buy three calves he could grow into bulls before selling for a good price. With the help of his neighbours, he built an additional room that he used as a barn for the animals.

They say time heals all wounds, and life has a ferocious way of forcing itself in – even in places that are paved with grief. It began with the small glances, the knowing smiles, the little jokes, the hand-holding, the night whispers, the touches, the embraces and . . . Khadija became pregnant a third time. This time, she carried her pregnancy like a secret. They didn't talk about it for many months until it became an inescapable reality, and the contractions began. Khadija gave birth to a beautiful baby girl. They named her Amal, meaning hope.

Amal was special. She was a fast learner. She walked and talked before she was two. She kept Khadija and the *sheikh* entertained with her endless chatter and her bird-like songs. One day, as the family was enjoying their evening by an open fire, Khadija placed a big pot of water on the stove to prepare for washing the laundry. She ran out of the room for seconds to grab the pile of dirty clothes in the yard, leaving the *sheikh* and Amal singing together.

It all happened too quickly. Amal stood up and started to dance. The *sheikh*, horrified, shouted at her to stop and to sit back down. This only frightened the little girl, and she took a few steps back. He tried to stand up, to run after her, but his legs were too weak and he fell face-down to the ground. The frightened child took one more step backwards and fell into the boiling pot. The *sheikh* smashed his face into the floor and wept. Khadija ran into the room, but she was too late. Fate had struck again. Loss and grief returned. Unable to withstand the pain, Khadija fainted.

When she woke, Khadija found herself in a hospital where she was kept for weeks in a special ward for the mentally ill. She spent her time there in complete silence. When she was finally released, and Moftiya took her home, Khadija stepped into the front yard and fell to her knees. She began to crawl and howl like a cat in pain, before she finally climbed up the sycamore tree and refused to come back down.

By the time Aziza arrived, Khadija had been in the tree for weeks. Aziza stood under the tree and called out to her:

'Come down, my child. Come down, piece of my flesh and fragment of my soul . . . My arms will carry your pain. My heart will share your sorrow. My eyes will cry your tears . . . Come down, my beloved. *Ya binty, ya habibty*, come down! *Mishan allah*, come down.'

There was a slight movement on the branch above as Khadija parted the leaves and looked down at her mother with eyes maddened by sorrow. 'I am not your daughter. I am a cat. I swallowed all my children.'

Months passed. No one knew for sure how Khadija survived in the sycamore tree. Some people say she must have descended from its branches into the garden, in the stillness of the night, to find sustenance in leftover foods and breadcrumbs. Others believed that her mother-in-law, Moftiya, hung baskets of food on the tree branches that kept Khadija alive. The *sheikh* shut down. He couldn't forgive himself for his helplessness. He could not save his daughter. He could not save his wife. He had nothing to offer his family. He wore his grief like a cloak, and plunged into silence.

Moftiya picked up Khadija's tasks around the heartbroken home, and made sure that the wheels of daily life continued to spin. Food was prepared, floors were cleaned, coals were burnt, clothes were washed and once in a blue moon, when guests came, she let them in with a deep sigh and a helpless eye.

Words wilted away and silence grew like nettle plants, stinging the hearts of everyone touched by them, until one night, Khadija's voice cut through the thick walls of quietude, echoing despair to the seventh sky.

'Dear God,' she howled, 'why didn't you create me in the shape of a worm? Why am I not a wooden branch from a cactus tree? Why didn't you make me a stone that has no feelings, that cannot hear or speak? Why didn't you make me infertile, never to carry a child in my womb or give birth or hold milk in my bosom? What have I done to be immersed in this intolerable suffering? Where is your mercy, God? *Where* is your mercy?'

It was said that Khadija saw a giant creature dressed in white descending from the clouds, his arms open wide ready to embrace her. He was so tall his head touched the moon, and so wide his chest covered the length of the cactus hedges that marked the boundaries of the Tuffah district. Khadija screamed, 'You are the angel of death! You took all my babies from me. Why have you returned? I have nothing more to give to you. You have taken them all.'

'I am not the angel of death,' the giant creature spoke. 'I am the angel of good fortune. There will be no more loss, death or grief in your life. You will give birth to many boys, and will not suffer the loss of any of them in your lifetime; neither will you suffer the loss of any of your grandchildren. Your sons and their children will travel far and wide on this earth.'

The giant wrapped Khadija in his light until she felt a calmness and a peace she had not known her entire life.

'Peace be upon you from the God of mercy!' he said, as his bright light slowly began to fade into the fog of night. 'Peace be upon you from the God of mercy! Peace be upon you from the God of mercy!'

Khadija felt God's mercy wash over her. She felt light enter her body, warm like the first rays of sun. She came down from the sycamore tree. She washed her neglected body and put on clean clothes. She rubbed jasmine flowers on her neck and into the palm of her hands. She drew black eyeliner on the edges of her eyes, and she went to sleep under the covers next to her husband.

Khadija tossed and turned on the mattress. It had been weeks since she had come down from the tree, yet still the *sheikh* had made no attempt to touch her. She was beginning to fear that he might have chosen to abandon her love forever. Loud bellowing from the barn interrupted her thoughts. The bulls were growing restless and intolerant of one another. She waited for the noise to die down, but it only escalated as the animals locked horns fighting over territory, waking the *sheikh* from his deep slumber.

'God give us strength,' the *sheikh* said, as he sat up and gestured for Khadija to bring him his cane.

'Our calves have grown into bulls,' he said. 'Now they want to fight till the death. We must sell them first thing in the morning.'

Khadija helped the *sheikh* to his feet. Her trembling hands gave away her fear. She was petrified of what the angry bulls might do to her husband. Seeing the fear in her eyes, the *sheikh* gently wrapped his arms around her for the first time in what seemed like an eternity.

'Don't worry about me,' he gave her an assuring smile. 'It's the bulls you should be worried about.'

They stood outside the barn. 'I'm going inside,' he instructed. 'You must stay out here and make sure you lock the door. Don't unlock it or try to come in until I call you.'

'No!' Khadija protested.

The *sheikh* looked at her as if seeing her for the first time. Never throughout the years of their marriage had she protested against any decision he had made. Her concern for his safety and her doubt in his ability to deal with the animals only filled his heart with more determination and courage.

'You heard me,' he snapped with an authoritative voice. 'Stand outside and keep this door locked until I call you.'

The *sheikh* slowly pushed the barn door open and quietly stepped inside. Khadija shut the door, pulled the latch across the iron bar and waited. Seconds that lasted for decades passed before she heard the *sheikh* roar so loudly he instilled fear into the hearts of the restless beasts, and all the living creatures in Palestine and beyond. A silence followed. The *sheikh* finally called Khadija to come in.

Inside the barn, Khadija's eyes surveyed the scene with amazement and adoration while the *sheikh*'s eyes surveyed Khadija's body with infinite desire. The bulls were cowered in separate corners, heads bowed down like frightened puppies. It was a glorious triumph that filled the *sheikh* with pride and brought back his confidence. He asked Khadija to tie the bulls up with steel chains, and when she hesitated, he coaxed her, 'Come on. Do it. Don't be afraid.'

'Afraid?' Khadija responded playfully, 'why would I be afraid? I have a lion to protect me.'

The *sheikh* could barely contain his desire.

That night, Khadija and the *sheikh* rushed back to their mattress, exhilarated by the victory and seduced by the sweet tingly feeling in their guts. That night, the *sheikh*'s manhood was fully restored and Khadija's womanhood was thoroughly savoured. That night, hope forced itself back into their lives and love soared high above their home. That night, Karim began to grow in Khadija's womb.

5

THE GENEROUS GOD

GAZA, PALESTINE, DECEMBER 1942

Gaza's railway station was bustling. The train from Jaffa unloaded a fusion of merchants, local travellers, and British and Australian soldiers. Vendors shouting the prices of cardamom coffee, *za'ater* pies and ceramic souvenirs competed for attention. Aziza stood on the platform next to her suitcase, relieved to have her feet finally planted on still ground after the long journey. She gestured to a scrawny, young porter to pick up her suitcase, but the boy ignored her and chased after an Australian soldier instead, yelling a chorus of 'Hello, hello! . . . G'day, mate . . . Hello! . . . Give me . . . give me . . . I carry . . . I carry for you!'

Aziza shook her head and hissed at the young boy's lack of manners. Times had changed. In the old days, the boy would have been ashamed to let an older woman carry such a load by herself; he might even have offered to help her free of charge. But since the beginning of the Second World War and the upsurge of soldiers from the Allied forces, the wartime economy provided a boost for local businesses, including street vendors and porters, turning them away from the service of the less-fortunate locals.

Aziza cursed under her breath as she balanced the heavy suitcase on top of her head, and began the long walk from the railway station to her daughter's home in Tuffah. She missed the days when she was able to ride her donkey along the coastal roads from Salama. That simple trip was no longer possible. Armed Jewish gangs had set up training camps along the way, and British forces had set up checkpoints – not to subdue the Jewish gangs but to target Palestinian resistance to both the British forces and the increasingly powerful Jewish gangs. Travelling by train was the safest option. What else was Aziza to do? Her daughter was ready to have her baby and, given Khadija's track record of tragedy in bearing children, Aziza knew she had to be there. A mother must always be there for her daughter, especially when it comes to matters of the womb.

Moftiya greeted Aziza with a jug of water and a cold smile. She didn't like how other women made themselves at home in her house. Since the *sheikh* married Khadija, not only did Moftiya lose her special bond with her son, having to share him now with another woman, she also lost territory and space. Khadija's mother became a regular staying guest and, if this wasn't enough, other women from the neighbourhood had come and gone freely to check up on Khadija throughout her pregnancy.

When Moftiya saw Khadija offering her mother pomegranates fresh from their garden, she was adamant it was time to draw the line. She appealed to her son to intervene.

'You must talk to your wife. This is not acceptable. We must have order and rules. We cannot squander our food like this. Does her mother really need to be here all this time? We would have sent for her when Khadija was in labour.'

The *sheikh* listened to his mother respectfully and promised he would talk to Khadija. But on that cold December night, after the last guest had left the *sheikh*'s room and as Khadija leaned forward to blow out the kerosene lamp, the *sheikh* could not remember a word his mother had said. His entire focus shifted to other more urgent and far more pleasant matters.

Moftiya, who shared the adjoining room with Aziza, expected to hear her son's voice through the thin mud walls telling his wife she must not be so wasteful. But instead she heard a different type of rhythm, marked by hard breathing and occasional outbursts of joyful laughter.

Aziza giggled on her mattress. 'My God reward the *sheikh*, and give him strength upon strength. All this work will surely induce labour. Khadija will have a baby suckling on her breast by tomorrow night, *Inshallah*.'

Moftiya smiled secretly. She was accustomed to these nightly sounds, and much to her surprise, they always filled her heart with delight. She couldn't be happier for her son.

The morning after, Khadija's contractions began. Aziza assumed her God-given duty as her mother to assist her. 'We need more coal to keep Khadija and her baby warm,' she told Moftiya.

Moftiya was horrified. Coal cost money, and there was no need to have more coal than what was already available.

'There is a mountain of coal right here.' She pointed to the corner of the room.

Aziza looked at the small pile and let out a sarcastic laugh. 'A mountain? That's barely enough for one night. As the saying goes, if you can't afford the horse, don't bother buying a saddle.'

'This is what we have,' Moftiya shot back with the proverbial insult, 'if you don't like it, you can drink the sea.'

Aziza was outraged. 'I am a guest in the *sheikh*'s home! I have no interest in drinking the sea.' She stormed out and headed across the yard to complain to the *sheikh* about his mother's ungracious behaviour. But the *sheikh* was engaged in a deep conversation with some of the men from the neighbourhood about things that were far removed from the lives of the women in the family.

The *sheikh* addressed his guests in a measured tone: 'The British forces only practise their strength against us. They arrest our activists and turn a blind eye to Jewish terrorism.'

Aziza was well aware of the growing number of European Jewish immigrants near her hometown, Salama, and had seen with her own eyes how the British authorities had forcefully evicted the Palestinian peasants from their farms, only to hand the land over to the new Jewish arrivals. She swallowed hard and tried to push away her growing anxiety that her own family might suffer the same fate.

'Soon, it will be over for Great Britain,' Abu-Sa'adah said. 'Germany will win the war and we will win our freedom from the *Engleese*.'

'And what makes you think Hitler will be any better?' The *sheikh*'s voice gave away his frustration. 'We cannot rely on one occupation to free us from another, or one tyrant to free us from another. We fought with the British against the Ottomans, and they betrayed us and promised to give our land to the Jews. Haven't we learned our lesson? Freedom will not come to us through an external power. We have to earn it ourselves.'

Aziza smiled at her daughter's good fortune. The *sheikh* was such a charismatic and articulate man amongst men – and from what she had heard the night before, he was also very pleasing to his woman.

Aziza decided to wait until the men left to bring up her complaint to the *sheikh*. When she did, the *sheikh* sided with her and told his mother there had to be enough heat to ensure the comfort and survival of Khadija and the expected baby. He ordered more bags of coal, enough to heat the room throughout the rest of the winter months.

At night, the coal arrived – and so did he.

He didn't wait for the midwife. He raced through the birth canal and landed straight into the hands of his grandmother. Surprised to receive him so quickly, Aziza cut the umbilical cord cheerfully, praising God for his gift.

'*Mashallah*, he's a healthy baby boy, who obviously has no patience at all!' She wrapped him in a blanket, handed him over to his mother and ran out the door to tell the *sheikh* the good news.

The *sheikh* was already outside the door, leaning on his walking stick. He shuffled into the room as quickly as his legs would allow. When he saw his baby boy, tiny hand wrapped around Khadija's finger and hungry mouth latched on to her breast, the *sheikh*'s heart split open.

'He's not impatient,' the *sheikh* smiled. 'He is a good boy. He knows how long we have waited for him. That's why he came quickly!'

It didn't take long for news of the birth to travel. The first to congratulate the proud parents were Abu-Awny and Fatima. Fatima had grown close to Khadija over the years. They borrowed from each other everything from brooms and pots to clothes and scarves. This time, Fatima brought with her a wicker basket. Her youngest child was now too big to sleep in it. She knew Khadija had thrown out the old basket that she had used in the past for her deceased children, and with that she had hoped to have thrown out the evil that inhabited their home and claimed their children's lives.

'You can keep this basket for now, so your baby has a good place to sleep,' Fatima said, as she placed the basket next to Khadija's mattress. 'But,' she added with a wink, 'you'll have to give it back in seven months.'

Khadija grinned, and squeezed Fatima's hand. 'No way! Seven months? Are you pregnant again? Congratulations! That's wonderful news!'

Fatima kissed Khadija on the cheek and declared with the confidence of a clairvoyant, 'I am hoping for a girl this time, and she is going to steal your son's heart. Just you wait and see.'

'Indeed. God is generous. *Allah karim*,' said the *sheikh*.

The baby was received as a gift from a generous God to a couple who for years experienced the bitterness of loss and grief. What else could the *sheikh* have named him but *Abdul Karim*, worshipper of the generous God.

6

ILLNESS

GAZA, PALESTINE, 1947

Darkness draped the Tuffah district. Cold December winds blew through its narrow walkways and along its dusty roads. Karim rolled out his mattress to the flickering light of the kerosene lamp. He had just turned five and was proud to be old enough to prepare his own bedding.

The family slept in the same order every night. The *sheikh*'s mattress next to the wall, beside him Khadija's, and next to her Rahim's, who had just turned four, followed by Karim's. When their baby brother Muti wasn't suckling on Khadija's breast, the *sheikh* cradled him in his arm. Sometimes in the morning, Karim and Rahim woke up to find baby Muti sleeping on the *sheikh*'s face, a sight that always sent them into a fit of giggles.

Rahim and Karim were only a year apart but looked like they were born to different families. Karim inherited his grandmother Moftiya's dark skin and sharp features, while Rahim had his grandfather's and father's round face, white skin and blue eyes. This was not uncommon in Palestine, where centuries of conquests and occupations played havoc with gene pools, producing families with mixed skin tones and eye colours.

The boys slipped under the covers, their eyes wide open and their ears intently tuned in, in anticipation of their nightly bedtime story, ready to imagine and capture every word their father was about to utter. The *sheikh* began, as always, with '*Bismillah alrahman alraheem*, in the name of God, the merciful, the compassionate,' before he went on to tell the story.

'*Kan ya ma kan fi qadeem alzaman*, once upon a time long ago, a hunter caught a small bird and held him in his hand. The small bird was clever. He said to the hunter, "You are a big man, and I am too small to satisfy your hunger. But, if you spare my life, I promise I can offer you three pearls of wisdom that are guaranteed to bring you great fortune." The hunter looked at the small bird with suspicion, but the bird assured him, "I will tell you the first one while I am still in your grip, and the second, if you let me fly to this low branch here, still within your reach. But the third, I will only tell you if you let me fly to the top of this tree." The hunter pondered the offer, then nodded for the bird to speak. "The first pearl of wisdom is this," the bird chirped. "Never believe what cannot be." The hunter smiled with satisfaction, and placed the bird on the low branch so he may continue. "The second pearl of wisdom," chirped the clever bird, "is to never waste time on regret." The hunter stepped back and let the bird fly to the top of the tree. Perched on the highest branch, the bird sang, "I swallowed a gem that weighs 200 grams. Had you cut me open, you could have become a very rich man." The hunter fell to his knees, cursing himself for his stupidity, for letting the bird out of his grip. When he finally calmed down, he stood up and demanded that the bird tell him the third pearl of wisdom. The bird shook his beak, and said, "Why should I?

You have learned nothing from the first two pearls of wisdom I gave you: you believed what could not be, and you regretted letting me go. How could you believe a bird as small as me, could swallow a 200-gram gem? You are a foolish man, and you are not worthy of my wisdom!"'

'They fell asleep,' Khadija whispered.

The *sheikh* waited a few moments before he reached his arm across and gently placed his hand first under Karim's nose, then under Rahim's. Scarred by the losses they had endured and by the cruelty of death, the *sheikh* could not trust that the wicked angel would not return to steal another one of their precious children. He had become obsessed with the boys' breathing, sometimes waking up several times during the night just to seek comfort in the warmth of the air his boys exhaled.

But illness arrived in the middle of the night. The *sheikh* woke up to Karim coughing once, then twice, then three times. The *sheikh*'s heart sank. 'Wake up!' he nudged Khadija. 'Karim is coughing!'

Khadija got up and gave Karim water, and went back to sleep. An hour later, the *sheikh* nudged her again. 'He's still coughing. Maybe the air is too dry. Why don't you boil some water to dampen the air in this room.'

Khadija rubbed her eyes and stood up again, half asleep. She felt her way in the darkness until she found the gas canister. She lit a fire and boiled a big pot of water, letting the steam fill up the air until it all evaporated. She switched off the gas fire and went back to sleep. But in the morning, Karim's cough had worsened. Panic ensued.

The *sheikh* held Karim in his arm, placed his hand on his forehead and recited from the Quran: 'We send down in the Quran that which is a healing and a mercy for the believers.' He read many more verses from the holy book, but still the cough persisted.

By noon, Khadija asked Moftiya for help. The matriarch had been waiting impatiently for this request. After all, if she didn't show her skills at times like these then what good was she to anyone? She marched with purpose towards the sick child, took one look at him and immediately began to work on the remedy.

Khadija watched as Moftiya chopped fresh mint leaves and mixed them with tahini and olive oil. She massaged the paste onto the boy's chest, then wrapped him in soft, cotton fabric, all the while explaining each step in a dispassionate voice that carried the confidence of generations of knowledge. Once she had finished, she told Khadija, 'The boy's skin needs to breathe out the toxins, so you must use only Egyptian sheer cotton until he's better.'

It was a very impressive performance but, much to Moftiya's disappointment, even the wisdom of a thousand and one ancestors was not enough to heal the boy.

By nightfall their neighbour Fatima came and presented Khadija with a pouch of herbs collected from her garden. 'Fresh thyme, sage and mint leaves,' she advised Khadija. 'Put them in boiling water and let Karim breathe the steam. He will leap like a horse in the morning.'

Fatima looked at the *sheikh* who sat helplessly, clutching the boy in his arms, and was moved to tears. She wanted to lighten the mood a little. 'If this doesn't work, just tell Karim if he's not better soon I will have to find another groom for my daughter Souhailah to marry.'

Karim opened his eyes and tried to sit up at the mention of Souhailah's name. This made everyone laugh.

'Oh, Karim,' Fatima said. 'Souhailah is not here. My beautiful princess does not chase after boys. If you want to see her, you'll have to get better and chase after her.'

Khadija laughed. 'He takes everything seriously. You know he is convinced Souhailah is his bride.'

'Let's pray he gets better and grows up to be a strong and healthy man. When he is old enough, he can choose for himself any bride he wants,' the *sheikh* said.

Fatima glared at the *sheikh*, who quickly had to adjust what he had said. 'And, of course, what better bride could there be for him than your daughter, Souhailah?'

Later that night Khadija boiled the herbs Fatima had brought, and placed a towel over Karim's head to trap the steam. The boy inhaled the vapor for ten minutes before he fell asleep.

But the *sheikh* did not sleep. He watched over his son, who coughed through the night, and by the next morning he called for a doctor.

A young Jerusalemite doctor arrived with some medicine and disturbing news.

'Jewish gangs are being armed by the British forces,' he told the *sheikh*, as he took Karim's temperature. 'Since the United Nations adopted the partition plan, these gangs have increased their attacks against Palestinians – especially those of us within the areas they want to claim for a Jewish state.'

'The UN only adopted the plan knowing that there is no way anyone in their right mind would accept it,' the *sheikh* said. 'Besides,' he added, 'how can there be a Jewish state if they still don't have a majority, even with the increased migration from Europe?'

'My dear *sheikh*,' the doctor sighed, 'they plan to create a majority by terrorising us and driving us out.'

'You are a learned doctor.' The *sheikh*'s tone was reproachful. 'You should not be spreading panic. There is no way the newcomers will drive the Palestinians out of their homes. There is such a thing as international law. The world would not stand for it.'

The doctor gave the *sheikh* a tired smile and a compassionate response. '*Inshallah*. From your mouth to God's ears!'

The *sheikh* assured the young doctor that the resistance would win in the end. In return, the doctor assured the *sheikh* that Karim would get better soon.

Another week passed. The resistance was not winning. Karim was not getting any better. Tearful, the *sheikh* implored Khadija to take him away. 'Take him to your mother's house in Salama,' he pleaded. 'Let him die away from here. Please forgive me. I cannot bear to witness the death of another child. I cannot endure another loss.'

Khadija was sympathetic to her husband, but she did not share his concern. Since that night up in the sycamore tree, the words of the angel of good fortune rang in her ears like the bells of Gaza's Saint Porphyrius on the eve of Easter: 'There will be no more loss, death or grief in your life,' the angel had promised her, and her heart was filled with faith. Though she did not believe Karim to be dying, she did love the *sheikh*'s idea of taking him to Salama. She had not been back in her family home since she had married the *sheikh*, and she was excited about returning and spending time with her mother. She packed a bag, planted baby Muti on her hip and asked Moftiya to care for Rahim in her absence.

Karim kissed his father's hand goodbye and turned around to kiss his grandmother's hand, but Moftiya came down on her knees and threw her arms around him. Karim was surprised to see his grandmother's face soften, a rare occurrence that was becoming rarer with the passing of time.

'Be a good boy, Karim,' Moftiya's tears came down. 'Come back to us. I will cook for you some of my chickens' special eggs when you return.'

Khadija and the *sheikh* exchanged glances. Moftiya never allowed anyone to touch the eggs her chickens laid. These eggs were her only source of personal income. Even though her son was taking care of her, she maintained her independence and her earnings from the chickens' eggs, a symbol of her autonomy and independence. How heartbroken she must have been over Karim's departure to promise him eggs from her chickens.

A new bus line was running directly from Gaza to Salama. Its interior was shiny, and the upholstery of the seats smelled like fresh soap. Karim's curiosity and sense of adventure overpowered his illness. He sat up in his seat exhilarated by the newness of the experience, and looked around him at the other passengers. An assortment of headgear was on display: Jewish kippahs, English hats, Turkish fezzes, Islamic veils and – ever so popular now – the Palestinian *keffiyeh*. Regardless of head cover, most men and women dressed in western-style clothes. Only the older generation of Palestinian men and women, and some younger Palestinian peasants, he noticed, were dressed in more traditional clothing – like his mother, Khadija.

Karim stuck his face to the glass window and watched as the bus drove out of the ancient part of Gaza and through the newly paved wide streets of Gaza City. He had never left Tuffah before. He was dazzled by the automobiles parked outside the double-storey houses in Gaza's main street. He saw restaurants and cafes for the first time, lining the road along the beach. He saw the shiny shop windows along the strip of Omar Al-Mukhtar Street. A whole world – a different world – was there, only a couple of kilometres away from the dusty roads, fields and valleys he knew. A world existed of wealthy homes with running water and electricity. A world with hardly any donkeys in sight. Karim looked at his mother in her long, black dress, white veil and old flat pair of shoes, and for the first time in his young life he realised that his family was actually very poor. Tired by the weight of his discovery, the young boy closed his eyes and fell asleep.

7

WHERE DID ALL THE MEN GO?

SALAMA, PALESTINE, 1947

In Salama, Aziza woke up alone. She rolled up her mattress, wrapped her shawl tightly around her body and stepped outside. She embraced the cool morning breeze, breathed it into her chest, allowed it to travel through her veins, all the way down to her toes. She held her breath and thought of all the wonders this new day may bring, then she lifted her head and exhaled, scattering all her fears and worries across a cloudy winter sky.

'*Sabahna we sabah almolk liliah*,' she greeted the almighty in the sky. 'God of mercy,' she prayed, 'bring our men home, victorious and free!'

She remembered only a year ago when Ibrahim sought her permission to enlist her sons Hafez and Marwan into the underground resistance. 'The Jewish settlements are strangling Salama. They are expanding across our agricultural lands, usurping our water, restricting our movement. The British forces help them and arrest us for protesting. They give them guns and give us prison cells.

We can't watch idly – we must fight back. The boys are now young men. We need them to protect their land.'

Aziza placed her hand on her aching heart. At first she tried to object, but her words came out soft and irrational. 'They are young men,' she said to Ibrahim, 'but they are *my* young men.' Of course, she knew her sons would not have a future if they had no land and no country. And so, she let them go.

Aziza took another deep breath. She smiled. I smell the scent of a loved one. But who? Who will come to see me? She went into the chicken coop and picked up the youngest and fattest chicken. 'I'm sorry,' she said, as she looked for the slaughter knife, 'but my heart tells me someone dear will be here to eat you, and my heart never lies!'

Aziza slaughtered the bird, plucked its feathers, stuffed it with rice and nuts and placed it into the oven. She had no idea whom she was cooking for; all she knew was that she had to be prepared to feed a loved one.

'*Yumma!*' she heard Khadija's voice calling for her. Aziza turned around and there was her daughter, back in her family home for the first time since she married the *sheikh*. At first Aziza was delighted, but fear and doubt quickly took hold of her. 'What did you do, Khadija? Did the *sheikh* send you home?'

Khadija smiled. 'The *sheikh* loves me,' she assured her mother, 'and he sends his regards. We came here for Karim. He's sick.'

Aziza hugged Khadija and Karim and fussed over Muti, who gurgled and smiled as babies do. She sat them down and fed them. Khadija tore into the stuffed chicken. Even with the *sheikh*'s income from teaching, they could not dream of eating this well. Aziza poured soup for her sick grandson.

'There is nothing more healing than chicken soup!' She spoonfed him, noticing how ravenous the boy was and how loosely his shirt hung over his bony body. 'Your other grandmother Moftiya can keep her eggs and her chickens,' she laughed.

Karim ate every drop of the hearty soup. His stomach was as full as his heart. He fell asleep and when he woke, he found himself lying on a mattress, Aziza towering above him, puffing on a cigarette. He could not believe his eyes – he had never seen a woman smoke before. In Tuffah, only men puffed smoke like dragons.

'*Yallah* Khadija, let's get him ready. We'll find him a mystic healer at the tomb of Salama Abu-Hashim.'

'Shouldn't we wait for the men to come home?' asked Khadija. 'Maybe one of my brothers can carry Karim to the tomb? He is too tired to walk, and too big for me to carry.'

Aziza put out her cigarette. 'The men can't come home. If they did, the British dogs would arrest them. Your brothers, like most men in this town, have joined the resistance.'

Khadija stared at her mother, her mind searching for an appropriate response. Did she really want an explanation? Or should she just let her mother's words fall, like she did all things that she found too difficult to comprehend, and too ugly to absorb? Images flashed in her mind's eye of such things that she let go without questioning. Like the *sheikh*'s mysterious midnight guests who hid their faces behind *keffiyehs*. Like the guns she knew they buried beneath the rocks in their backyard. Like the constant harassment of British forces, and the random checks for identity cards, like people disappearing from daily life, like riots, like gunshots, like tanks, like knowing but not knowing that the world is changing. Should she, Khadija, the woman with the simple mind, ask why this peaceful town where she had grown up was now empty of its men? Did she want to know?

Aziza didn't wait for Khadija's response. '*Ya binty*,' she began, 'there are things you need to know and be prepared for. Your brothers and . . .'

'*Yumma*,' Khadija's heart was pounding. What if the British soldiers stopped her and asked her where her brothers were? She was never good at lying. '*Yumma*, please, let's just go to the tomb.'

At the tomb the mystic holy man, dressed in a red robe and a turban, sat cross-legged on a prayer mat. Khadija and Aziza sat on the floor across from him, holding Karim and baby Muti in their arms. The mystic listened to Khadija with an exaggerated sense of importance and self-worth. He reached out, placed his holy hand on Karim's forehead and closed his eyes for a very long minute before he opened them again.

'You have no need to worry.' He sounded like a doctor diagnosing a familiar ailment. 'This boy's star is high in the sky. He will live a long life. He will prosper. This illness will pass, if you follow my instructions.'

Khadija squeezed Karim in a tight embrace, paying close attention to the mystic's prescription.

'You need to get a common nail, it doesn't matter if it is long or short. Burn it on an open fire until its iron turns red, then drop it in a glass of donkey's milk. Let it sit for a few minutes, then have your son drink the milk. Do this for a few days and your son will bounce back to good health, God willing. *Inshallah*.'

Aziza paid the holy man and walked out with her daughter, grandsons, and a new – albeit extreme – remedy. 'Fortunately,' she told her daughter, face beaming, 'our neighbour's donkey gave birth a few weeks ago. Surely, they'll be happy to volunteer the donkey's milk for the boy's medicine.'

It's not clear if Karim got better because of the mystic remedy, or because he could no longer stomach drinking the donkey's milk. What is important was that he recovered fast, and soon he, his mother and his baby brother Muti were ready to return to Gaza.

'*Yumma*, come with us,' Khadija urged her mother, as she kissed her goodbye. 'Don't stay here alone – it's not safe without the men.' Aziza shook her head and refused to leave. Her intuition was telling her to run from Salama as fast as she could, but her heart would not let her leave without knowing the fate of her men.

8

MADNESS, *JONOON*

GAZA, PALESTINE, 1948

Karim held on to the hem of Khadija's long, black dress, doubling his steps to keep up with her pace as she pulled the donkey away from Mohatta Street and into the farming fields that surrounded Tuffah. The aroma of hearty stews and freshly baked bread rising from communal ovens gradually dissipated, giving way to the scent of wild herbs and sweet fruit blossoms. '*Sobhan Allah!*' Khadija praised God for the stunning beauty that surrounded her – the small hills that stood in the distance, draped in green velvet and splashed with tenacious colours of red, yellow and purple wild-flowers. The spring of 1948 had arrived with a vengeance.

Since his return from Salama, Karim took on the role of accompanying his mother on these magical daily outings to fetch water from the wells in the fields. He savoured this time away from the cries and tantrums of his younger brothers and the never-ending house chores his grandmother Moftiya asked him to perform. He also revelled in the idea that he was old enough to be his mother's 'protector'. 'Look after your mother,' is what his father always told him as they left the house. 'You're strong now, aren't you?' his father would ask, and Karim never failed to roll up his sleeves and flex his tender muscles to prove he was the man for the job.

Khadija made use of the time it took to walk to the wells to remind Karim of some important rules: 'Don't run through the vegetable beds or pick fruits from the trees in these fields; these are privately owned properties, and we are only entitled to the water in the wells'; 'Always reply when someone greets you'; 'Don't forget to say *Alhamdulillahs*, praise be to God, if anyone asks how you're doing'.

Karim tried to remember and obey all these rules but some-times, in the excitement of chasing a flock of birds or a beautiful, coloured butterfly, some rules may have been broken.

When they arrived at the farming fields, Khadija looked at her little boy and began the usual challenge: '*Yallah*, Karim! Try to guess which well has its motor running?'

Karim loved playing this game! He listened until his ears picked up the humming sound of an engine before triumphantly pointing Khadija in the well's direction.

Those outings could have been amongst Karim's most treasured childhood memories if it weren't for this one incident that brought them to an abrupt ending. That spring day, when they arrived at the well, they saw a man sitting under a tree holding a clay water jug. Khadija froze, and squeezed her little boy's hand. '*Allah yoster*. God protect us. It's the *majnoon* of Tuffah.'

Majnoon is Arabic for madman, and it was how people referred to the son of the imam of Tuffah's local mosque. He was born with a delusional mind. His father tried to cure him with prayers and Quran readings, but the older the boy grew the more unstable he became. Desperate, the imam sought out magical cures and potions, but these methods, including beating the demons out of his son, only pushed the boy further into insanity. In the end, the imam took his son to the *sheikh*'s school in the hope education might stimulate his mind and counter his madness, but there was little that the *sheikh* could do.

The boy grew into a man who wandered the streets of Tuffah aimlessly. At times he spoke like a scholar reciting poetry and verses from the Quran he had learned at the *sheikh*'s school. Other times, he uttered nonsensical words twirled in circles and chanted in strange languages. His moods were unpredictable, changing from calm to violent to calm again in seconds. Sometimes during his fits of rage, the men in Tuffah would gather around him and tie him up to a tree to prevent him from hurting himself or others.

When the *majnoon* saw Khadija and Karim, he quickly put his clay jug aside and stood up to welcome them. 'The wife and son of our learned and noble teacher, the *sheikh*!'

Before Khadija could respond, the *majnoon* grabbed their empty jugs from the donkey saddlebag, climbed up the well, carefully filled the jugs with water, then came down and placed the full jugs back into the donkey saddlebag. He patted Karim on the head, then grabbed his own water jug and climbed back onto the well, chanting Quranic verses with a beautiful voice, *'And when he [Moses] arrived at the watering (place) in Madyan, he found there a group of men watering (their flocks), and besides them he found two women who were keeping back (their flocks). He said: "What is the matter with you?" They said: "We cannot water (our flocks) until the shepherds take back (their flocks): And our father is a very old man."'*

Khadija whispered to Karim, 'Oh, God! He thinks he's Moses. Let's get away from here fast.' She sealed the top of the jugs swiftly with banana leaves to avoid spillage, and let go of the donkey rope. The donkey always knew his way home, so he started walking in that direction.

Seeing them leave, the *majnoon* lifted his clay jug, smashed it on the side of the well and began to recite his own made-up Quranic verses. '*Barakeesh Barakeen*, the pigeon told me I was Haron's sister. Blond blonding brown browning black blacking terror terrifying terror terrifying terror terrifying.' He fell to the ground, spit foaming from his mouth, repeating 'Terror terrifying . . . terror terrifying . . .'

Karim ran for his life, abandoning his responsibility as his mother's protector. When he arrived at the house, he was too ashamed to look his father in the eye. He had left his mother behind. He sulked in his disgrace. Khadija arrived only minutes after he did.

That night the *majnoon* broke into the home of the Jabry family in Tuffah and severed the head of their new-born baby. Terrified, the people of Tuffah locked their doors for the first time in decades. The bravest of their men went out looking for him, but he was nowhere to be found.

That was the last day Karim and his mother ever went on that magical journey to the fields to fetch water. The *majnoon*'s senseless and ruthless violence gave Karim a taste of what was yet to come. Palestine was on the edge of *jonoon*, a madness that would last the rest of his life. A madness that would claim many of the lives he treasured, and send him disgraced into exile. The world changed that night. Karim just didn't know it yet.

9

BREATH, *NAFAS*

SALAMA, PALESTINE, 1948

Breath, *nafas*, is the most important ingredient in Palestinian cooking. Anyone can follow a recipe, but only a woman with *nafas* can prepare truly exceptional meals. Aziza had *nafas*.

Aziza placed a pot on the *kaz babur* stove and poured milk into it. She hadn't made *riz bi haleeb* since her first husband Ismael died more than twenty years ago in a work accident at the shipping docks in Yaffa, leaving her with two sons and one daughter to raise. This had been his favourite dessert, so when she mourned his death she'd made a pact with God that she would never make *riz bi haleeb* for another man. On this particular day she was determined to break that pact, certain she would have God's blessing.

Aziza added rice and sugar to the milk and as she began to stir, she looked around and contemplated every detail of her modest home. Ismael had built this house for her with his bare hands when she was his bride. Her eyes followed the sunbeams that came through the window to rest on the mattress beneath, and she recalled waking up to the gentle embrace of the sun on their first morning together. 'This is my house,' she sighed, as she watched the milk and rice begin to simmer.

After Ismael's death Aziza's family and friends surrounded her, offering food, love and support. But as the days passed, her brothers' wives grew weary of the burden of having more mouths to feed; her neighbours and friends became fearful that the young widow would steal their husbands; and her parents became worried about their daughter's reputation.

Aziza pushed aside those memories, wiped a tear, added a pinch of mastic gum to the pot and continued to stir. It was her brilliance in the kitchen that had enabled her to raise her children. Not long after Ismael's death, Aziza put her God-given *nafas* into a catering business. She stuffed clay pots with rice, spices and lamb and prepared the most exquisite *qidreh* for the elites of Salama. But despite the financial independence this allowed, her family continued to pressure her to marry a second time. 'Marriage is *sater*, a shield that protects a woman's reputation,' her mother insisted. And so when Ibrahim asked for her hand in marriage and she refused, her mother reminded her of the old adage: 'The shade of a man is better than the shade of a wall.'

Aziza inhaled the sweet-fragranced steam rising from the pot. Her *riz bi haleeb* was ready to be served. She turned off the heat and reached out for the small bowls in the kitchen cabinet. Her second husband Ibrahim had bought the bowls from the artisan market in Hebron – he had known she would love them. He was a rough man with hard edges, but he loved her in his own way. He was good to her boys, helping them grow into fine men. He never interfered with her choices or asked her to justify where she went, or why. When she visited her daughter in Tuffah, he never pressured her to come home. He supported her in so many ways. He loved her. And now . . .

Aziza held the bowls close to her heart and wept. She had never shown Ibrahim that she loved him. When he joined the resistance she was so proud of him, but said nothing. When he left the house the last time, with Hafez and Marwan, to fight against the Jewish gangs that were spreading terror throughout Palestine, she embraced them all and prayed for them. But she was too proud to beg them – especially Ibrahim – to stay. All she could do was pray for their victory and safe return. But God was not listening to her prayers. She remembered her mother's words, 'The shade of a man is better than the shade of a wall.' Now the men were gone, and the walls were about to be taken.

'This is my house,' Aziza spoke the words aloud, and wiped her tears. She began to scoop the thick, creamy dessert into the bowls. This was supposed to be her time to shine. Her oldest daughter Khadija was happily married to a *sheikh* in Gaza, her two sons were now fine young men. In a different life, Aziza would have found them wives and would have two young women under her roof to boss around – and possibly grandchildren, too. She would have sat on her throne, the matriarch of her kingdom, without any need to lift a finger. But the Jews came from Europe and now all was gone.

She sang louder again, 'This is my house!' Her song had no rhythm, but she didn't care – there was no one left in Salama to hear her. The Jewish paramilitary organisation Haganah had launched Operation Hametz, in a bid for the villages that surrounded Jaffa – and the city itself. Flyers were dropped on the houses, warning residents to leave their homes or face dire consequences. She had heard that many Palestinian towns and villages had already been emptied.

'This is *our house*,' she shouted, again and again.

Aziza crushed pistachios, mixed them with cinnamon and sprinkled them on top of the *riz bi haleeb*.

The night before, she had heard of the massacres. She had heard of the women, children and men who were slaughtered, their corpses piled onto trucks and paraded through the streets. She had seen these trucks drive through the streets of Salama. She had also seen, only that morning, the lines of cars leaving and others fleeing on foot, carrying whatever possessions they could manage. Some people ran barefooted, in fear of the terror that was to come.

They all locked their houses and took their keys.

'Run, Aziza!' her neighbours told her. 'Run, Aziza!' 'Run!' 'The Jews are on their way. Run!'

'But this is *my* house!' Aziza stood unable and unwilling to run.

She placed the dessert bowls of *riz bi haleeb* on the kitchen table and sat down and prayed for her men to return. As if this act of making the dessert she had denied them all these years would summon them back. She imagined their faces as they walked through the door, how happy they would be, especially Ibrahim – how he would finally know that she loves him as much as she did her late husband Ismael, or maybe even more.

Aziza waited for her loved ones to arrive. They did not. Instead, the Haganah arrived. She heard their tanks rolling in. She ran to the rooftop of her house and watched as the armed gang broke into each house in Salama and claimed it. She watched as they loaded people's possessions into trucks – books, rugs and whatever they deemed valuable was stolen. She saw the trucks heading towards her home, and she ran back down to the kitchen.

Two men with guns walked in. Surprised to find her there, they shouted, 'Why are you still here? Go!'

'This is my house,' Aziza cried.

One man held a rifle to her head and smiled, 'Repeat after me, "King Farouk is a bastard."'

Aziza couldn't care less for the King of Egypt and for all his men. 'Damn the king, and damn you!' she lashed out.

They dragged Aziza outside, laughing, amused by the fighting spirit of a helpless woman.

'You come back inside,' they threatened, 'and we will kill you.'

They turned around but Aziza followed, every inch of her body yearning to be in her home.

The armed men were annoyed. They pushed her to the ground. 'You are lucky you are still alive.' One of them barked. 'Now, go!' he shouted.

Unable to walk away from her home, Aziza dragged her feet, sobbing, to the side window, and watched as the armed men made themselves at home inside. She whimpered through sobs when she saw them sit at the kitchen table and eat the *riz bi haleeb* dessert. 'This is my house!' she shouted through the window. 'This is my house.'

One of the soldiers picked up his rifle and shot her.

They say *nafas* is the most important ingredient in Palestinian cooking. Aziza put her *nafas* in the sweet, thick dessert hoping it would bring back her men. But as she took her last *nafas* on earth, she prayed the invaders would never enjoy a breath of air in her homeland.

10

SUN SETS OVER THE BRITISH MANDATE

GAZA, PALESTINE, 1948

The nature of all things was altered. Daily routines were disrupted, schools closed, outings cancelled and offices raided. Streets filled with only two kinds of people: invaders in their tanks, and the dispossessed fleeing for their lives. The fabric of Palestinian society was torn into shreds as one nation was removed so that another could occupy its place.

The usually quiet Mohatta Street was turned into an evacuation artery. Thousands of desperate families fled on foot from the northern parts of Palestine, carrying nothing but stories of loss and grief. When the houses of Tuffah could no longer accommodate the endless stream of refugees, the stream continued to run through to the next neighbourhood, and the one after, and the one after, and so on, until they reached the sea.

The *sheikh* sat on a chair outside his home, while his sons Karim and Rahim played a game of marbles nearby. He could see many of his neighbours also sitting or standing outside their homes. Some offered water to the passing refugees, others shared food, most stood by in shock and helplessness observing the tragedy and bearing witness to the catastrophe.

Abu-Awny walked over to the *sheikh* holding his daughter Souhailah's hand, followed by his two sons Azmy and Awny. He nodded a silent greeting to the *sheikh*, and the *sheikh* nodded a broken greeting back. The boys joined Karim and Rahim on the ground, while Souhailah watched them from her vantage point standing next to her father.

Karim looked up at Souhailah and smiled at the beautiful girl in the frilly pink dress. His father watched him with tender eyes. The softness and innocence of the moment that passed between Karim and Souhailah gave the *sheikh* a little reprieve. He smiled to himself. Now that his sweetheart was here, Karim would definitely be more determined to win.

'No news from Salama?' Abu-Awny's sombre question dragged the *sheikh* from his momentary escape and thrusted him back into the morbid reality that was all around them.

'I've been sitting here since morning hoping to spot them,' the *sheikh* replied. 'Khadija had prepared mattresses and blankets; she had expected her entire family would stay with us. But so far, none of them have appeared.'

'It must be hard for Khadija, not knowing what happened to them,' Abu-Awny said, as he produced a folded newspaper from his pocket. 'Here,' he said, passing it to the *sheikh*. 'Read it. This is the last newspaper out of Yaffa, printed just before the Jewish gangs claimed the city.'

The *sheikh* read the front-page headline: '*Yaffa's mayor sends telegram to Arab leaders: Bury us in the sand, then bury your heads in the sand.*' His eyes watered up. 'I thought the day Britain left this land would be a day of joy, but the English dogs have handed over the keys of our country to European Jews. They gave them everything. They gave them the official government buildings, the airports, the seaports, the military equipment and even the training. Everything! And they gave us checkpoints, prison cells, torture chambers and targeted assassinations for any one of us who tries to resist.'

'This is the dawn of a darker era than what we were forced to bear under the Ottomans and the English.' Abu-Awny's voice sounded broken under the weight of anxiety building inside of him.

'No,' the *sheikh* insisted, 'we have to believe this will not last. What they are doing is insane. You cannot empty a country of its people and claim it, just like that. The world will soon see this.' He pointed to the refugees. 'You cannot hide a crime like this one. Justice will win in the end.'

The two men stood in silence for a few minutes, as the endless parade of loss and anguish continued to march down their street.

Allah akbar. Allah akbar. Allah akbar. Allah akbar.

The *muezzin* announced the *Maghrib* prayer with a sorrowful sweet melodic voice, which reminded everyone of the greatness of the divine.

'God is greater!' Abu-Awny affirmed. '*Allah akbar*! He is our victor and in him we trust.'

'God is greater!' echoed the *sheikh*.

As the sun set on the British Mandate for Palestine, a new kind of darkness descended.

'*Allah akbar*, God is greater', the *muezzin* continued to call.

The men headed to the mosque to pray, while the women and children went inside their homes. The refugees who were not able to find shelter for the night, stopped their journey wherever they were and waited for the inevitable coming of dawn.

11

CACTUS WALK

GAZA, PALESTINE, 1948

Moftiya's eye could not see through the bright light.

'Walk!' the voice commanded.

'How?' she shouted. 'I cannot see!'

'Walk!' the voice repeated.

Moftiya took a hesitant step forward into the light, her one eye squinted into focus, trying to make out the dark shapes ahead.

'Walk!' the voice commanded once more.

She took another step and could make out the outline of thick and thorny branches. 'It's a huge cactus bush,' she protested.

'Walk!' the voice insisted.

'I can't walk through a cactus bush.' Moftiya was scared and weary.

The branches swayed and ruffled, bended and stretched, folded and pointed away from each other, until they cleared a long, seemingly endless trail through the middle.

'Walk, Moftiya – this is the only way!' the voice said.

Moftiya took cautious, frightened steps. 'How long is this trail? I'm tired,' she said, her voice small.

No one answered.

'How long?' she asked again, and again she was met with only silence.

'How long?' she screamed, but her scream came out muffled as it warped into something else. Boom! The earth tremored, sending shock waves through Moftiya's body. The bright light disappeared, and the cactus trail vanished into darkness. Moftiya sat up on her mattress, breathless. It took her a few seconds to distinguish dream from reality. The cactus was a dream, but this, the bombing – yes, she was sure it was a bombing – that was reality.

Heart pounding out of her rib cage, Moftiya ran to her son's room praying for God's mercy.

The *sheikh* was woken by the raid. He tried to move his legs. He wanted to jump to his feet, grab his children and take them to safety, but as he woke up he was confronted by his disability. The boys woke screaming and clung to one another, trembling in fear. Khadija swiftly put Muti on her breast and stretched her arm out, touching her two older boys gently. 'Shhhh . . . don't be afraid. Don't cry,' she tried to soothe them.

'Dear God,' the *sheikh* prayed. 'What am I to do now that the sky is raining bombs and the streets are sprouting tanks and guns? How am I, an invalid, going to protect my family?'

Moftiya stood by the door of their room and breathed a sigh of relief when she saw her son and his family were not harmed. She threw her scarf over her hair and hurried out into the street to check on her neighbours and to find out what was behind the explosion.

Outside, the people of Tuffah stood in their pyjamas and slippers, their necks extending towards the horizon where they could see plumes of smoke and fire light up the night sky. 'They blew up the railway!' The words echoed from house to house and passed from mouth to mouth. 'And now, they are bombing Gaza.'

Moftiya returned to her son and his family with a heavy heart. 'The Jewish gangs bombed the railway station, and some of the houses nearby.' She paused for a few moments before she added, 'It seems all our neighbours have decided to leave for safer ground.'

The *sheikh* reached for his *keffiyeh*. 'Jewish *gangs*?' he repeated, with clear bitterness. 'They are no longer called Jewish gangs. They're now a state with an army and an airport and a parliament, and all with international legitimacy.' He looked at Khadija, Moftiya and his boys, and his mind was made up. 'We also should leave for a few days, just until the Arab armies arrive and hopefully bring this horror to an end.'

Moftiya's heart sank. They are leaving. She recalled her dream. 'How long?' she had asked the voice behind the bright light as she walked through the cactus bushes. In Arabic, the word for cactus is *sabr* – but it's also the word for enduring patience. God was telling her that the road ahead is long, and she needs to be patient. That is what her dream had meant. She could feel the sting of the cactus thorns pricking her skin and piercing her heart.

'This is not going to end quickly,' she whispered to herself, as she walked with heavy, determined steps towards the chicken coop.

Moftiya guarded her chickens like they were her own children. She protected them from all creatures great and small – especially the two rascals that were her grandsons, whom she forbade from going anywhere near her coop. And while Moftiya took great care of her chickens, her chickens took care of her. She kept them fed and clean, and they produced enough eggs for her to sell at the market. It was important for Moftiya to maintain financial autonomy.

That was who she was – a woman who always stood on her own feet, never needing to rely on anyone else. Not even her beloved son.

Moftiya grabbed one of her chickens, lifted it into her arms, brought it closer to her face and with her one good eye, cried until its feathers were wet. She grabbed hold of a sharp knife and recited the slaughter prayer. She thanked the creature for the life she gave, and she thanked God for giving her the creature. '*Bismillah, wa Allahu akhbar*!' She swiftly ran the knife across its neck. Blood coated the bird's feathers and covered the tracks of Moftiya's tears.

The *sheikh* helped the boys get dressed while Khadija packed for the road. She made sure they had enough clothes, flour, olives, dates, and she filled a container with dried sycamore figs from their tree.

The *sheikh* retrieved his money purse, which he kept hidden under his mattress for a rainy day. He tied it around his waist and gestured to Khadija to help him. It was time for them to leave.

Outside their room, in the garden, they saw Moftiya reigning over a breakfast like no other. Bewildered, they sat with their boys in a circle around a big tray and watched her scoop the broth over the rice and layer it with chicken pieces. The *sheikh* wiped a tear, imagining how hard it must have been for his mother to slaughter one of her beloved birds. Moftiya looked up, and saw a tear escape from her son's eyes.

'Eat.' She spoke with unusual tenderness. 'I want you to be strong as you take on —' her voice caught. There were no more words to say.

'*Bismillah*! In the name of God!' the *sheikh* said, and rolled up his sleeves.

'*Bismillah*!' everyone repeated, as they reached into the tray.

There, in between the chewing and the swallowing, conversation threads hung unfinished in the air. All future plans were suspended. Matters that seemed important only a day ago, evaporated into thin air.

With a full stomach and an aching heart, Khadija helped the *sheikh* up on the donkey, grabbed Muti into her arms and told Karim and Rahim to hold on to the hem of her dress and to never let go.

Abu-Awny came to say goodbye. He had already sent his wife, Fatima, and their children to Fatima's family home in Khan Yunis. 'I came to let you know that I have volunteered to stay in Tuffah,' he said. 'I will be here to look after the empty houses and the elderly who might be left behind.'

'May God bless you.' Moftiya was relieved. 'You will give me good company.'

The *sheikh* and Khadija stared at her. They didn't think for a moment that she would choose to stay behind.

'Why?' The *sheikh* already knew the answer, but still he asked.

'Son, you must leave to protect your children. But I am too old to walk with you, and only God knows how far you will have to travel and for how long you will be away. I will be all right here. This is my home. I will not leave.'

Tearful, the *sheikh* kissed her hand as she recited *Ayatul Kursi* from the Quran and prayed for their safe return. The boys kissed their grandmother's hand and hugged her tight. Khadija threw herself into Moftiya's arms, and cried, 'I still don't know what has become of my mother, and now you!'

Moftiya held her daughter-in-law's face in the palm of her hands, and smiled. '*Inshallah*, you will be back in no time. And you will find me standing here like the sycamore tree, waiting for you. Or do you think I am more like the cactus, thorny and hard?'

The *sheikh* and Khadija couldn't help but smile. Moftiya had never before in her life told a joke.

Karim held on tight to his mother's dress as the young family walked out of Tuffah and into the big world beyond the old city. He was determined he would never abandon her again, as he had done at the water well. He was convinced the *majnoon* was in the sky, making frightening noises, dropping balls of fire, following them from street to street.

Karim looked over at his brother Rahim, who clutched his mother's dress on the other side. 'I'm not afraid, are you?' he asked.

Rahim couldn't pretend to be brave if he wanted to. He just looked at his brother and then lowered his head in shame.

Karim understood they were leaving under strange circumstances that he couldn't fully comprehend. While his parents were packing, he worked up his courage and ran outside and waited under the pomegranate tree in the open yard between their home and Abu-Awny's home, hoping to catch a glimpse of Souhailah, the girl next door with the beautiful curls. But the angry sky roared as Israeli warplanes hovered above, and when he closed his eyes, all he could see was the image of the *majnoon*. 'Terror, terrifying,' the *majnoon* whispered, and Karim ran back inside.

They walked for two hours at the speed of their youngest pair of feet, but eventually Rahim's four-year-old feet were too tired. Exhausted, he began to cry. The *sheikh* told Khadija and the boys to sit down and rest by the side of the road, and he rode away on his donkey.

The boys watched their father leave and held on even tighter to their mother's dress. Minutes later, the *sheikh* returned with a cart attached to his donkey. The boys clapped happily, delighted to see their father reappear, and even more thrilled by the sight of the cart. They climbed on board, and instantly their journey became more than tolerable – it became exciting! They were distracted from their fear by the newness of the adventure. They had never gone out with both their parents before, and certainly never this far from home. With their father riding the donkey, they could pretend they were a normal family that went out on picnics every Friday afternoon.

They travelled south, making lots of stops along the way. Spring was turning into a hot summer. The trees were loaded with fruit, and many farmers opened up their groves for the refugees to eat whatever they needed. They refilled their clay pots with water every time they passed a well, shared meals with groups of strangers in the fields and played with new friends at every opportunity. The boys' ears grew accustomed to the different dialects they encountered as they met families from all the different parts of Palestine. At the end of each day they giggled as they tried to mimic other children they had met, stretching their words like the boys from Yaffa or pronouncing the 'q' as a 'k' like the peasants. Sometimes they slept in rented rooms, sometimes in the fields under the stars. But no matter where they went, the Israeli warplanes followed – and they were forced to move again.

For the most part, the boys coped well. For them, all was right with the world so long as they had their mother's dress to hold on to, and their father's wisdom to provide them with a sense of security.

They finally arrived south of Khan Yunis, where most families from Tuffah had agreed to gather. Abu-Awny, who made regular trips back and forth from Khan Yunis to Tuffah to keep an eye on Fatima and his children, was there to greet them. He handed the *sheikh* a bag full of sycamore figs that Moftiya had sent to replenish their supplies, and told him that Israel had bombed a few sites in Tuffah, but that their home – so far – had been spared.

Karim was very happy to find Souhailah in Khan Yunis, and even more so when their family and Abu-Awny's family made plans to spend the night together in the same house. But his happiness did not last. The *majnoon* appeared in the sky over Rafah and, once again, sowed fear deep into the hearts of the defenceless families trying to find shelter on the ground beneath.

Abu-Awny was on his way back to Tuffah when he heard the bombing of Rafah. He rushed back to move his family to a safer place – but the question was, where would they all go? The men gathered around the *sheikh*, hoping their wise learned *sheikh* could tell them what to do. The *sheikh* weighed their limited options, and then said, 'We have no other choices – we should head towards the coast. There is no infrastructure there for Israel to bomb, and we could survive there on the fruits of the sea.'

The people of Tuffah carried their children and what few belongings they had, and once again were on the move.

This time the *sheikh*'s family travelled with Abu-Awny's family, and together they made their way towards the coast. But as soon as they left the boundaries of Khan Yunis, they were confronted by another challenge. The landscape changed from rich farming soil to dry desert sand, and the wheels of the donkey cart sank and refused to spin. The *sheikh* decided to trade the cart for two camels that could carry the children the rest of the journey.

At first the idea of travelling in a camel caravan led by the *sheikh*'s donkey captured the children's imagination, and filled their hearts with anticipation. But when the animals arrived, the children took one look at their big lips, large teeth and long legs and were petrified. They had never seen such beasts before.

Aware of Souhailah's presence, and of his need to impress her, Karim was the first to step forward. 'There is nothing to be afraid of,' he assured his brothers. 'Watch me, I'll be the first to sit on the camel.'

The young boy mounted the camel with an exaggerated show of courage, and called out: 'Souhailah, come sit behind me. I'll take care of you.'

Fatima and Khadija smiled broadly, and Fatima quickly picked-up her daughter and sat her behind Karim. Souhailah's heart was beating fast, both in fear and shyness. She kept quiet, and did not protest.

Not to be outdone by Karim, Awny, Azmy and Rahim bravely sat on the other camel's back, masking their obvious anxiety behind false, frozen smiles.

Karim's camel was in the lead. Once all the children were seated, his camel stood up on its hind legs and jolted forward. Karim threw courage to the wind, and let out a terrified scream. 'Let me down!' he cried. 'Please, let me down!'

The rest of the children joined his screaming and crying. Their parents tried to convince them to stay on the camels, but to no avail. The camels were returned, and the two families continued their journey on foot, led by the *sheikh* riding his donkey, while Khadija, Fatima, and Abu-Awny took turns carrying the children who grew too tired along the way.

At first they were relieved to see the blue line of the sea on the horizon, but as they got closer their eyes filled with the scale of the disaster that had befallen their people. Relief gave way to shock and grief. Fatima fell to her knees, and sobbed. Abu-Awny prayed, '*Hasbi allah we nam alwakeel*, God will suffice, and in him I trust.'

As far as the eye could see, the entire coast of the Gaza Strip – stretching from Jabalia in the north, to where they stood in Al-Mawasi, to the south of Khan Yunis – was covered with tents to accommodate the hundreds of thousands of Palestinian refugees who had been driven at gunpoint out of their homes in order to create a Jewish state for the Jewish people.

The *sheikh* glanced at Khadija who stood still, tears falling and mind churning with questions she was too afraid to ask. 'Your family is probably here,' he consoled her. 'We will find them.'

The refugees organised themselves into camps according to the villages and cities they came from, and erected signs to help people find each other. There was a camp for people who had fled from Lydda; a camp for people who had fled from Jaffa; and a camp for the people who had fled from 'Be'er Sheva'. The signs were endless, the scope of the crime committed unimaginable.

Khadija's eyes gleamed with hope every time they saw a sign, but they did not pass a sign that said Salama.

'So, this is it?' Abu-Awny said to no one. 'We are now a nation of refugees?'

'Yes,' said the *sheikh*. 'The wealthy mansion owners and the poor peasants, the farmers and the doctors, the educated and the illiterate – all of us, an entire nation, we are all refugees looking for shelter in the farthest corner of our homeland.'

The *sheikh* and Abu-Awny stopped when the last of the refugee camps ended.

'Where is the Tuffah camp?' the *sheikh* wondered out loud.

'Knowing the men from our district, they probably didn't want to be close to the other refugees. They probably walked further south and set up camp next to the Egyptian borders.'

'What idiots.' The *sheikh* was not impressed.

'They think their women are so beautiful, they don't want the modern men from Haifa to be seduced by them.' Abu-Awny spoke through his teeth.

'Or maybe they just wanted to be as close to the Egyptian border as possible?' the *sheikh* said with resignation.

They walked south of Tel Zo'reb. There on an empty and desolate stretch of beach they found the sign that read '*Tuffah*', and knew that was where their people had gathered. It was far from all the other camps, right next to the Egyptian border fence.

'Having endured the air bombardment,' the *sheikh* said, 'the people of Tuffah wanted to be close to a fast exit through the Egyptian border.'

Abu-Awny helped set up a tent for the two families and, after a short rest, told them he needed to head back to Tuffah, promising he would return regularly to check on them.

Abu-Awny opened his arms to Fatima to bid her well, but she exploded. 'Wait!' her voice carried all the anger and all the fear she had kept locked inside. 'Don't you dare leave me here! Take me back to my family home in Khan Yunis. I would rather die with my parents than be left here in this desolate camp without you, and without them.'

Karim was stung by Fatima's words. He couldn't bear to think he would have to say goodbye to Souhailah. But there was nothing he could do but watch Abu-Awny's family walk away, Souhailah sitting on her father's shoulders, blonde curls flying in the breeze.

12

AL-NAKBA

GAZA, PALESTINE, 1948–1949

The Tuffah refugee camp was run with great efficiency. Tasks and duties were clearly assigned, and schedules were put in place. Some men went into the sea each day at dawn and came back with nets full of sardines. Others were responsible for keeping the peace in and around the camp. They checked on everyone, and made sure there were enough blankets and water. Women gathered in circles around cooking pots or washing loads. The *sheikh*, too, needed to fulfil his role. Much to his students' dismay, he decided to resume his classes.

'Education must not stop until one's heart stops,' he told his disappointed students, who were hoping they would not need to study for a while. 'Without education, we will lose everything.'

At the end of each day, while the women put the children to sleep, the men gathered outside the *sheikh*'s tent to listen to the news on the only radio they had. After the broadcast, the *sheikh* would share with the circle his analysis. During this time Karim always sat next to his father, his head resting on his father's knee until he fell asleep.

Summer gave way to autumn and the cold winter breeze brought further unrest and fear of a future fraught with more hardship. The men and women became restless. One night, as they gathered outside the *sheikh*'s tent, someone asked, 'How long must we sit here while this disaster unfolds?'

The *sheikh* did not have a definitive answer. All he could do was explain that by the time the Arab armies arrived with their outdated weapons, their poor coordination and lack of training, two thirds of the Palestinian population were already ethnically cleansed from their homes.

'What we see here in Gaza is only a fraction of the disaster that has befallen our people,' he explained. 'Hundreds of thousands of Palestinian refugees were literally pushed into the sea in Akka and Haifa. They climbed into overcrowded boats and sailed away to Lebanon. Others travelled by foot to Syria and Jordan. Two thirds of our people were dispossessed of everything they own, their homes handed over to Jewish immigrants from Europe.'

The *sheikh* stopped talking, distracted by the figure of a man walking along the beach in their direction. When the man got closer, the *sheikh* recognised him. It was Ibrahim, Khadija's stepfather. Ibrahim greeted the men and sat quietly next to the *sheikh*. The *sheikh* took in a deep breath before he asked, 'How is your family?'

Ibrahim looked into the fire, his face hardened by the horrors he had witnessed. 'Salama put up a good fight,' he said, 'but we were poorly equipped, with one rifle for every four fighters. We took turns guarding our town but the flight of Palestinians from Jewish gangs and the horror stories that spread about the massacres caused great panic. Everyone in Salama locked their homes, grabbed their keys and ran.'

'Aziza?' the *sheikh* asked.

'We weren't there when it happened,' Ibrahim continued. 'We, the fighters, were told to wait for the Egyptian authorities at a designated meeting place. They were supposed to give us more weapons. We were ready to fight with them, and the other Arab forces. But the Egyptian forces came and took our weapons from us and told us to go home. They didn't want local militias interfering with their operations. They disarmed us and left us there with nothing. Unarmed, we rushed back to Salama, but by then it was under Israeli control. The soldiers forced us to keep walking south towards Gaza.'

'What happened to Aziza?' the *sheikh* asked again.

'On the way, I ran into one of our neighbours. She told me Aziza did not leave. No one has seen or heard from her since.'

A gut-wrenching scream was heard inside the *sheikh*'s tent. '*Yumma! Yumma!*' Khadija wailed into the night. Her heart shattered into a million pieces.

The bleak winter of 1948 was unbearable. Icy wind blew water from the sea over the camps, cloaking the refugees' tents with salt and sand. But as the people of Tuffah, and other refugees along Gaza's shore, huddled under UN blankets and around camp fires, they said a prayer in gratitude of God's mercy. They had heard of worse stories befalling their brothers and sisters, who were herded into refugee camps in neighbouring countries, where heavy snowfall flattened their thin UN tents. They reminded themselves that they were still on Palestinian soil, at least – they were still breathing the air of their homeland.

The eventual arrival of the disjointed and weak Arab armies failed to raise hope or lift spirits. It was too little, too late. They came after gruesome acts of terror and massacres by the Jewish gangs had been committed. They came after more than 400 Palestinian cities and villages had been emptied of their populations. They came without a coordinated strategy and without shared diplomatic goals. The Arab armies came after the facts were established on the ground, and after Israel, backed by powerful international allies, had become a member state of the United Nations. The Arab armies waged war after two thirds of the Palestinian population were driven off their lands to pave the way for the arrival of Jewish immigrants from Europe who were desperate to believe that God had given them a land without a people for a people without a land.

The people of the Tuffah camp gathered on a cold winter's night in a circle around the camp fire and waited for Abu-Sa'adah to fix the radio so they could listen to the news. Abu-Sa'adah fiddled with the antenna with a sense of urgency. At that moment he felt he had the most important job in the camp, tasked with the miracle of producing sound through metal. The men shifted from side to side, rubbed their hands together, clicked their tongues, coughed, sighed, huffed and puffed, until . . .

'Whooooosh . . . Radio al-Arab . . .' the sombre, deep voice of the newsreader came through.

Like sunflowers turn to the sun, the men stretched their necks and pointed their ears in the radio's direction.

'The Zionists' aggression . . . whoooooosh . . .' Cold wind gusts

delivered the voice of the announcer in waves. 'Whoooooosh . . .
air force . . . whooooooosh . . . Egypt . . . whooooooosh spokesper-
son . . . whooooooosh . . . air raid . . . . whooooooosh . . . Rafah . . .
whoosh . . .'

The men looked at each other, frustrated and unable to make
sense of what they heard. Abu-Sa'adah slowly touched the antenna
with the tip of his finger, and the signal returned. '. . . condemned
the actions of the Zionist state.'

Excited to hear the presenter so clearly, the men shouted
instructions at Abu-Sa'adah: 'Don't move! Keep your finger there!'
Abu-Sa'adah froze, and the men returned to their listening position.
That was when they heard the radio announcer say clearly, 'Gaza
has fallen!'

Abu-Sa'adah lifted his finger and shouted, 'No!'

Fear and panic ensued. Voices grew from whispers to shouts.

'Gaza has fallen?'

'Have we just lost our homes?'

'Where do we go now?'

'We can't stay here.'

'Run. We must run!'

Kerosene lamps were lit, tents ruffled, pots clanked, sleeping
children woke. Questions were asked.

'Where do we go?'

'What's the plan?'

'Does anyone have a plan?'

Tents were emptied, cleaned, dismantled and folded.

'We are near the Egyptian border. We must run into Egypt.'

'Egypt!'

'Egypt!'

'Egypt!'

At first the *sheikh* watched in silence, unable to stop the spread of panic. But when he heard the men from Tuffah talk of crossing into Egypt, he could no longer keep his mouth shut.

'Are you out of your minds?' he shouted. 'You want to cross the border? To leave? This is what Israel wants you to do; leave your country!'

No one paid the *sheikh* any attention. They all continued to pack and talk amongst themselves.

The *sheikh* raised his voice higher. 'Israel is not allowing any of the refugees to return. You will not be allowed back into Gaza.'

Still, no one was looking at him. The *sheikh* roared with anger. 'You want to run into the Sinai Desert? It is a desert – you will die in it!' But even that seemed to fall on deaf ears. No one listened. Not even his own wife, Khadija, who was inside their tent packing for the journey.

With everyone rushing to pack and leave, the *sheikh* found himself left alone. He struggled to rise on his wobbly feet, unassisted, and to shuffle his way into his tent, leaning the weight of his body onto his walking stick. Once inside, he let his knees fold and fell onto the mattress. He called to Khadija, but his wife was so focused on packing she didn't even see him come into the tent.

'Khadija,' he called again. 'Come, sit next to me.'

Khadija folded the last piece of clothing into the travel sack and sat next to the *sheikh*.

'Don't pack.' His words made no sense to her. 'We're not leaving.'

Khadija was confused. 'How do we stay here alone? How will we survive without the others? Who will bring us food? Who will fish for us? Who will . . .' The more questions she asked, the more afraid she became.

The *sheikh* wrapped his arm around her.

'We don't have our donkey cart to carry the children, and Abu-Awny is not here to help us.'

'But,' Khadija argued, 'we can ask others to —'

'No,' the *sheikh* interrupted with a firm voice. 'Khadija, we cannot burden others with our load. Everyone has their own families, children and burdens to carry. I'm sorry. I know how much you want to join them. But I wish . . .' the *sheikh*'s voice caught. He ran his hands over his legs, feeling a surge of anger rise like a tide inside of him. He grabbed his walking stick and threw it across the tent. The stick bounced off the tarp before it fell only a few steps away from him.

Shocked to see the *sheikh* lose control, Khadija's eyes filled with tears.

'Go without me,' the *sheikh*'s voice trembled. 'You can walk and use the donkey to carry the children in turns.'

Khadija threw her arms around him. 'Don't!' she said, kissing his forehead. 'Don't think that way. I can't leave you. Don't ever say this nonsense again. We will all stay together – live or die *together.*'

They lay down on the mattress and pulled their three sleeping boys tightly into their embrace.

'They are leaving without us.' The *sheikh*'s voice carried more disappointment and sorrow than Khadija's heart could handle.

'They didn't even say goodbye,' she whispered in disbelief.

'We must forgive them. They have their own families to look after.' The *sheikh* stroked her hair.

If abandonment has a sound, Khadija and the *sheikh* heard it that night as they listened to their friends and neighbours packing up their tents and belongings and leaving them behind.

Khadija opened up her eyes at dawn, and slowly adjusted to the shadows inside the tent. A heaviness weighed upon her chest, and a sense of foreboding hung in the air. She held her breath momentarily as she tried desperately to hear a familiar sound outside, but there were none. No calling for the dawn prayer, no sleepy footsteps, no clumsy clinking of pots, no water running, no tarps fluttering or tents zipping or unzipping, no whispers, hushes, humming, singing, coughing or sneezing. There was nothing but the sound of the waves whooshing upon the shore, and the soft, cold wind blowing.

'We're the only ones left here!' she gasped, as she came to terms with this daunting new reality. She sat up on her mattress and ran her hand softly over her sleeping boys' faces. She turned to her husband and watched him inhale and exhale deeply in his sleep. 'We're the only ones left here!' she repeated, in urgent whispers.

Afraid, her heart pounded, her breathing became faster, her tears started to fall. Muti, ever tuned in to his mother's moods, began to stir. At first, Khadija did not hear him over the loud drumming of her heart, but when the toddler moved into her arms and reached into her dress with his tiny fingers, she could no longer ignore him. Her heartbeat slowed down, her breathing returned to normal and her anxiety disappeared as she watched, with adoring eyes, her youngest help himself to her breast, latching with his open mouth onto her nipple. Muti curled his hand around Khadija's finger and gazed into her eyes. Khadija's milk flowed, and she felt a powerful surge of love and faith engulf her. The image of the angel of good fortune appeared in her mind's eye. He had promised that her boys would have a long life. He had promised she would live to see her grandchildren. 'Dear God of mercy,' she prayed, 'don't abandon us!'

At first, the *sheikh*'s family survived on what remained of the sycamore figs and dates they still had, while they waited patiently for Abu-Awny's visit, dreaming of the fresh supplies he would bring. But days passed, and Abu-Awny never came.

A few sunrises later, Khadija cautioned the *sheikh*, 'We only have a few dates left. There is nothing else to feed the boys. What will we do tomorrow?'

The *sheikh* took her hand gently. 'Abu-Awny is probably on his way,' he assured her. The *sheikh* and Khadija gave the last few dates they had to Rahim and Karim, and they went to sleep on an empty stomach.

That night, strong wind gusts rattled their tent while an angry sea whipped it with foam and sand. Lightning struck, illuminating tired, cold faces too hungry to scream. Thunder roared and the sea heaved. The boys moved closer, each tightening their grip on the part of their parents' garment that they had access to. The family huddled together, deserted, floating through the night, in an angry cold ocean of hunger and uncertainty.

The *sheikh* turned to prayer. 'Repeat after me,' he instructed his children. '*Bismillah alrahman alraheem*, in the name of Allah the merciful, the compassionate.' He recited one *surah* from the Quran after another, his wife and children echoing his words and amplifying his prayers. When the storm finally ended, exhausted from fear, hunger, cold and anxiety, the family huddled under the blankets and surrendered to sleep.

Of course they knew the sun had risen, but they wanted to stay under the blankets anyway. After all the horror they had experienced during the previous night's storm, they wanted to savour the comfort and warmth. Besides, what was there to get up for? Nothing new. No one came. No food to eat.

The *sheikh* resumed his prayers from the previous night in hushed, slight whispers. The boys stared at the tent ceiling, too tired to say a word.

Khadija was the first to speak. 'Birds,' she said. 'Do you hear them? Birds are chirping!'

'Birds!' Karim's curious voice responded. 'Chirping. I hear them too.'

The *sheikh* smiled and kept praying under the covers. Rahim did not move. He closed his eyes and tried to go back to sleep. But Muti had a much more enthusiastic response. He lifted his head off his mother's breast and looked around. '*Foor*,' birds, he babbled. '*Foor*.' He pointed to the door of the tent. When no one took him outside to see the birds, he got angry and babbled an endless stream of '*Foor* blab lo *foor* dh dha *foor* o *foor* a *foor*!'

Smiles turned to giggles inside the tent. A positive energy ran through them, touching them one by one.

Karim rose to his feet. 'I'll take you outside to see the birds.' He reached for baby Muti and scooped him into his arms. Muti clapped as they both stepped outside the tent. Only seconds later Karim was shouting for Rahim. 'Rahim! Rahim! Come outside!'

Rahim opened his eyes and willed himself to move slowly.

'Rahim!' Karim shouted again and again. '*Yallah*, come outside!'

The *sheikh* and Khadija watched as Rahim dragged himself from under the blankets and followed his brother outside. Seconds later, they heard Rahim's energised voice rising with excitement and joyful laughter. '*Yumma*,' he called out to his mother. '*Yumma*, come out! You must see this!'

Khadija dragged herself from under the warm blankets and wrapped herself in her woollen shawl. She stepped out, and screamed. '*Ya allah!*'

She ran back into the tent to rouse the *sheikh*. 'Get up!' she insisted, and pulled the blankets off him. 'You have to see this!' Khadija handed the *sheikh* his cane. 'Our prayers have been answered. God is listening. Get up!'

Khadija helped her husband to his feet and out of the tent. The two of them stood bewildered by the tens of red, rounded objects that spread along the shore, breaking the monotony of the blue and beige seascape.

'What, in God's name?'

The *sheikh* did not finish, when Karim ran to him yelling, 'Look! Delicious red apples are everywhere!' Karim took a big bite out of a red, ripe apple, letting its juice run down his hand all the way to his elbow.

It seemed that the night's storm had knocked off dozens of apple crates from a trading boat, and washed them ashore – a true act of divine intervention.

The neighbours returned.

They carried their belongings, their children, their broken egos and humiliation, and returned to the camp south of Tel Zo'reb. One by one they greeted the *sheikh* and Khadija, who returned the greetings with smiles of relief.

'*Alhamdulillah*, thank God you look well!' the neighbours said, as they tried awkwardly to hide their shame. How could they have done this? How did they have the heart to leave their beloved *sheikh* and his family behind?

But the *sheikh* and Khadija had no time for sadness or reproach, and they certainly had no patience for pity.

'We were not abandoned,' the *sheikh* corrected his neighbours. 'God looked after us.' He pointed at the apple crates. 'Help yourselves,' he offered.

And help themselves they did. Young and old, they fell on the apples like a swarm of locusts on a field of wheat.

'We are not here to stay,' Abu-Sa'adah said, as he wiped the apple juice dripping down his chin. 'We came back for you. So we can all return together.'

'Return home?' Khadija shouted, unable to contain her excitement.

'Yes,' said Abu-Sa'adah. 'In Sinai we met Egyptian soldiers who were surprised to hear that we ran from Gaza. They told us a ceasefire had been struck between Israel and Egypt. The war is over. And, the best part is, Gaza did not fall under Israel's occupation.'

'We did not lose Gaza?' The *sheikh* breathed a sigh of relief.

'No, and we did not lose our homes!' Abu-Sa'adah said. 'It turns out, we reached the wrong conclusion based on bad radio reception.'

'So, who controls Gaza now?' inquired the *sheikh*.

'The Egyptian army. It has full control.'

The *sheikh* sighed deeply. 'Still, we are not the ones in charge of our land. And we are not the ones in charge of our own destiny.'

Abu-Sa'adah's son, Salem, hoisted a Palestinian flag on a stick, raised it high in the air and began the march home, followed closely by the *sheikh* on his donkey, and the rest of the Tuffah families behind. The journey home was bittersweet. For hours the families of Tuffah rode along the coast, passing refugee camps filled with those who had been driven away from their homes inland, now claimed as Israel. Hundreds of thousands of refugees languished, suspended in misery, their homes stolen, their land taken, their national identities forever denied.

As they passed them by, the people of Tuffah thought of how fortunate they were not to have lost their homes, and prayed their brothers and sisters in these camps along the coastline of Palestine would one day return to theirs. That day is yet to come.

Sorrow hung thick in the air as the community from Tuffah dragged their feet in silence past clusters of dispossession and misery. Karim and Rahim clung to their mother's dress, afraid of being lost – after all, it seemed everything was getting lost. That's what the adults kept saying. '*Kol shey dha'a*, everything is lost.' What was *everything*? The children did not understand. Their mother's dress was there, their parents were there, everyone they knew from Tuffah was there, baby brother Muti and the donkey and Abu-Sa'adah . . . and . . . *everything*. Yet their own father kept saying, 'We've lost everything.'

The procession passed through Deir Al Balah, a Palestinian city in the central Gaza Strip, fourteen kilometres south of Gaza City, famous for its date palms. Local volunteers greeted them and offered them plates of dates and cups of coffee and water. They ate with no appetite for food or conversation. Beneath the trees, the earth was planted with refugees. Some slept in tents, some on blankets, some lay on the bare ground. A woman called out the name of a child she could not find. A man wept under a tree. Tearful eyes stared at them and stared through them. Lips trembled prayers: '*Hasbi allah we nam alwakeel*, God will suffice, and in him we trust.'

They continued their walk until finally they reached Tuffah. The *sheikh*'s family turned into the small alleyway that led to their home. They were confronted by the passage of time and the tyranny of neglect. The gate to their house was almost completely concealed behind a thick façade of tall grass and wild plants, with only a narrow clearing on the side, used by Moftiya to get in and out of their home.

The boys cut through the wild grass and green vines. Karim pushed open the gate and Moftiya ran across the garden to welcome them home.

'*Alhamdulillah*, praise be to God! You are back!' Moftiya's thin bony arms stretched so wide, they drew the entire family within her embrace.

As the family slowly disentangled from Moftiya's arms, smiles on faces and laughter on lips, Moftiya turned her focus to her daughter-in-law.

'You have another baby on the way,' she said with delight.

Khadija nodded.

'Good!' Moftiya allowed a smile to stretch across her face. She placed her hand on Khadija's belly. '*Inshallah*, this one will arrive by the start of the winter.' She turned to her son. 'I see nothing stops you. Not even the war!'

An awkward moment passed before all three adults laughed so deeply and so wholeheartedly, it felt like they had reached into the depth of their bellies, pulled out long-forgotten joy and stretched it on their faces, softening features that had been hardened over months of dejection.

Moftiya plucked fresh zucchinis, onions, lemons and hot chillies from the garden and sat down with her son, chopping and dicing vegetables while catching up on nine months of separation. With Khadija outside washing and dressing the boys, Moftiya had her son all to herself – or so she hoped.

'*Dastoor!*' came Abu-Awny's voice, announcing his and Fatima's arrival.

Fatima stood by the door, a cheeky smile spreading across her face as she watched the *sheikh* chopping onions earnestly. Next to her, Abu-Awny was clearly disturbed by the *sheikh*'s domesticity. 'You really shouldn't be doing this,' he rebuked him. 'This is women's work!'

The *sheikh* raised his eyebrows but said nothing. Abu-Awny felt he may have upset him with his remark, and wanted to lighten the air around them with a joke. 'Truth is, I'm just worried you'll open Fatima's eyes to the possibility that she can add chopping onions to my list of chores.'

'Oh, believe me my dear,' Fatima teased, 'my eyes are already open wide!' Everyone laughed. 'May God give you a long life, *Sheikh* Hussein,' Fatima added in a deliberate tone. 'And may he keep you, a crown above the heads of *all men*.' She glanced at her husband when she said 'all men', and he was quick to respond with an 'Ouch!'

Still laughing, the *sheikh* wanted to steer away from this dangerous conversation. One never knew when humour turned to drama between Abu-Awny and Fatima.

'You know what would go well with these vegetables?' he asked.

'*Khobeeza* from the garden.' Fatima was quick with an answer. 'That's what everyone in Gaza is cooking today.'

During the war, *khobeeza*, a wild, edible weed, fiercely took over the uncultivated and neglected lands of Palestine. It grew in the fields, on the sides of roads, in pathways, in domestic gardens and in the cracks of the mud homes. *Khobeeza* covered the entire grounds of the shared garden between the two households.

'*Khobeeza*!' Khadija echoed, as she walked into the room. All eyes went to her. Her face was relaxed, her smile was glowing and her eyes were gleaming, finally free of fear and anxiety. Finally at home.

Fatima and Khadija hugged one another, and giggled like two schoolgirls as they checked each other out.

'*Hamdellah, alsalamah.*'

'Thank God you're all safe!'

Khadija shrieked with joy when she saw Fatima's belly. 'Oh my God! You're expecting too?'

Arm in arm, the two women went into the garden to harvest *khobeeza*. They took their time, picking out the best leaves while they swapped stories of relentless husbands who managed to steal private moments of pleasure even in the worst of times – or, as Fatima put it, '*especially* in the worst of times! Isn't it always when they need *it* the most!'

While Fatima and Khadija giggled, calculated due dates and rubbed one another's bellies, they noticed Karim reclaiming his romantic spot under the pomegranate tree quietly, waiting patiently for Souhailah to emerge. The women squatted in the high *khobeeza* grass behind the lemon tree, and waited to see what would happen next.

Souhailah finally came out and joined Karim under the pomegranate tree. The boy, nervous, offered her a handshake. She hesitated.

'Good girl,' her mother whispered to Khadija, as they watched on from the distance.

'You know,' Khadija shot back, 'the God who created her, has also created others. She's not the only girl in the world!'

Fatima was about to answer Khadija's insolence when they saw a shy Souhailah stretch out her hand to take Karim's. The women giggled quietly. Karim held on to Souhailah's hand and wouldn't

Fatima and Khadija, c. 1958.

let go. Souhailah was not impressed. She panicked. She pulled her hand away and ran back into her home.

Khadija and Fatima laughed to their heart's content. 'She's her mother's daughter,' Fatima bragged, 'a truly virtuous girl!'

Karim heard his mother and Fatima's laughter and looked in their direction. He discovered them crouching awkwardly under the lemon tree. He knew they were laughing at him, but he did not care. He was utterly content – at last, he had touched the hand of the girl of his dreams.

By nightfall, the smell of *khobeeza* stew rose from every house in Tuffah, and mingled in the air over Mohatta Street, marking a celebration of a return to life. The *sheikh*'s family went to sleep in the same order as before, but after the *sheikh* told them their bedtime story, and the kerosene lamp was dimmed, Karim could not sleep. His mind raced with an endless stream of disturbing thoughts. *What had happened?*

Karim would learn many years later that what his young eyes had witnessed since the spring of 1948 was *Al-Nakba*, the catastrophe that marked the establishment of an Israeli–Jewish state on the soil of his homeland. But while it was happening, there was no name for it. There were no words to explain it. The images of that year flashed before his eyes. Unforgettable, sad faces in ragged tents, homeless families in the fields, young mothers and children sleeping under the trees, Khadija crying on an empty beach praying for God's mercy – and always, the fear of the *majnoon* in the sky and the possibility of senseless terror on the ground. These images and these memories would haunt him forever.

1948 and 1949 were years of *osra*, hardships. They were also years of resilience, and many acts of kindness. Palestinian locals in Gaza were kind and hospitable to the refugees, who were double their own population. And Gaza was kind and hospitable to all its inhabitants. Its earth gifted them with nutritious wild plants like mallow, endives and sorrel. Its sea filled the nets of its fishermen with more sardines than any other time. Hunger and mass starvation were kept at bay. The old, formidable city, accustomed to rising and falling only to rise again was, once more, well on its way to its resurrection.

13

RITE OF PASSAGE

GAZA, PALESTINE, SUMMER, 1949

Karim, Rahim and Muti took turns stepping in and out of the portable iron tub. Khadija filled a jug with water and poured it onto her sons' heads, savouring the sensation of the cool droplets that bounced onto her dress and offered a much-welcomed reprieve from the heat.

'*Mashallah*, they have grown so much!' A familiar voice filled Khadija's heart with joy. She dropped the water jug and turned around, screaming, '*Yumma!*'

The boys laughed and thought their mother was playing a game. But Khadija wasn't playing. She saw her mother Aziza standing with her arms open calling her to fall into her embrace. There was so much catching up to do! Khadija wanted to know what had happened to her mother in Salama, and she wanted to tell her about their time in the camp by the sea – and that she was pregnant again and hoping for her help, like every other time. But her mother's image faded away.

Her three sons stood naked in the iron tub, and their skin had begun to turn blue. 'Come on, *Yumma!*' Karim called her attention.

Moftiya, who had heard Khadija's cry, rushed in and offered to help her get the boys dressed. She had heard Khadija calling her mother a few times before, and her heart ached every time.

The boys were ready wearing their long white garments, their *thawbs*. Khadija combed their hair and gazed at them with adoring eyes.

'Karim,' she spoke softly. 'You are the eldest. You must be a good role model for your brothers, Rahim and Muti. Everyone we know is coming to celebrate with us and to congratulate you all, so be polite and welcoming to our guests.'

In the six-and-a-half years he had been alive, Karim had never seen his home become the centre of such a lavish celebration. Even during *Eid*, visitors only came for short periods, dropping in and out quickly after having a sip of coffee and a bite of something sweet. But this was different – something much bigger. Karim and his brothers were too swept up in the excitement of it, too distracted by the sweet aroma of the *ghoraybeh* shortbread that Khadija and Moftiya baked, too overwhelmed by the guests who were arriving, that they never asked what the purpose of the celebration was, or why they seemed to be at the centre of it.

Dozens of lanterns lit up the garden. Guests sat in big circles. Some brought sweets, others brought musical instruments: an oud, a couple of flutes, tambourines and *tablas*.

The women's song and laughter outside in the garden permeated the snorting and guffawing of the *sheikh*'s companions, as trays of sweets and juice were extended.

'You will have to start with Karim,' the *sheikh* whispered to his neighbour, Hamada, who was busy sharpening his knife. 'If you start with his younger brothers Karim will bolt, and there will be no one in this neighbourhood fast enough to catch him.'

Fatima was thrilled to see her friend Salwa and her bags of wonders arrive at the party. She helped her find a well-lit spot in the garden where she set up her rug and her bowls and brushes. Salwa lived nearby, just off Mohatta Street, not far from the Gaza railway station. She had refused a few marriage proposals, insisting she was waiting for 'the prince of her dreams to arrive'. Her love for fashion trends and the latest beauty products made her Tuffah's most called-upon hairdresser, beautician and henna artist. Her popularity rivalled only Fatima's, with both women always invited to attend every party in the district.

'Souhailah,' Fatima called out, as soon as Salwa was ready to begin. 'Quick, come get your hands done!'

Souhailah sat on the rug, her frilly pink hoop dress falling in a perfect circle around her. She extended her small hands to Salwa and patiently watched as the henna artist drew elaborate patterns. When she was finished, Salwa winked at her, and said, 'Your hands are so pretty now, everyone will think you are a bride tonight!'

Souhailah hid a shy smile and rose slowly to her feet, mindful not to smear the wet henna paste that drew cold lines on the palms of her hand. She took careful steps, her arms stretched forward away from her fancy pink dress, and sat next to her mother. Fatima, always the life of any party, drummed on her *tabla* and sang, the women joining her during the chorus of each song.

'With joy your days be filled

Eyes turned with joy to see

    the face of the beautiful one

With joy your days be filled

White horses and red roses

    await the beautiful one.'

A soft, fluttering rose petal landed on Souhailah's dress. She looked up and saw Karim perched on the tree branch above her. She looked down again quickly, pretending not to have seen the petal – or the boy who had thrown it.

Khadija finally emerged from the house with the sweet trays, passing them to the guests who offered their congratulations. Like a monkey, Karim quickly climbed down the tree and pushed himself into the vacant spot right next to Souhailah, ready to reach into the oncoming tray of sweets.

'It's your lucky night,' Khadija teased him. 'You get to sit next to the most beautiful girl at this party.'

The women laughed, and Fatima sang.

'With henna from Mecca I'll draw on your hand

Your beauty is more radiant than the full moon . . .'

Karim grabbed a piece of *ghoraybeh* shortbread and devoured it. He turned to Souhailah to see if she, too, was enjoying the sweets. Instead, Souhailah sat sulking, her eyes fixed on the *ghoraybeh*, her hands still covered in wet Henna paste, totally unusable. Karim grabbed another piece of *ghoraybeh* and placed it into Souhailah's mouth. This romantic gesture was not lost on Fatima and Khadija, who exchanged tender, sweet smiles.

The songs continued, and the sweets kept coming. Things were going so well, until Khadija stood up and said, '*Yallah*, Karim. It's time.'

Khadija took her son's hand and walked him to where the men were gathered. 'Remember, you are big and strong. Show them you are a man!' she said, as she let go of his hand and propelled him into the room. Karim stepped forward, turning back a few times to look at his mother who stood by the door, smiling nervously.

Inside the *sheikh*'s room, Karim was ambushed. Hamada whisked him up and pinned him to a chair, right opposite the neighbourhood barber. The two men grabbed his legs, one on each side, and parted them. The barber swiftly lifted his *thawb* and reached for his penis. Karim was mortified, unable to understand how all these respectable men could be so dirty and crass. This behaviour went against everything he had been taught about honour and shame, but there was no time to process anything. The barber, with one wave of his blade, cut off the foreskin around his penis, and gave him a hot water bottle to soothe the pain. Karim, wounded with shame and relieved it was over, pressed the hot water bottle against his throbbing penis and sat in shock. He did not cry. He watched as the men cheered and congratulated him.

'You're a man now,' they said. 'Be brave. Don't let your brothers see you cry! Show them how brave you are.'

Karim put on a brave face, first for Rahim, then for Muti. It only took a minute, and all three boys were circumcised.

14

BORROWED

GAZA, PALESTINE, SUMMER, 1949

The boys were kept at home for a few weeks to recover from the circumcision, but Karim felt as though he was imprisoned with his brothers for an eternity. When the *sheikh* finally announced it was time for them to take a dip in the salty waters of the Mediterranean to ensure they were totally healed, Karim, Rahim and Muti were ecstatic.

They joined the large group of women and children from Tuffah who were also going for a swim. Fatima was always the instigator of such fun outings. She organised who got invited, who brought the food pots, who cooked the stews, who baked the bread, who brought the watermelons, and all the other fine details needed to ensure a beautiful day on the white, sandy Gazan beach.

The women's laughter and the children's shrieks were drowned out by the occasional singing that reverberated from their caravan of donkey carts that headed to the coast. Along the way, the women turned their headscarves into canopies to shelter their children from the burning sun above, as they sang:

'Why is the sea laughing

As I walk seductively

To fill my water jugs'

It only took a few minutes to unload the carts and organise the blankets and picnic pots on the sand before everyone ran into the water. Women and children, young and old, bounced off the burning sand straight into the sea. Karim, Rahim and Muti were allowed in the water up to Karim's waist and Muti's shoulders. Moftiya and Khadija stood in the shallows watching over them.

'*Yumma!* Come!' Karim called out to his mother. 'We'll look after you.'

Khadija was melting from the heat and didn't need much convincing. She lifted her long dress up to her knees and waded in, exhilarated by the cool waves that crushed against her large, pregnant body. She laughed so loudly Moftiya wondered if the *sheikh* could hear her in Tuffah.

The water came up to Khadija's hips when she reached her boys. She lowered herself to her knees, her headscarf forming a perfect white circle around her, and her dress inflated like a balloon. Her boys chuckled and in the excitement of the moment, they forgot their boundaries, and took to splashing her so hard, she was terrified. She screamed and cursed at them. Moftiya looked on with disapproval. How silly it was of her daughter-in-law to behave like a child, she thought. Moftiya never ventured into the water – she didn't trust the waves, and was petrified of the deep. But above all else, she was afraid she would lose her composure, her iron-fist self-control, and become as silly as everyone else seemed to become when they threw themselves into the playful waves of the Mediterranean.

In the late afternoon the boys played a game of skipping waves while the girls took to building sandcastles, or decorating one another's hair with crowns made of seaweed. Karim's hunger pangs led him away from the games in search of something to eat. He spotted his mother sitting on the picnic rug with the other women, preparing food. When he got close he overheard a conversation that would later keep him up all night.

'What do you mean Khadija isn't coming to the wedding?' Fatima sounded surprised.

'She has nothing to wear,' Moftiya explained in a matter-of-fact tone. 'Her only good dress is too worn out – it has holes in it.'

'It's okay,' Khadija said, sadness evident in her tone. 'I don't have to go. I'm not like you, Fatima. I don't sing or dance or even know how to put colours on my face! Weddings and parties are wasted on me. I don't mind staying home, really. I am happy for you and Moftiya to go without me.'

Karim felt a sharp pain in his heart for his mother. That night he thought hard until he came up with a plan that would enable her to go to the neighbour's wedding. It was not purely an act of selfless love – there was more to it. Karim wanted to go to the wedding too, and he knew that if his mother did not go, he wouldn't be allowed to go either. He thought of all the food that he would be missing out on if Khadija didn't go. All the scrumptious desserts he would never taste. He resolved that he simply was not going to miss out, and neither was his mother.

The next morning, Karim went over to Fatima's house and asked her if she could lend his mother one of her many beautiful maternity dresses. Fatima had a dazzling collection, but none of her dresses fitted Khadija's large, pregnant body. She didn't want Karim to leave empty handed, so she offered to lend him a fancy evening *abaya* for Khadija to wear over whatever dress he might find for her.

Karim spent the remainder of that day going door to door, looking for an outfit his mother could borrow. Om Sa'adah, Abu-Sa'adah's wife, offered a pair of shoes. Om Zaki from the Jarro family offered a blue satin dress, and Salwa, Tuffah's favourite beautician, offered a matching handbag and accessories. 'And that's not all,' she said to the zealous young boy. 'I'll even come by and do your mother's make-up and hair.' Karim hesitated, but she quickly added, 'Don't worry. It is free of charge!'

At home, Karim watched his mother clean the floor of the *sheikh*'s classroom, collecting every paper scrap containing written words, and gathering them in a pile before burning them into ashes.

'Why do you do this?'

'Do what?' Khadija drew a deep breath, and blew the ashes into the air, repeating the Quranic verse, '*Salamun qawlan min rub'en raheem*, words of peace from the Lord of mercy.'

'Why do you do this?' Karim repeated. 'Why do you burn the scraps of paper the students leave behind?'

'Your father told me God created this universe with one word – a word that is so small, it only has two letters in it: Be. Can you imagine the power of all these words and all these letters combined on all these scraps of paper?'

'But these are . . .' Karim wanted to say scribbles and silly words written by students, but he decided not to argue with his mother.

She had her superstitions, and he had a more important agenda in mind.

'It's not important,' he said. 'I come to you with exciting news.' Karim led his mother to the front yard, where he put on display the items he had collected. 'I managed to get everything you need to wear tonight at the wedding.'

Khadija's jaw dropped when she saw the dress, the shoes, the handbag and the accessories. Karim was filled with pride. 'Also, Salwa has offered to come over and help make you up.' Khadija beamed with joy. Even though she hated the idea of borrowing clothes from neighbours, this was different. It was her son who had taken the trouble of doing this for her. It was an act of love. She didn't want to let him down.

A couple of hours later, with Salwa's help, Khadija's hair was gathered in a stylish bun on top of her head, and her plain face was concealed behind a thick layer of make-up. Excited by her transformation, Khadija wore Fatima's evening *abaya* over her borrowed, knee-length blue swing satin dress. Leaning on Karim's shoulder, and with eyes fixed on the ground beneath her feet, she carefully balanced herself on Om Zaki's high heels. She kept looking at herself in the mirror with a smile and a look of disbelief. Karim had to pull her away.

Before leaving, the *sheikh* instructed Khadija to keep her *abaya* on and to cover her made-up face with a scarf until she was inside the women-only wedding party. He didn't want any men to catch a glimpse of her. He then added with a mischievous wink, 'And keep your make-up on until after the boys fall asleep tonight. I think I will need to take a closer look at it!'

Khadija had never walked in heels before. She leaned on Karim's shoulder all the way, finding it impossible to gain her balance. But as they approached the wedding party she decided to let go – she wanted to walk through the door unassisted, like all the other women. She took a few steps, her head held high, feeling confident and beautiful – but her borrowed shoes betrayed her. Khadija came tumbling down into a puddle of muddy water in full view of all the wedding guests.

The women ran to Khadija to assist her inside. Fatima and Salwa helped her wash the mud off her face and change into another dress they borrowed from the bride's family. Karim felt guilty for encouraging his mother to wear high heels, and for pushing her to come to the party. So guilty, in fact, that only the taste of tender cuts of lamb on spicy rice covered with pine nuts had the power to ease his tormented soul.

15

SCHOOL WALK

GAZA, PALESTINE, 1949

On a late-summer morning, the *sheikh* asked his wife to bring him his best outfit, and to dress Karim in his finest. 'Today is a special day,' he proclaimed. 'I will teach Karim how to make his way to school.'

Karim's eyes widened, and his smile stretched from ear to ear. Khadija jumped to her feet and let out a shriek that echoed throughout the Tuffah district and beyond. They had finally made it. Their firstborn had reached this magnificent milestone, ready for school.

Khadija washed Karim's face, combed his hair, dusted off his worn-out sandals and tied their broken leather straps into a double knot. She planted a kiss on his cheek and went outside to untie the donkey, but the *sheikh* stopped her. 'You don't have to do this anymore, Khadija,' he said. 'From this day on, it is Karim's job. He's a big boy now.'

Karim was happy to be trusted with such responsibility. He untied the donkey, brought it over to the *sheikh* and helped his father push his foot into the stirrup. The *sheikh* lifted his weight onto the donkey's back, and together, father and son left the house. Khadija and Moftiya stood at the door waving goodbye, tears of joy filling their eyes as immeasurable pride overflowed in their hearts.

Karim took fast steps to keep up with his father's donkey, curling his toes to ensure his feet remained inside his sandals. Along Mohatta Street they passed the vegetable sellers who set up their boxes and carts under the giant tamarix tree. The vendors shouted as they walked on by: 'Watermelon . . . watermelon, ready for your knife!'; 'Red tomatoes, sweet and ripe!'; 'Eggplants! Eggplants! Grill them! Stuff them! Marinate them! Fry them!'

The shouts of the vendors faded into the distance, as father and son reached the farming fields where Karim and his mother used to fill their water jugs. Karim hastened his steps along the dusty road, terrified of the memory of the *majnoon*. When they reached the *sidra*, an ancient tree that stood at the centre of a fork in the road, they stopped for a short rest under the tree's cool shade. Karim sat on the grass and leaned his back on the tree's wide trunk. The donkey immediately began to feast on the grass.

'Make sure you remember this tree – it's an important landmark on your way to school,' the *sheikh* said. 'You know, this tree has a very special story!' he added, with a slight smile.

'What story?' Karim asked, as he fiddled with his broken sandal strap.

'Centuries ago,' the *sheikh* began, 'there was a holy man, a *wallee*, a servant of Sayyed Hashim, the grandfather of Prophet Muhammad, peace be upon him.'

'Peace be upon him,' Karim repeated, as he was taught to do every time the name of the prophet was mentioned. The *sheikh* nodded in approval.

'This holy man,' the *sheikh* continued, 'he sat under this tree, just like you're sitting now, and he fell asleep right there.' The *sheikh* pointed at the ground beneath Karim. 'And . . .' the *sheikh* paused for dramatic effect.

Karim's curiosity got the better of him. 'And *what*? Tell me! What?'

The *sheikh* drew a deep breath. 'And the holy man never woke up again. When the locals found him, sitting there, dead, they buried him in this same spot. Right there. In the exact spot where you are sitting.'

Startled, Karim jumped to his feet and stepped away from the tree. The *sheikh* laughed as he coaxed the donkey to start moving again. 'I guess you've had enough rest, son – follow me!'

They continued up the hill along the rubble of Gaza's ancient city walls, past the mosque of Sayyed Hashim where it is believed that the prophet Muhammad's grandfather was buried, and entered a dazzling arched street. Karim held his breath in amazement as he observed the upper floors of the large, historic houses hanging overhead on both sides of the street. Each house had an imposing wooden door, beside it, a big circular stone tub and iron poles that his father explained were used, once upon a time, to tie up the horses.

'We call these houses *sobat*,' the *sheikh* explained. 'They were built during the Mamluk era, hundreds of years ago. Nowadays they belong to the families of the rich merchants of Gaza City'.

Karim looked at the balconies hanging above, and their intricate, carved wooden exteriors, and wondered if anyone was inside watching the passers-by beneath. Just in case it was so, he didn't want to be taken for a child. So he straightened up his shoulders, lifted his head high and strutted in the way he thought grown men walked.

At the end of the street their destination appeared before them, perched on top of the hill – the School of Hashim-Ibn-Abd-Manaf. They began the upward climb towards its front steps.

'What do you think?' the *sheikh* asked from atop his donkey, as they approached the bottom step.

'*Yubba*, it looks so beautiful!' Karim shouted.

'This beautiful building was a palace built by the Ottomans during the period of their occupation,' the *sheikh* explained. 'The English transformed it into a police station. Now that Gaza is officially under Egypt's control, the Egyptians have turned it into a primary school.'

The *sheikh* was hardly at the end of his sentence when Karim ran up the stairs, shouting, 'I am a schoolboy!'

The *sheikh* laughed, and waited for Karim to come down. Eventually, he did. He ran back to his father, panting with exhilaration.

'Tell me,' the *sheikh* smiled, 'what do you see when you stand with your back to the school?'

Karim looked into the distance. 'A dome,' he said.

'Yes,' the *sheikh* stared into his son's eyes. 'But this is not any dome. This is the shrine of Abualazzem, the father of courage!' The *sheikh* turned his head towards the dome and continued. 'People believe Abualazzem is Samson, the Israelite who had superpowers in ancient times. Abualazzem snuck into the city of Gaza to destroy its temple but he fell in love with a Gazan woman named Delilah. She discovered his weakness and betrayed him. In the end, he destroyed the temple and killed himself in the process. Gazans built this shrine on top of what they believe are the remains of the old temple that Samson destroyed.'

The *sheikh* turned his head back to look at his son, but the boy was not listening. In fact, he was no longer there. He had run off to the top of the stairs once again and was trying to get a good look at the school through the gate. The *sheikh* laughed. 'Maybe I've burdened the boy with the weight of four thousand years of history.' He patted his donkey and coaxed it to move. 'Karim, come down. Let's keep going, son. There is one last surprise in store for you.'

The *sheikh* took Karim to the nearby Fehmy Beek Street, a street named after the first mayor of Gaza who ruled under the Ottoman Empire. Karim's appetite was taunted by the delicious aroma of food and the sweet fragrance of dessert emanating from the endless cafes that lined the street. The *sheikh* felt inside his purse. He knew money was a scarce commodity he must not spend on frivolous things, but he couldn't resist the desire to make this outing with his son as special as possible. He knew, with his declining ability to walk – even aided by a walking stick – that he would probably never be able to make another trip like this one again. And so, he simply decided.

'I'm going to invite you to a cafe.'

Of all the lessons Karim had learned on that day, the one that brought him to his knees was discovering the taste of *shish kebab* – the delicious grilled minced lamb, mixed with onions and parsley, arranged on sticks and barbecued. He could not conceive of such succulent flavour or creative presentation. Even in the best of times, meat was rare in the mostly vegetarian diet that the poor people of Tuffah were accustomed to – more usual fare was vegetable stews out of shared pots with only a side of bread used for dipping. Father and son enjoyed their meal with relish.

As the sun began to set, Karim helped his father back onto the donkey. Teary eyed, the *sheikh* pleaded with his son, 'I wanted to bring you here, and to share this special meal with you. But you must promise me you will not come back to this street again by yourself. Look, you can see how many automobiles use this street! They are dangerous machines! They can kill you. So, I want you to swear to me, on God's name, you will not come to Fehmy Beek Street without my permission.'

'I swear, *wallahi*!' Karim responded affectionately, understanding his father's worry.

But as they made their way home Karim kept looking behind him, fighting the urge to run back to the cafe and order more of the delicious *shish kebabs*.

16

THE BOY, THE MAN

GAZA, PALESTINE, 1949

Karim opened his eyes before the Tuffah roosters began to crow. He wasn't sure if the surge of emotions washing over him came from anxiety or anticipation. He wished he could sneak over to his mother's mattress and dive into her arms, but he knew if he did, she would scold him and push him away, reminding him that he was a young man now. A six-and-a-half-year-old young man!

The call for the dawn prayer announced the beginning of a new day. Karim was relieved it was finally time for everyone else to wake up. Khadija and the *sheikh* stretched and yawned and, in a synchronised pattern practised for years, Khadija stood and helped the *sheikh* to his feet. She fetched the water jug and together they began the timeless ritual of *wudu*, the ablution in preparation for prayer. In keeping with the teachings of Prophet Muhammad, may peace be upon him, they stated their intention to cleanse for prayer. They washed their hands, arms, face and feet. Each time beginning with the right side, repeating three times, before moving to the left. All the while their lips were set in rhythm, uttering words of grace and gratitude to the great almighty. Karim happily joined his parents for the first time. Khadija and the *sheikh* smiled at him with approval. Karim mimicked their actions, repeated their words, desperately hoping his fast-beating heart would find comfort and solace in connecting with God.

The *sheikh* led the prayer seated on a chair; behind him, Khadija and Karim stood, bowed, prostrated and humbly touched their foreheads to the ground as they contemplated the greatness of the one God. After prayer, Khadija lit the *saj* stove and began to bake the dough she had kneaded the previous night. The *sheikh* asked Karim to fetch three red chillies, two ripe tomatoes, four basil leaves and one lemon from the tree in the garden.

It was still dark outside, but Karim told himself he was not afraid. To prove it, he courageously confronted the pesky Gekkonidae lizards that inhabited the exterior walls of his home. Hands planted on his waist, feet rooted in the ground, he stood close to the lizards and glared into their eyes. The reptiles responded to his act of insolence by shaking their heads sideways and rolling out their tongues.

Karim raised his eyebrows. 'You think that scares me? It doesn't. I am a man now,' he told the creatures. 'I'm so grown-up I'm going to government school. So . . .' he stuck his tongue back out at them, shook his head sideways, and walked away triumphantly.

Karim watched his father crush the fresh, hot chillies in the clay mortar with a pestle. '*Yubba*, why are you sending me to a government school?'

The *sheikh* was never one to give an answer without taking his time to dig deep into his lore and to arrange an eloquent and informative response.

'The prophet Muhammad, peace be upon him.'

'Peace be upon him,' repeated Karim.

'He said we must seek knowledge from the cradle to the grave.' The *sheikh* added lemon and fresh basil into the mortar and continued to crush the ingredients into a fine paste.

'But *Yubba*, I am learning here, at your school. You have taught me how to write and read. You have taught me Quran and classical poetry and —'

'Son,' the *sheikh* interrupted with a smile, 'above every scholar there is a higher scholar. I can only teach you what I know. I may know many things, but I do not know everything. Learning is a lifetime quest, and a good student is one who seeks knowledge from a variety of sources. The Muslim scholar Imam Al-Shafi'i said that a man is only knowledgeable for as long as he seeks knowledge. Once a man believes he knows everything, it is then that he falls into ignorance.'

Karim surrendered, annoyed by his father's constant lecturing. He washed and put on his school uniform, a white shirt and black, knee-long shorts. He ate his breakfast with his brothers quietly, washing down the burning chillies and tomato salad with water, and stuffing as much bread as he could into his mouth.

When it was time to leave, Khadija smiled broadly as she instructed Karim to put on his brand-new pair of black leather shoes. She was expecting him to express excitement and gratitude – after all, the shoes would have cost a fortune, if not for her brother's help. 'The UN is distributing school shoes and uniforms at the camp,' Marwan had told her a few days earlier. 'So I secured these for my nephew!'

But Karim was anything but grateful. He squeezed his feet into the hard leather and was instantly uncomfortable. Never before in his life had he worn anything but open sandals. Disgruntled, he tried to walk a few steps but felt the hard heel collar dig into his flesh. He wanted to protest, but his mother's stare and his father's glare made him reconsider.

Karim sucked in the discomfort, picked up his knapsack, kissed his mother's and father's hands goodbye, who in turn showered him with blessings and prayers. He took a step to the door, hesitated for a second, then stopped. He filled his chest with air and his heart with courage, and decided to make just one, simple request. '*Yubba*,' he turned to his father, pleading, 'may I have some money for a *felafel* sandwich?' His voice was overly polite and deeply hopeful. 'Awny told me they sell delicious *felafel* sandwiches at school.'

The *sheikh* knew he would start making money once his teaching classes resumed later that morning. But at that moment, as his son stood before him, he had no money to give – he had spent all his savings on Karim's uniform, school fees and supplies. Not to mention that he'd splurged with whatever remained on the *shish kebab* he'd bought Karim in Fehmy Beek Street a few days earlier. He couldn't tell this to his son. He couldn't say they had no money. He never wanted his children to ever feel that he could not provide for them. So, instead, he simply said 'Your mother made a *za'ater* sandwich for you. She packed it inside your schoolbag.'

That was it! Karim's supressed anxiety, discomfort and fear finally erupted in a spectacular explosion. He threw his schoolbag on the floor, shouting, 'I've been eating *za'ater* sandwiches every day my whole life!' He stomped his feet. '*Za'ater, za'ater, za'ater* . . . I am sick of *za'ater*! I want to taste *felafel*. I want to be like the other children. Why is everyone else better than we are?' And with that, he stormed out into the front yard and out the front gate. 'I am not going to school!' he shouted, as he ran out into the alley.

Khadija stood frozen, shocked by her son's unexpected behaviour and insolence. He had never acted this badly before. But her husband was smiling. 'Did you see what your son just did?' she asked, glaring at him. 'Why are you smiling?' she snapped.

'He believes he is a man now,' the *sheikh*'s smile gave way to laughter. 'Make us some tea. The boy is growing up, and he has much to learn. His lesson for today has already begun.'

Unlike the government schoolchildren who marched that morning in neat uniforms, schoolbags slung across their shoulders and feet in shiny black leather, raising clouds of dust in their trail, the *sheikh*'s students shuffled in slowly, feet hanging loosely inside worn-out sandless, patched-up shirts tucked into faded trousers and faces unwashed, still holding on to the previous night's sleep. The morning *kottab* students were an eclectic mix of hardworking sons of farmers, and older kids who fell out of the regular school system.

The eldest was Salem, Abu-Sa'adah's son. The almost fifteen-year-old had been appointed by the *sheikh* as keeper of order and discipline in his *kottab*. As soon as he arrived, the *sheikh* gave him the instruction.

'Find Karim, and bring him to me.'

Salem did not have to look for Karim. He had seen him as he came into the *sheikh*'s home, sulking in the alley just outside the front gate.

When Karim saw Salem walk towards him, he knew his civil disobedience stunt was over.

Karim stood before his father, head lowered in shame, trying, in his mind, to guess which punishment he was most likely to receive. Would his father order him to stretch out his hand for a smack with the walking stick, or would he order him to stand disgraced in the corner while he taught his morning class? Would it be pain or humiliation – or both?

'I will not punish you.' The *sheikh*'s voice was calm. 'You're not on my watch right now. You're a student at a government school. The time you have wasted this morning belongs to them. It is the responsibility of the school's principal to decide what to do with you.'

The *sheikh* turned to Salem. 'Take Karim to school and hand him over to the principal. Tell the principal that you found him sitting in the street and refusing to go to school.'

'No!' Karim was horrified. '*Yubba*, this is the worst punishment ever. The principal will think I am a bad student who runs away from school, and if he thinks that on the first day he will always believe I'm bad. Please!' he begged.

'Well,' the *sheikh* said calmly. 'Don't waste your time with me. You are not going to make a good impression on the principal if you're not at school. Run!'

Karim ran. He did not think about his sore feet inside the weird, new leather shoes that dug into his skin. He did not think of the delicious taste of *felafel* that was no longer within his reach. He did not think of how angry or sad or tired or anxious he felt. Karim just ran. The only thought on his mind was that he needed to outrun Salem and get to the school before the first bell rang.

Salem chased Karim, half-heartedly, allowing him to stay in the lead the entire way. They reached the school gate just in time before the students lined up for their first class.

Karim turned to Salem, pleading, 'Please don't take me to the principal.'

Salem nodded his agreement and watched as the son of the *sheikh* of Tuffah climbed up the school steps and walked into a whole new world.

'Rise!' The teacher picked up his long wooden ruler and waved it upwards, like a maestro directing an orchestra. 'You must stand up whenever a teacher walks into the classroom.'

Eyes glued to the ruler, and imaginations wild with the severity of pain its sharp, thin edges could inflict, the students stood up at once.

The teacher scribbled his name on the blackboard. 'My name is Ostath Na'eem.' He turned around and faced the students. 'We always begin with the morning greeting. I say, "Good morning, class," and you say . . .?' He pointed his ear in their direction.

'Good morning, Ostath Na'eem!' the nervous students shouted back, and the ostath appeared pleased.

Ostath Na'eem picked up his ruler, and spent the entire first period of the first day of school instilling fear in the hearts of his first-grade students. He lectured them about school rules, teacher expectations and, most importantly, the system of rewards and punishments they should expect.

'You are here to learn,' he repeated, as he paced between the desks, inspecting the children's uniforms and books. 'This is a school. You will not misbehave here, as you do at home. You are here to do what?'

Silence. The children were too scared to speak. Ostath Na'eem tapped his ruler on the nearest desk to him. The boy sitting at that desk raised his head slowly, and swallowed hard.

'What is your name?' Ostath Na'eem barked at him.

The boy stood up. His voice trembled. 'My name is Isa Saba.'

Ostath Na'eem's features softened as he considered the student for a moment. Unlike most of the boys in his classroom this boy's hair was well groomed and his nails were neatly clipped and cleaned. Also, the boy's Christian name gave Ostath Na'eem cause to pause.

I need to be gentle with this boy, he thought to himself. He might be related to the school principal – they are both Christian. But more importantly, he looks like a child of wealthy parents who would pay lots of money for private lessons.

Ostath Na'eem smiled at the prospect of private lessons. Using his softest and most polite voice, he said, 'It is a pleasure to meet you, Mr Isa Saba. Now tell me, why are you here?'

'I am here to learn!' Isa answered.

'Good. Now, sit down.' Satisfied, Ostath Na'eem returned to his desk. Somewhere along the way he was able to jump back into character and resume his earlier performance of shock and awe. 'Your mothers will not come in here to save you.' He raised his ruler and smashed it hard against a stack of books on his desk. The students cringed in fear. 'So, I suggest you obey your teachers. You pay attention to your lessons. You do your homework. You study hard . . . or . . .'

Ostath Na'eem did not need to strike the desk again with his ruler – he merely waved it this time, and the children gasped and tried to swallow the hard knot that had formed inside their tiny throats.

By the time the bell rang announcing the beginning of the second period, Ostath Na'eem was exhausted, albeit pleased with his overall morning performance. He had clearly set rules and boundaries, and drew disciplinary lines that would ensure the students' good behaviour for the entire year. Now, it was time for him to sit down and try to get to know his students and their level of intelligence and education.

'Class,' he said, as he lowered himself on a chair behind his desk, 'it is your turn to speak. Show me how much you know. Have you learned a song or a poem you can recite by heart? If so, it means you are ready for this class. But if you haven't learned a simple song by now it means you don't belong here, and that maybe you need to be placed in a *kottab* instead.'

Karim's ears prickled at hearing the word *kottab*. That's what people called his father's school. Why was Ostath Na'eem saying *kottab* like it's a bad word? He wanted to tell his teacher and everyone in the classroom that his father's *kottab* is actually good, and that everyone in his neighbourhood gathers there. He raised his hand, but his heart fell and melted into a puddle beneath his feet when he saw the ostath fix his gaze upon him.

'Do you have something you want to say?'

Karim felt his blood run cold. Courage abandoned him. 'No, Ostath,' was all he could muster as he sat back down again.

'Raise your hand if you have memorised any ballads, poems or songs,' Ostath Na'eem commanded, and every student in the class-room raised their hand. He expected as much. They were six- and seven-year-old boys – of course they had memorised something by now, and what they chose to share with him would reveal their upbringing and level of intelligence.

The young boy from Tuffah raised his hand, along with all his classmates. He was seething from the insult the teacher had directed at his father and at his family's *kottab*, albeit unintention-ally, and he really wanted to prove a point and to show his teacher how much he had learned in his father's school. He watched as boy after boy got up and sang a simple nursery rhyme or a short ballad from the popular Arabic folklore, his heart burning with the desire to outshine them all. When eventually Ostath Na'eem pointed at Karim and nodded for him to stand up, the little boy, son of *Sheikh* Hussein and former student of his *kottab*, rose to his feet, lifted his head up high, closed his eyes to keep his focus, and began:

> 'Stop, oh my friends, let us pause to weep over the remembrance of my beloved
> Here was her abode on the edge of the sandy desert between Dakhool and Howmal.'

'What are you doing?' Ostath Na'eem sat up in his chair.

Karim's heart fell. He opened his eyes, sweat trickled down his back. Did the teacher hate his recitation? 'Ostath Na'eem, I have not finished yet. I can recite the whole poem.'

Ostath Na'eem's eyes widened. A slight smile formed on his face and a sparkle escaped from his eyes. 'Imru' al-Qais? You have memorised Imru' al-Qais' poetry?'

'Yes.' Karim's heart quickened. He did not know what to make of his teacher's reaction.

'Well, go on!' Ostath Na'eem's face was now unmistakably a happy one.

Karim continued, eyes shut and heart beating fast, reciting with perfect grammatical pronunciation until he reached the twentieth stanza.

> 'Has anything deceived you about me, that your love is killing, me,

And that verily as often as you order my heart, it will do
what you order?'

The bell rang announcing the first recess. Students began to shuffle
in their seats. Karim opened his eyes and was encouraged by the
teacher's wide smile. 'Would you like me to continue, Ostath
Na'eem? I know this poem till the end.'

'You have memorised all sixty stanzas?'

'No Ostath, the poem has sixty-three. I have memorised sixty-
three stanzas.'

'Sit down,' the teacher ordered him. 'The rest of you,' he said to
the other students, 'must take out your snacks and eat them outside
in the schoolyard. I will see you all back here when the next bell
rings.'

As soon as the last student left the classroom, Ostath Na'eem
grabbed Karim's hand and led him to Principal Hanna Farah's
office.

Karim was mortified. He didn't understand what he had done
wrong or why his teacher was taking him to the principal's office.
Awny had told him that only bad boys get called to the principal's office. The door was open, and Hanna Farah was engaged in a
heated discussion with three other teachers who sat on chairs across
the desk from him.

'Ahem . . .' Ostath Na'eem cleared his throat. 'I am sorry to
interrupt your meeting, but —'

'But what?' Principal Farah barked, as he considered Ostath
Na'eem and the little boy he had brought with him. 'Isn't it too
soon to start bringing me your misbehaved students? It is the first
day, Ostath Na'eem. Cut them some slack!'

'No,' Na'eem smiled. 'It's not like that. Please, let me show you.'

Ostath Na'eem suddenly swooped Karim off the floor and stood him on a chair across from the principal's desk, enthusiastically gesturing to the little boy to continue the poem.

'Go on. Continue the poem from where you left it. Show them.' Ostath Na'eem smiled, his face transforming into that of a different man from the teacher who ignited fear in the hearts of students in the first period.

Karim took in a deep breath, and he continued to recite the long, challenging poem, in perfect form, until the end.

Principal Farah could not believe his ears. How could a boy so young memorise such a difficult poem, and how did he learn to pronounce it with such perfect grammar?

'Where did you learn all of that?' the astonished principal asked.

'I am *Sheikh* Hussein's son,' Karim answered simply. But neither the principal nor any of the teachers who had gathered around him had ever heard of the *sheikh*. This came as a shock to the boy, who believed his father was the most important scholar on the planet.

'Did your father, the *sheikh*, teach you any other classical poetry?' Principal Farah inquired.

'Yes, I know many.' Karim shared his list of favourite classical Arabic poets whom he admired – Al-Mutanabbi, Al-Ma'arri, Abu Nuwas . . .

The principal seemed to be enjoying himself. He handed Karim a newspaper. 'Can you read?'

Karim picked up the newspaper and read with outstanding fluency.

'Unbelievable.' Principle Farah scratched his head. 'How is this possible?'

'I told you. I am *Sheikh* Hussein's son. My father runs a *kottab*, a school in our house. It is called *Madrasat Sorour Al-Atfal*.'

'So, your home is a school!' the principal smiled. 'Well, that explains it!'

'That's why I have brought him to you. He doesn't belong in my classroom.' Ostath Na'eem said.

The principal thought for a few moments. 'Let's put him in grade four.'

Karim squeezed Ostath Na'eem's hand as they stood outside the grade-four classroom. Through the open door they could see the much older, tougher-looking boys filling up the spaces between chairs and desks. Ostath Na'eem looked at the small boy whose hand he was holding, and something tugged at his heart when he saw Karim touching the skin above his upper lip. The boy was searching desperately with the tips of his fingers for any signs of a potential moustache growth, but there was none. Karim was a long way from looking like the grade-four students who had begun to grow facial hair and muscles. He was just a skinny, vulnerable little boy, and both Karim and Ostath Na'eem knew it. Tears began to well up in Karim's eyes. Ostath Na'eem didn't have the heart to leave him in such company, so he returned to the principal's office. There, after a long discussion, it was decided that Karim would begin his school journey in grade two instead.

When the last bell rang announcing the end of the first day of school, Karim took off his leather shoes, tied their straps together, slung them over his neck and ran barefoot all the way home. He was so eager to share the triumphs and tribulations of his first day with his parents, he ignored the discomfort and pain of the sharp stones and twigs that dug into the soles of his feet as he ran.

When he finally stepped through the front gate and into the garden, his grandmother, Moftiya, intercepted him.

'Karim, come over here!' Moftiya was fixing the wiring of her chicken coop. The *sheikh* had promised to give her money to buy new chickens as soon as he collected the fees from his students. Karim let out a big sigh, threw his bag under the pomegranate tree and ran over to help his grandmother.

'Karim!' he heard his mother shout from the house, 'Come inside! Your grandmother's coop can wait.'

Outraged, Moftiya shot back, 'Karim will finish helping me first.'

Khadija, heavy with her fourth pregnancy, waddled out of the house, panting for breath. 'The boy just came back from his first day of school,' she yelled. 'Have a heart!'

As Khadija's belly grew, so did her temper. Every day that brought her closer to her due date was another reminder of her mother's absence. She wondered who would be there for her when she had the baby. Who would stand up to Moftiya to ensure she got enough rest? Who would offer her the comfort and wisdom of generations of women? She became defiant of Moftiya and ready for a fight all the time.

Moftiya saw the simmering rage in Khadija's eyes and made a rational decision to de-escalate. She had become accustomed to her daughter-in-law's emotional storms, and knew it was best not to engage. She gestured to Karim to go and returned her focus to the chicken coop, mumbling under her breath the proverbial wisdom, 'They asked the pharaoh, "How did you become a tyrant?" He said, "No one tried to stop me."'

That evening, the family gathered in a circle over a pot of okra stew. Karim was at the centre of everyone's attention, as he talked, non-stop, about his teacher Ostath Na'eem – how impressed his teacher had been with his poetry recital, how he took him to the principal's office, and how Karim had ended up in grade two. His parents and grandmother listened, their hearts expanding with every word Karim spoke, and pride illuminating their faces with radiant smiles.

It wasn't until they had finished their dinner, and began sipping on their *meramieh* tea, that something shifted in the air. An unmistakable sense of foreboding hung thick in the spaces between them, and settled itself in the room like an uninvited guest who kept returning. Pride and joy gave way to an irrational but real fear of loss. That was how this family had become. That is what life had shaped them into. Happiness was always a reminder of grief; pride a reminder of disappointment; and joy always brought his evil cousin, foreboding.

It was Khadija who spoke first. She lifted her hand and pointed her right index finger upward towards the sky, waving it five times in circular motion as she repeated, 'God protect our Karim from the evil eye.' This superstitious gesture, passed down through the generations, is believed to fend off all kinds of evil – big, and small.

As if on cue, Moftiya reached out her palm and placed it on Karim's forehead and began performing a more sophisticated *rukiah*. Karim surrendered to the ritual he was by now accustomed to. Pressing her palms on Karim's forehead, Moftiya whispered the verse of *Ayatul Kursi*: 'Allah! There is no God but He – the Living, the Self-subsisting, Eternal. No slumber can seize Him, nor Sleep. His are all things in the heavens and on earth.

Who is there that can intercede in His presence, except as He permitteth?'

The *sheikh* waited for Moftiya to finish before he addressed his son. 'Karim, the best way to fend off envy from others is by keeping yourself humble. You must promise me that you will not boast of your intelligence or use it to put down others. The love of those around you will be the greatest protection, after that of God's. *Inshallah*.'

The *sheikh* reached into his purse, now finally replenished after the return of the school year, and handed Karim a coin. 'This,' he said smiling, 'is for your *felafel* sandwich tomorrow!'

17

MOTHERS

GAZA, PALESTINE, 1949

On the second day of school, Karim managed to run all the way with his clenched hand firmly stuck in his pocket clasping the coin, dreaming of the taste of the *felafel* sandwich that awaited him.

Karim's eyes were fixed on the big clock that hung over the green-painted wall of the classroom. His mouth felt as dry as the Sinai Desert, his stomach as hollow as Fatima's *tabla*. He sat still and waited. The two morning periods passed in agonising slow motion. Teachers came and went. Words were scribbled on the blackboard. Words were erased from the blackboard. Questions were asked. Answers were given. Faint giggles, hushed whispers, inhales, exhales . . . Nothing interrupted his thoughts or drew his eyes away from the clock. He sat still in a perfect quiet state of anticipation, until finally the hands of the clock settled into the desired slots. Karim wet his lips with his tongue as the lunch bell rang. He bolted out of the classroom and into his long-awaited *felafel* moment.

Karim loved food. His body demanded it, his mind dreamed of it and he was in a constant state of craving it. But the road between himself and a good meal was filled with obstacles. Not only was his family poor, limiting the ingredients of any meal they had to grains and vegetables, but his mother, Khadija, was a terrible cook. She had not inherited her mother Aziza's good *nafas*. Karim believed that if it weren't for his father's added touches to his mother's bland, over- or under-cooked stews, he and his brothers would have starved to death.

Karim was the first to arrive at his school canteen. He held out his coin and ordered his first ever *felafel* wrap, shifting the weight of his body from leg to leg as he waited impatiently to trade his coin for the culinary treasure.

Sandwich in hand, Karim ran out into the schoolyard where he settled into a vacant spot on a bench next to his classmates, Raja'a and William. Karim said a quick hello to the boys, not wanting to waste too much time on conversation, before devouring his lunch. But the exact moment Karim opened his mouth, two long, rough hands reached out gesturing for him to hand over the sandwich. He looked up, mouth still open, to see Ahmad AlJaro towering above him. Ahmad, a boy in his mid-teens, turned school thug, was a former student of *Sheikh* Hussein's *kottab*. Karim swallowed a lump that had begun to form in his throat. He took in a deep breath.

'No,' he said, 'this is my sandwich.'

William and Raja'a groaned, as if they could feel the pain they anticipated Karim was about to experience.

'What?' Ahmad brought his face closer to Karim's. 'Say it again?'

'No,' Karim said, bravely. 'You can do whatever you want – you can beat me, but I will not give you my *felafel*.'

More students gathered around the boy on the bench and the thug that towered above him.

'No, I will not beat you,' the boy barked. 'I have something better.'

'What?' Karim closed his eyes fearing the worst that was to come.

Ahmad leaned forward and whispered into Karim's ear the one word that broke Karim's resolve.

'Khadija.'

Ahmad straightened up and laughed as he snatched the still-warm *felafel* sandwich and walked away. No one around them heard what he had whispered, but everyone knew it had to be Karim's mother's name.

Karim knew there was nothing shameful about his mother's name. In fact, Khadija is also the name of the wife of the prophet of Islam, Mohammad (peace be upon him). Karim also knew there was nothing shameful about being a mother. In fact, God said in the holy Quran, 'Heaven is at the feet of mothers.' But Karim also knew how the name of a mother can be weaponised in the schoolyard. If word of his mother's name got out, he would be condemned to endless taunts. Students would never call him by his first name again – they would call him Khadija. Such irrational but real disgrace is one that could not be redeemed with a thousand and one felafels, even the ones coated in roasted sesame seeds.

When Raja'a and William, the boys sitting next to him on the bench, offered to share their lunch with him, Karim was too upset and far too humiliated to accept their kindness. So they both dug into their lunches, and he was left to watch with eyes filled with regret. Why did he reject their offer? Raja'a was slurping on long white strings that Karim later learned was called spaghetti, while

William was stuffing his mouth with rice and lamb. He wished they would notice that he was staring at their food and make him an offer again, but they didn't. If only his pride had not gotten in the way. He swallowed his bitter saliva and simmered with resentment for the rest of the day.

When he returned home, he threw his knapsack on the floor and sat in the corner sulking. Khadija was stirring small pieces of white, cotton fabric in a big pot of boiling water, in preparation for the arrival of the new baby.

'What is wrong with you?' she inquired, as she used a big, wooden spoon to lift the steaming nappies from the pot, in order to hang them to dry.

'Ahmad AlJaro. He took my *felafel* sandwich.' Karim choked on his words. He lifted his head and exploded with anger. 'He knew your name. He knew it. He said "Khadija",' he shouted dramatically, expecting his mother to fall apart, to cry, to share the burden of the shame of it all. Instead, Khadija continued to lift the nappies out of the boiling pot, suppressing a faint smile.

'Ahmad has always been a bully,' she said, finally. 'He is just like his mother. The woman is so rude, she has a long tongue that stretches from here to the *sidra* tree.' Khadija turned to Karim, looking into his eyes, as if handing him a very dangerous weapon. 'Do you want to know the name of that intolerable woman?'

'You mean Ahmad's mother's name?' Karim's eyes opened wide to make room for all the possibilities.

'Yes,' Khadija nodded. 'Ahmad's mother's name is Moty'a. Just whisper that in his ear next time he tries to take your *felafel* sandwich.'

The following day, armed and ready, Karim bought a *felafel* sandwich and sat down on the bench with his friends and waited.

Within seconds, Ahmad showed up and gestured to Karim to hand it over. Karim stood on the bench so he could be taller than Ahmad. Slowly, he bent down and whispered into Ahmad's ear: 'Moty'a.' Nothing more needed to be said or done – Ahmad quickly fled the scene. Wild horses could not have dragged him back. Karim savoured his *felafel*, grateful for his mother and for how she had saved the day!

Autumn made way for the arrival of a cold and temperamental winter. The rainstorm began with a few drops in the morning while armies of children made their way to school. Karim lifted his bag over his head and smiled at the sight of younger boys in the street who stuck out their tongues to taste the rain.

By the time Karim arrived at school, the rain had become a downpour. The morning assembly in the schoolyard was cancelled and students were rushed into the classrooms. Karim's first period was Quran studies, but the religion teacher, Ostath Rabah Al-Rayes, was caught up in the heavy rain and never made it to school. Principal Hanna Farah stepped in to replace him. Even though the principal was Christian, he was known for his flawless recitation of the verses of the holy Quran, and for his ability to bring out the beauty, rhythm and poetry of the sacred text.

The principal's eyes were drawn to the window, watching the rainwater accumulate into puddles in the schoolyard.

'Good morning, class!' he muttered.

The students, standing, responded in one voice, 'Good morning, Principal Hanna.'

The principal sat down and so did the students. He reached out for the Quran, his mind already made up. 'I believe it is most appropriate today to learn the story of Prophet Noah, may Allah's blessings and mercy be upon him.'

The principal used his storytelling charm to keep the students' focus from wandering outside. But when he began to recite the verse, 'O earth! Swallow up your water, and O sky! Withhold (your rain)' the sound of the rain outside drowned his melodic voice, and the cascade of water falling against the glass windows warned of flooded streets and falling mud roofs. The principal had no choice but to declare emergency measures. He announced a total school closure and told the students to go home until further notice.

Karim walked out of the classroom with his closest friends, Raja'a and William. The grade-two students were excited by the magnitude of the rain and the interruption to their school routine. It all seemed exhilarating and wonderful, and it threw the day open to all kinds of new adventures.

When they reached the school gate, Principal Hanna Farah told them to wait at the top of the stairs until adults claimed them. The crowd of fathers swelled in number below, arriving to rescue their sons from the floods. Some came in cars, others came on foot – all stood in the rain, eyes searching for their own. Karim stared at the worried faces as they called out names, and the excited younger faces who responded gleefully. His heart grew heavy. Never would he share such moments with his crippled father.

William spotted his father in the crowd. 'Let's go!' He gestured to Karim and Raja'a. The boys started to move, but Principal Hanna Farah stopped them.

'Are your fathers here?' he asked.

'Yes,' said William. 'My father is down there, he's in the red Buick Roadmaster. I'm sure he won't mind driving my friends – Karim and Raja'a – home.'

'All right,' said the principal. 'Off you go. Be safe!'

The three boys ran down the steps and towards the Buick. Karim's mind was hard at work. He had never told Raja'a and William how poor his neighbourhood was. He never told them that the roads into Tuffah were not fit for cars and that the narrow alleyways that branched off Mohatta Street only welcomed feet, hooves and donkey carts.

William's father quickly rolled down the passenger-side window and shouted at the boys through the downpour: 'Come on boys, get in the car.'

William jumped into the passenger seat, Raja'a into the back. Karim stood in the rain, unmoving.

'Karim, get in!' William's father's impatience grew. 'We need to drive now before the streets become completely flooded.'

Karim wished the earth would open and swallow him. He knew that his friend's fancy car would no doubt get stuck in the muddy streets of Tuffah. 'Thank you,' he said, finally, 'but my father is on his way to pick me up, and he will worry if he doesn't find me here.'

It all happened so fast. The car moved away, Raja'a and William's hands waving goodbye through fogged-up windows. Suddenly, everyone was gone. The teachers and the students and the parents, they all disappeared. Only Karim stood alone outside the school. He gathered his courage and began running down the hill. At the bottom, his feet became immersed in a torrent of cold water. He repeated to himself, 'I am a man. I am not afraid. I am a man. I am not afraid.' But Karim was not a man, he was a child – trembling, cold and very much afraid.

When he reached the fork near the *sidra* tree, the water became deeper. He closed his eyes and prayed as he waded into it. It reached his waist. His vision became blurry. He wiped his eyes, but still he could not see past the tears that kept falling, and the rain that kept pouring. He took more steps forward until he felt he was too tired to take any more. His knees folded. Only his head remained above the water. His eyes closed. Too cold. Too tired. He could not swim.

The water splashed heavy footsteps in his direction. Was he dreaming, or was that the sound of her? The one who always came to his rescue. He drew in a deep breath and released it into the rain. Wet scent of garlic, *za'ater*, sumac and olives warmed his heart. That was unmistakably the scent of her. That was her. She had come for him.

Two arms, like angel wings, scooped him up into a blanket and lifted him to her bosom. His legs could feel the shape of her pregnant belly. She squeezed him tight. He shivered a smile. Her lips pressed hard against his forehead. '*Habeeby ya ibny*, my beloved son,' Khadija's voice whispered into his ear as she waded into the water, one son in her belly and another in her arms, and carried him all the way home. 'I've got you. *Alhamdulillah*, I've got you.'

Once home, Khadija changed Karim into warm clothes and cradled him in her arms as they sat by the fire. He had never experienced such tenderness. He had never known such heroism.

Khadija extracted herself from Karim's embrace and stood up, with a look of pain on her face. 'I think carrying Karim home from the flooded streets might have triggered my contractions,' she said to Moftiya. 'I think it's time.'

Moftiya, mindful of the absence of Khadija's mother, did not hesitate to step in to help. She boiled cinnamon tea and watched as Khadija began to pace back and forth, rubbing her back occasionally to give her some comfort. The boys went to sleep inhaling the sweet smell of cinnamon and thinking with excitement of the new addition to the family who seemed well on the way. The *sheikh* drank cinnamon tea, and watched how his wife and his mother were transformed into intimate allies. There was not a hint of resentment between them, only love and care as two mothers worked together, one giving comfort to the other, reciting prayers and hoping to welcome a new life into the world.

The rain only stopped by giving way to snow. White fluff covered the mud homes and green cactus hedges for the first time in decades. Karim, who was woken up at dawn, was mesmerised by the beauty and uniqueness of each falling snowflake, and how the sheets of snow transformed old familiar sites into new, magical ones. Most of all, he was struck by the way the snow turned the still, dark sky into day.

'Run, Karim,' his father rushed him. 'Try not to fall on the way – the snow is slippery.'

Karim ran with careful steps along Mohatta Street. He was on a mission to fetch the midwife. His mother's contractions had become short and regular, and although the midwife arrived quickly, the baby was still in no hurry at all.

Khadija's labour lasted a few more hours, and so did the snowfall. Tired of the waiting, the *sheikh* stepped outside, leaned on his cane and breathed in the crisp, winter morning. His sons were enjoying a snow fight against the neighbours' boys. Their joyous cries blended with Khadija's screams for mercy, and the midwife's cheers: '*Yallah! Yallah!* Push! We're almost there!'

The *sheikh* looked at his donkey. The loyal beast was in high spirits, shaking his head while savouring the snow with heightened pleasure.

'Et tu, Brute!' the *sheikh* reprimanded the donkey. 'How could you be enjoying the snow, and ignoring what it means to our brothers and sisters still in tents in refugee camps?'

The *sheikh* took in a deep breath and sighed. He remembered that he must always be grateful for the kindness of God. '*Alhamdulillah! Praise be to Allah.*' He was grateful to the almighty who in times of hardship had given them a warm home, healthy sons and plenty of coal to keep their fire burning on this cold day. God's kindness washed over him.

By noon, the *sheikh* and Khadija welcomed a newborn, another baby boy. They named him Abdul Latif, worshipper of the kind God.

18

GROWING PAINS

GAZA, PALESTINE, SUMMER, 1950

Gaza's population tripled as refugees from other parts of Palestine, who remained stuck and unable to return to their homes, crowded its landscape. Everyone, including the locals, struggled to find work and to adjust to the new reality. The local economy, cut off from the rest of Palestine, was devastated. Merchants in Gaza could no longer travel to, or trade with, cities that fell inside the new borders of what was the newly created state of Israel. Many *fellaheen* – farmers – lost access to their fields, as most of Gaza's agricultural land was also taken by force into what became Israel. Hardships touched everyone equally as jobs became scarce and the cost of living soared.

With less farmers sending their children to the *sheikh*'s school, together with the ending of the school year, the *sheikh*'s heart was heavy with worries. His mind raced to find ways to make ends meet during the summer holidays. Friends and neighbours who gathered around him for the nightly circle shared his sombre mood. Khadija's stepfather, Ibrahim, and her brothers Hafez and

Marwan, sat quietly next to him, also crushed by the weight of the world.

'Is everything all right, brother?' the *sheikh* asked with an absent mind.

'The sons of bitches . . .' Ibrahim's voice trembled, as he attempted to control his anger. 'They forced us to leave Salama, prevented us from returning to our homes, and now claim we are absentees and under this guise, they've taken our properties and given them to Jewish settlers.'

'Absentees!' Hafez grunted. 'Just one more label to add to our collection. It's not enough they made us refugees, stateless, internally displaced and exiled – now we can also be called absentees.'

The *sheikh* nodded. 'I know. But this law was passed in the Israeli Knesset a few months ago.'

Ibrahim's voice caught in his throat as tears welled up in his eyes. 'So, what? I should get over it by now?'

'I didn't mean . . .' the *sheikh* began, but Ibrahim interrupted him.

'Easy for you to say that. You have remained on your land, in your home, in Gaza. Your city. You have the luxury of counting time by days and months and years. But for us, since they forced us out of our homes and into refugee camps, every day is still 1948.'

Marwan placed his hand gently on his stepfather's knee to calm him down.

'Ibrahim,' the *sheikh* spoke softly. 'I didn't mean to be insensitive. You are still on your homeland. This is still Palestine. And one day, we will have all of Palestine back and you will return to your home in Salama.'

'The *sheikh* is right.' Hafez spoke with practised precision. 'From this part of Palestine, we will return to it all. The choice is clear: return or martyrdom.'

The *sheikh*'s eyes filled with tears. 'Whatever you need brothers, we are all with you!'

The guests joined in, one by one: 'We are with you!'

A moment of silence passed, as the men reflected on the predicament of the refugees: how much time had passed; how the refugee camps in Gaza were growing into permanent-looking structures. How the world had not done enough to ensure their return to their homes. Would they be destined to remain in such limbo for much longer?

One of the *sheikh*'s guests that night was Qasem, a man famous for his sorrowful voice. He wanted to change the mood in the room, so he coughed a few times to clear his throat, sipped on some water, sat up straight, closed his eyes, and began to sing a melody written and composed by Egyptian musician Mohamad Abdel Wahab.

> No I'm not one to cry
> No I'm not one to complain
> Even when your love hurts me
> And I'm not one to chase
> And beg and plead with you
> When I have done nothing wrong
> It is you who have abandoned me
> And you who have wounded me
> And you think I will beg you?
> I have one thing to say
> Everything is fated
> And this is my fate with you

Qasem was showered with praise and sighs.

'That was not uplifting at all!' the *sheikh* laughed. 'But good job on the singing.'

'You're laughing, so it must have done something,' Qasem retorted.

'I can listen to Abdel Wahab's songs all day!' Ibrahim-Hamada mused.

'What about you, *sheikh*?' Abu-Sa'ada asked. 'Who do you listen to?'

The *sheikh* did not own a radio but, with much prompting from Fatima, Abu-Awny had offered to extend a cable that could run across their shared garden connecting his radio to a speaker at the *sheikh*'s house. From then on, whenever Abu-Awny was listening to his radio, the *sheikh* was listening too.

Officially, the *sheikh* said he needed to listen to the radio so he could hear the news reports. But the unofficial truth was that the *sheikh* also loved listening to popular music, especially songs sung by women such as Umm Kulthum, Asmahan and Samira Tewfik. For all his enlightened views, the *sheikh* of Tuffah didn't like the idea of men singing their hearts out. Men, in his opinion, should not be exhibiting their sensitivity, or publicly expressing their sentiments of heartache and yearning to the world.

Abu-Sa'ada repeated the question, '*Sheikh*, who do you listen to?'

The *sheikh* thought carefully. He was a respected *sheikh*, a teacher, a man of religion – he had to craft a delicate response, one that conveyed his love for music in a respectable, dignified way. But before he was able to open his mouth, Karim jumped in and offered the worst answer there was.

'My father likes women,' Karim said. The men laughed and Karim, aware he had put his foot in his mouth, tried to correct his answer. 'I mean, he only likes listening to women.'

The *sheikh* swallowed his embarrassment and allowed his friends to have a hearty laugh at his expense.

A few minutes later, Mohamad Khodry, a successful Gaza merchant who sometimes joined these nightly gatherings, asked the *sheikh* if he thought Karim was old enough to work for him. The *sheikh* hesitated. He knew how much Karim was looking forward to the holidays. But he also knew how much the extra income would help the family, and how important it would be for Karim to stay out of trouble and to learn the ethics of hard labour.

'I think Karim is a fine young man who is ready for hard work,' the *sheikh* answered, looking at his son.

Karim, stunned by the turn in conversation, nodded in agreement. Deep down, he wasn't sure how to react. He had dreamed of spending his summer days reading poetry and swimming in the Gaza Sea, but he saw the look in his father's eyes and understood that he had no choice but to accept.

Later that night, the *sheikh* dragged his feet, leaning on Karim and Rahim, away from his classroom where his daytime lessons and nightly gatherings took place, across the garden, to the other room that was the centre of his family's life. The room where they slept, cooked, showered and prayed. The room that was their entire home.

In that room, he rested on the floor mattress under the window. Rahim, assisted by Muti, pushed aside the large cooking pot, and Karim helped his mother, Khadija – who was pregnant once again – take out the washing tub and the gas stove. Baby Latif crawled to his father, drool covering his entire face, ripe apricot dripping its juice down his hand and onto the floor.

'Feed me – I'm hungry,' the *sheikh* said, opening his mouth playfully, his head stretched forward. Baby Latif took a bite out of the ripe apricot and stuffed the rest of it into his father's mouth. The *sheikh* grabbed Latif and tickled his belly, sending him into a fit of giggles, spreading smiles on everyone's faces.

Once the floor was cleared, the boys and their mother each rolled out their own mattress and arranged their sheets and pillows. The growing family maintained the same sleeping order every night. The *sheikh*'s mattress always next to the wall under the window, Khadija's mattress next to the *sheikh*'s and the boys' mattresses arranged from youngest to oldest next to Khadija. With the birth of each new baby, Karim's mattress was pushed further away, touching the opposite wall.

'*Yumma*,' Karim warned his mother. 'This baby in your belly right now had better be the last one. If I get any closer to the wall I will suffocate.'

Khadija didn't pay Karim any attention, but the *sheikh* eyed him with concern. Karim had spoken out of order with his mother, and had earlier embarrassed his father in front of the men. He worried that his eldest son might have become wasteful with his words.

When the boys were all under the sheets and ready for their bedtime story, the *sheikh* knew which one he was going to tell.

'In the name of God, the merciful, the compassionate!' he began. '*Kan ya ma kan fi qadeem alzaman*, a powerful king ruled over a vast kingdom. One night, the king dreamed he lost all his teeth. In the morning he called his most trusted advisors to interpret the dream. The first advisor told him, "You will lose something precious, your majesty." The second advisor said, "You will face disgrace, your majesty." And the third advisor said, "You will lose your loved ones, your majesty." The king didn't like any of these interpretations, so he banished the advisors forever from his kingdom. A wise man heard of the king's dream and offered to stand before him. The king agreed. The wise man told the king, "Your majesty, your dream means that you will have a very long life – so long you will live after all your teeth are gone." The king was very happy with this interpretation. He rewarded the wise man with lots of gold and appointed him as his top advisor.'

The *sheikh* paused for a moment to signal the end of the story. 'My sons,' he then said, 'your words are precious. They can lead you to success or to failure. They are key to your fortune. Use your words wisely.'

Karim knew the story was directed at him. He had noticed his father's glare of disapproval earlier. '*Hader Yubba*,' he promised. 'I will!'

At just seven years old, Karim – the eldest son to a crippled father – knew how heavy his burden was and how lucky he was to have a job that could keep food on his family's table. He no longer thought of summer days sitting on the beach with friends, reading books, practising writing poetry, and chasing beautiful Armenian girls who always frequented the beach during the summer. Those fantasies were behind him. He was prepared for hard work. What he wasn't prepared for was how much he would end up enjoying it.

First of all, working meant that Karim no longer had to run around all day completing endless lists of chores and errands. 'Karim, trim the branches in the yard!' 'Karim, take your brothers to the shoe mender.' 'Karim, help your grandmother clean the chicken coop.' 'Karim, watch over your brothers.' 'Karim.' 'Karim.'

'Karim.' Secondly, at home, Karim had three bosses: his mother, his grandmother, and his father. But at work, he only had one boss. One voice telling him what to do. But the best part of his job was the job itself!

Mohamad Khodry, the merchant, assigned Karim the task of guarding the inventory during its transportation from Gaza's railway station to the store near Suq al-Qaysariyya, Gaza's gold market bazaar. Every morning Karim would walk to the station and wait for the train to arrive from Cairo. He would then watch as large sacks of flour, sugar and coffee, destined for his boss's store, were unloaded onto a flatbed truck. Once the truck was full, Karim would climb over the sacks and lie down on his back on top of the pile. It was his job to ensure that no one would cut open any of the sacks along the way and steal any of the goods. The only training he was given was a brief warning not to sit or stand up along the way, or else he would be entangled in the low-lying electrical wires – apparently, a fatal mistake that had claimed the lives of others before him – and to shout and knock on the truck window if he saw anyone, other than the driver, approaching the load.

The drive from the station to the Suq al-Qaysariyya took only fifteen minutes, but Karim wished it would last longer. He loved sleeping on top of the sacks and relished the sensation of the wind brushing against his skin when the truck moved fast. He enjoyed inhaling the scents of coffee, flour and sugar, and losing himself to the vivid and numerous daydreams that filled the space between his eyes and the deep-blue sky above. It was on top of the truck that he began to stitch together his first poetic verses. None of them materialised into poems, but he knew if he kept on trying, one day they would.

At home, Karim's relationship with his brothers evolved. They looked up to him with added respect, as did the elders in his family. They ran to him when he came home at the end of the day smelling like a delicious, sweet blend of roasted coffee. They smiled and even giggled when he greeted his parents and grandmother with 'Salam alaykom' in an exaggerated deep voice. And, when he placed his daily earnings into the palm of his father's hand, his brothers watched on with reverence.

'Bless you, my son!' the *sheikh* said every night, as he took a small amount of Karim's money and gave it to him. 'This, you will need for your own spending.'

The summer came to an end in the blink of an eye. School uniforms were prepared. Notebooks, bags and shoes were sourced. Karim worked until the last day of his summer holiday. He came home from work exhausted and was ambushed by his grandmother Moftiya shouting '*Mabrouk!* Another boy! *Mashallah!* Another boy!'

At first, Karim was puzzled. He had spent so little time at home during the summer, he hadn't paid much attention to his mother's growing belly and never thought to ask when the baby was due. He ran past the cluster of children in the front yard and into his parents' room. There, he saw Khadija asleep and the *sheikh* seated on his mattress across from her, holding the baby in his arms.

'We are so blessed,' said the *sheikh* to Karim.

'Praise be to God!' Karim sat next to his father and smiled at the sight of the newborn.

'I have five sons now,' the *sheikh* said, almost in disbelief.

'I have four brothers now,' Karim said with a hint of panic.

The *sheikh* reached for Karim's hand. 'Each child brings its own fortune. You are the eldest, my second in command. Your brothers are your responsibility. But you will find my son, they are also your tribe, your helpers, your protectors and your allies in this life.'

A moment of silence passed between them.

'What is his name?' Karim asked, as he gestured to his father to hand his new baby brother over.

The *sheikh* placed the tiny human bundle into Karim's arms. 'We have been so fortunate this year, with you working and making us proud. So we named him Abdul Razak, worshipper of the God of fortune.'

Karim could barely toss or turn on his mattress. He had grown, and so had the family. There were now too many sharing the floor. Starting from the other wall across, where the *sheikh* went to sleep, followed by Khadija, and his brothers. Karim, firmly now pushed into the wall on the other side.

When he kicked off the cover and sat up, feeling thirsty, he sensed a strange movement in the room. He looked across his sleeping brothers to the other side, and there in the faint light of night, he could make out his mother's figure, sitting – no, rocking – over his father, the *sheikh*.

'*Yumma*, what are you doing? Why are you sitting on top of our father?' Karim asked with innocent curiosity.

Khadija and the *sheikh* froze. They held their breath for what seemed like an eternity.

'She is helping me get into a warm sweater,' the *sheikh* finally said. It was the first thought that had come to his mind. 'Now, go back to sleep before you wake up your brothers.'

Karim had no reason to doubt his father's explanation. He took a sip out of the water jug and went back to sleep.

The following morning, while they were eating their breakfast, Karim noticed his parents were looking at him, smiling.

'Son,' his father said finally. 'You are now a young man, and you shouldn't be sleeping in your parents' room anymore. It is too small anyway. So, if you want, you can clean up the barn, and get your brothers to help you make it your own space!'

'It's not fair!' Rahim immediately objected.

Karim did not object. He was so excited – this was a huge milestone. It took him a few days, with the help of his brother Rahim, to clean the barn and claim it as his own. It took him years to understand what that smile his parents had shared that morning was really about.

The *Sheikh* with his sons Abdul Karim, Abdul Rahim, Abdul Muti and Abdul Latif, in the Tuffah district, Gaza, Palestine c. 1952.

19

GOD IS ALIVE

GAZA, PALESTINE, 1951

'Christ is risen!' William shouted, as he raced Raja'a to the Tuffah district, leaving a trail of dust behind him.

Raja'a yelled back, 'Indeed, he has . . . Stop running! I said, stop!' William did not stop; he wanted to get to Karim first to show him his smart Easter outfit.

Karim waited for his friends in the shade of the ancient *sidra*, resting against its wide trunk, his mind transported into the world of *Magdalen*, a novel by Mustafa Lutfi al-Manfaluti. At eight years of age, Karim was no longer afraid of the spirit of the holy man buried beneath the famous tree. He had made a pact to co-exist with the spirit in peace.

'Karim!' 'Karim!' his friends shouted, as they raced down the hill towards him, but he seemed oblivious to their calls. When they finally reached the *sidra*, William kicked Karim's leg, shouting, 'Well? What do you think?'

Karim looked up and smiled at the sight of his friends in their three-piece suits, hair meticulously kept on the side by a generous amount of oil, and shoes almost shining like a mirror – until the dust of Tuffah had its way with them.

'You look like the Egyptian movie stars Anwar Wagdi and Rushdy Abaza,' Karim told his friends, but the boys were not satisfied by the compliment.

'Of course, we do,' William said. 'But the important question is, which one of us looks better?'

Karim examined his friends closely. 'A wise man once said, he who feeds his friends the sweetest Easter *ka'ak* is the handsomest of them all!'

The boys laughed. Karim stood up, dusted off his pants and tucked his shirt in. He didn't mind that his worn-out white shirt and black pants were not as impressive as his friends' attire. After all, this was not his celebration; this special day belonged to his Christian friends.

'Happy Easter!' he said, as he shook their hands and hugged them. 'Thank you for inviting me to your celebrations!'

'We wanted to give your miserable students a break!' William teased.

Karim had just started to help his father out by offering after-school tutoring.

'That's so Christian of you,' Karim shot back. The boys laughed, and walked arm-in-arm towards the Zaytun Quarter in the old city where the oldest Christian church in Gaza, the world's third-oldest Church, the Church of Saint Porphyrius, stood.

Karim's life could not have been more different to that of most other boys his age. At school, his advanced learning skills, his sense of humour and his flair for public speaking always placed him at the centre of attention, winning him favours with his teachers and fellow students alike.

After school, while most boys lingered on their way home to buy treats from the local store or to compete over who could climb the highest tree, Karim raced home so he could take advantage of every drop of precious daylight in a district that still had no electricity. The *sheikh*'s school *Madrasat Sorour Al-Atfal* ran all its classes before sunset, and Karim had become his father's reliable assistant and tutor, preparing lessons, tutoring students and marking papers. Karim was proud of sharing this responsibility and of contributing to his growing family's income.

When William and Raja'a invited Karim to join their Easter celebration, Karim was reluctant to accept. He feared that cancelling his lessons that night would create a shortage in the family budget, but his father encouraged him to go. In fact, the *sheikh* went beyond encouragement; he evoked the much-revered word *wajeb* – meaning duty. He told his son, 'Christianity is part of our Palestinian heritage and an integral part of our identity. It is your *wajeb*, son, to visit your Christian brothers and sisters on their important day of festivities.'

Karim knew that his city was home to a host of saints and martyrs from the early years of Christianity, but this would be his first time to personally witness the most celebrated Christian ceremony in Palestine, the holy fire on the eve of Easter.

'You are going to witness a real miracle, my friend!' William announced, with much excitement, on the way to the Church of Saint Porphyrius. 'Each year this miracle happens on the eve of Easter. It starts when BOOM, a fire comes out from the tomb of Jesus Christ at the Church of the Holy Sepulchre in East Jerusalem.'

'That's the church where Jesus was crucified,' Raja'a interjected.

'Wait. What? Do you mean to say that BOOM, and the fire comes out?' Karim asked. 'Who lights the fire?'

'It is a miracle!' both Raja'a and William respond in one voice, a slight smile on the tip of their lips.

William continued, in high spirits, with the rest of the story. 'Our fathers, the Orthodox priests, emerge from the antechamber with the holy fire, and pass its light by igniting the torches of all the other priests who come from far and wide. Our holy father is on the way back from Jerusalem right now carrying the holy flame in his hands.'

Karim liked the image of Roman Orthodox priests carrying holy fire torches across the land and the seas, and was excited at the prospect of bearing witness to the arrival of the holy flame to Gaza.

At the church's external gate in the Zaytun district, the boys joined a growing crowd from Gaza's Orthodox Christian community. Some stood with crucifixes decorated with Orthodox icons, others sang to the beat of drums and many in the crowd danced *dabke* and waved their swords and olive wood crosses in the air. Raja'a and William joined the dancing circles; Karim watched on happily as more people arrived and greeted one another with '*Al Massih qam*, Christ is risen.'

After the dancing, the faithful filed into the ancient church where prayers were held until the midnight arrival of the holy fire. Karim sat on the wooden bench next to his friends, his eyes wide open, expanding, as he tried to fit in all the details of the golden frames and beautifully coloured icons that adorned the church walls. His heart soared when the choir began to sing. He looked around him and caught a glimpse of his principal, Hanna Farah, sitting across the aisle. The principal smiled at the young Muslim boy from Tuffah, and the boy smiled back.

At midnight, the archbishop appeared in his bejewelled crown holding the holy fire. He walked in a procession with altar boys and the church choir igniting the candles held by the congregation to the joyous clamouring of church bells and the chanting of the faithful praising the glory of Christ.

Karim woke up late the next day, and was sluggish during homework time. He sat with his brother Rahim on the rug across from the *sheikh*, struggling to maintain his focus. Rahim was deeply immersed in his Arabic calligraphy assignment. Although he was only in first grade, with a strike of a pen he could turn ordinary text into stunning masterpieces. Rahim had developed a taste for beautiful patterns. He had a creative mind that was able to turn ordinary lines and dots into dramatic curves and waves that rose and fell like a cappella, a *mawwal* sung from the heart.

Karim, on the other hand, was not at all inspired by his homework. His English notebook sat unopened in his hand while his ears strained to decipher the details of a conversation that Fatima and Khadija were having outside in the garden.

The *sheikh* struck the floor with his stick three times to get Karim's attention, before he ambushed him with a command: 'Spell "cat".'

Karim was quick. 'C A T.' He sounded out the letters mechanically. English was his least enjoyable subject, but he could not escape it, as it was mandatory in grade four. The *sheikh*, who had limited English language skills, had ordered *Morris 1* and *Morris 2 English for Beginners* at the end of the previous school year, and had spent the entire summer battling the stifling heat and arduous nonsensical spelling of words like 'picture', 'pen' and 'cat'. By the time Karim started grade four, the *sheikh* had a basic understanding of the language – enough to supervise his son's homework.

'Karrriiiim!' The *sheikh* spoke louder and with more emphasis. 'Stay with me! Spell "apple".'

'A B B L E.'

The *sheikh* couldn't tell if Karim had the right letter. There is no 'p' sound in Arabic, only 'b'. The *sheikh* needed to find a way to distinguish the letter 'p' from the letter 'b'. 'Which one?' he asked. 'Is it the one with the stick pointing downwards, or the one with the stick pointing upwards?'

'The one . . . with the . . . stick pointing . . .' Karim's answer came in dribbles. He heard Fatima and Khadija outside saying his name, and later mentioning Souhailah's name. He desperately wanted to know what they were talking about. The *sheikh* lost his patience, and reached out for his stick.

Rahim elbowed his brother. 'Hey, I think it is the one with the stick pointing at you.'

The *sheikh* suppressed his smile. His sons were growing fast, and so was their sense of humour.

'Go!' he told Karim, as he threw the stick aside. Karim was puzzled. The *sheikh* explained, 'I too could hear the negotiations taking place outside. Fatima will not rest until you take Souhailah to see the doctor.'

The *sheikh* was right – Fatima was relentless. And whenever Souhailah needed to see the doctor, Fatima always came to the *sheikh* or Khadija, and asked if Karim could take her.

Karim and Souhailah walked through the alleyway and into Mohatta Street. Karim's pace was always inconsistent on such walks. He would take big strides, notice she was not next to him, run back to her, pounce around her and, at times, stand still and watch her walk ahead. Souhailah never felt she needed to change her pace for him. She took graceful consistent steps, savouring each moment along the way. Her feet struck the ground like the hand of a clock, always moving to the same measured rhythm. Their differences were clear for anyone to see. Karim was always animated, she was always calm; he was bold, she was shy; he could speak all day, and she never got tired of listening. He composed poetic phrases, she was like poetry – composed.

Along the way to the clinic, Karim described in detail the Easter ceremony he had attended with his friends – the suits and knee-length dresses, the opulence of the church on the inside, the singing of the choir and the magnificent lighting of the sacred fire. Souhailah listened quietly, smiling and nodding. She waited until there was a moment of silence, when Karim paused to take a breath, to ask, 'You didn't bring me anything?'

'I did!' Karim flashed a boyish smile. 'I brought you a decorative wreath made of wheat. It would have looked beautiful on your head, like a crown, it really would have!'

'Would have?'

'Would have. *Sitty* Moftiya found it and fed it to her chickens.'

'Some crown!'

They laughed, and talked all the way to the clinic.

The doctor could not find anything wrong with Souhailah. 'It could be you had a mild heat stroke,' he guessed, 'but it seems to have passed now. Just drink lots of water,' he added, 'and go home at once, before it gets too dark.'

Karim's smile illuminated his dark face, and his eyes danced to the beat of his joyful heart. He was certain now beyond any doubt that Souhailah had faked being sick knowing this would afford her more time with him. He understood how Fatima fell for it. Souhailah's father and brothers were at work. Who else to take her, but Karim? The quiet girl next door had grown and was now weaving her own romantic threads.

They didn't pay too much heed to the doctor's instructions and instead of going home at once, they dragged their feet back towards Mohatta Street. Walking together, as slowly as was humanly possible, breathing in the cool breeze that comes with the glorious Gaza sunsets, and witnessing together the thick blanket of night draping over their world, hiding every secret and every desire.

They were approaching the streetlight at the corner of Mohatta Street. Nervous the night was coming to an end, Karim gathered his bravery and reached out with the tip of his finger, ever so slightly, and touched the back of Souhailah's hand. He meant it as an invitation for her to hold his hand. He did not mean to start a fire. But there it was. Hot flames ran through him and stung her delicate skin. Quickly, they stepped away from each other. Souhailah hastened her pace home, and Karim ran behind her. Nothing needed to be said. His eyes were lost in her long, wild hair as it bounced to the rhythm of her steps, her curls perfectly catching the streetlight, illuminated like a burning flame. Souhailah was his sacred fire. She, his holy flame.

Karim and Rahim elbowed their way through the crowd, squinting their eyes as they tried to see past the colourful bright flashlights that adorned the walls of the Mosque of Sayed al-Hashim. Rahim tugged on his brother's shirt. He was petrified to lose sight of him in the sea of people who had gathered to celebrate the birthday of Sayyed al-Hashim, Prophet Muhammad's great-grandfather, who was buried in the city that forever cherished his name, known to many as Gaza of Sayed al-Hashim.

'Hurry up!' Karim shouted at his brother. 'We will miss the *khalifah*.'

'I can't go any faster.' Rahim's voice was strained. He was scared and tired. His hands gripped harder to Karim's shirt.

Karim stopped and turned around. 'Rahim, do not tug on my shirt. You will rip it.'

'I don't want to get lost.'

Karim remembered his father's words. 'Keep your eye on your brother. Do not let go of him.' This was the first time Rahim was allowed to go outside their neighbourhood with his brother and without an adult.

'So hold on to my hand.' Karim stretched his hand out to his brother.

'No!' Rahim shouted stubbornly. 'No way. I am not a baby. I don't need to hold my big brother's hand.'

'Fine,' Karim muttered through his clenched teeth. 'I will pull you instead.'

Karim grabbed the hem of Rahim's shirt and resumed his fast walk, dragging Rahim behind.

'What is the big deal?' Rahim yelled. 'Why do we have to see the *khalifah*?'

'Because he is a great horseman. Because I want to see the huge white turban on his head. Because he is a maker of miracles. Because I SAID SO.'

They squeezed through clusters of people. Boy scouts marched in their uniforms. Sufis whirled in multi-coloured skirts. Dervishes led people into *dhikr* circles. Men swayed to the beat of large drums and danced to the point of exhaustion, chanting '*Allah hay*, God is alive' as they impelled their bodies and minds into an ecstatic trance, reaching for oneness with God.

Suddenly, the sky turned green. The two brothers lifted their heads and above them they saw dervishes on horses waving large green flags over the heads of the spectators. The flags were inscribed with *La Ilaha illa Allah*, there is no God but the one God. Smiles on the boys' faces grew into laughter as they stared at one another. Their complexions reflected the colour of the flags above them, turning their skin green as peas. The boys ran under the rows of flags, laughing, keeping a safe distance from the horses while they flapped their green arms, pretending they were soaring and fluttering with the wind.

They ran until they reached the centre of the crowd. There, the two boys stood shoulder to shoulder in absolute reverence. In the middle of the circle was the main attraction, the man with the impressive white turban, the leader of devout Sufis and mystical maker of miracles – the *khalifah* himself, riding his splendid, white horse.

'You see!' Karim threw his arm around his brother's shoulder and drew him close. 'Aren't you glad we made it?'

'Yes!' said a bedazzled Rahim. 'Do you think we will see a miracle?'

At that exact moment, the *khalifah* turned his head towards them, nodded, then coaxed his horse in their direction. The boys were stunned. They caught their breath, their shoulders tightened and their chests exploded to the wild drumming of their nervous hearts. The *khalifah* was only inches away. He towered above them, on his majestic horse. They squinted through the flashing lights trying to make out the features of the face beneath the big, white turban.

'Sons of *Sheikh* Hussein!' His voice was familiar. '*Mashallah!*' he sang. 'The *sheikh* now allows you to go out at night without an adult? You do have his permission to be here, don't you?'

Confused as to why the *khalifah* would care, the boys answered, 'Yes, sir!' Karim hesitated for a second before he added, 'You know our father?'

The *khalifah* laughed. 'You don't recognise me?' He lowered his head closer to them and their eyes nearly popped out of their sockets.

'*Sheikh* Soluman Haneyah?' The boys' voices carried both disbelief and disappointment.

This man was no maker of miracles. *Sheikh* Soluman was an ordinary man, a regular visitor to their father's evening circles and a good friend to the family. They never thought of him as anyone special. Yet there he was, the man of the hour, the highlight of the festival – a distinguished, respectable *khalifah* wearing a big, white turban, riding a big, white horse.

'Look after yourselves,' the man said, 'and say hello to your father!' he added, as he rode back into the centre of the circle.

Karim looked at his younger brother, who seemed deflated and let down. He decided to bring some magic and wonder back into the night. 'Hey,' Karim said. 'You know, we are very lucky that we now know the real identity of *Sheikh* Soluman. But we must keep it a secret.'

'What do you mean?' Rahim was clinging to hope again.

'The *khalifah* trusted us enough to show us who he is. But not everyone can know that he is a *khalifah*. If word got out, everyone would bother him. Everyone would be asking for miracles. He would never be left to rest. He's like a superhero, you know — they, too, always have a secret identity.'

Rahim's face beamed. 'So, *Sheikh* Soluman is really a maker of miracles?'

'Shhhhh.' Karim hushed his little brother. 'Not so loud. Of course, he is.'

The boys returned their attention to the dervish circle. Rahim's faith in the *khalifah* restored and miracles were happening all around. Dervishes ran swords through their faces, walked smiling on hot coals, juggled fire torches, swallowed burning flames and floated on invisible chairs. Karim enjoyed watching his little brother's reactions to the miracles, but in his heart, he was old enough to recognise them as tricks. For Karim, the greatest miracle he witnessed that night was that of language threaded in exquisite poetry and chanted by the dervishes to the beat of drums.

For many days that followed, Karim watched his younger brothers as they re-enacted with other children in Mohatta Street the Festival of Miracles.

'Join us, Karim.' Rahim tugged at his brother's arm. 'We need someone taller to play the part of the *khalifah*, *Sheikh* Soluman.'

Karim laughed. 'Have you heard the conversation between the wind and the sea?'

'What conversation?' asked Rahim.

'Well,' Karim began with a sly smile. 'Last night, I heard the wind whisper to the sea, "I have a secret. The *khalifah*, the Sufi *sheikh* of miracles, the man on the big, white horse, the man in the big, white turban, is no other than *Sheikh* Soluman!" and the sea roared with laughter and said to the wind, "What you think is a secret is no more than an old song slipping off the tongues of all the children of Tuffah."'

Rahim didn't have his brother's eloquence and imagination, but he understood when he was being mocked. He admitted to himself that the burden of keeping the secret of the *khalifah*'s identity was too hard for him to bear. He only whispered it to a few of his most trusted friends, and they, in turn, whispered it to a few of theirs, and now was it really his fault that every child in Tuffah knew of it?

'I don't think *Sheikh* Soluman cares if children know he is a *khalifah*,' Rahim said defiantly. 'You'll see. He will arrive soon, and you will see.'

No sooner did Rahim say that, a ripple of excitement swept the children who started to shout 'The *khalifah* is here! The *khalifah* is here!'

Much to Rahim's relief, the Sufi *sheikh* laughed joyfully at the sight of the young crowd who had formed a circle around him. 'Children of Tuffah, from this day on you are my little dervishes!' proclaimed *Sheikh* Soluman. 'We will take the oath together, so you are inducted into the Sufi path.'

Sheikh Soluman raised his head to the sky and howled, 'My dervishes!' and the boys whirled around him, swinging their heads and chanting, noisily, '*Allah hay*, God is alive!' '*Allah hay*!'

Sheikh Soluman took advantage of the chaos as the boys tried to form their own *dhikr* circles, and he made his way towards *Sheikh* Hussein's home. Karim, who had been watching on, followed him with eager steps.

'Welcome,' Karim said out loud, hoping to get *Sheikh* Soluman's attention. 'My father will be happy to see you.'

Sheikh Soluman smiled to himself, revelling in all the newly acquired attention. He made way for Karim to pass him in the narrow alleyway and announce his arrival at the *sheikh*'s home.

'Did you enjoy the festival?' *Sheikh* Soluman asked.

'Yes, very much,' Karim replied.

'What did you enjoy the most?'

'The songs and the poetry.'

Sheikh Soluman was intrigued. He had expected the boy to say the fire-eater or the snake charmer. He would never have guessed that a boy of Karim's age would be more impressed by songs and poetry. 'Was there any particular song, or poem?'

'Yes,' said Karim, as he swung open the front gate to their home. 'Please, come in.'

'*Ya sater!*' *Sheikh* Soluman shouted, announcing his presence, as he walked into the front yard. This was customary, intended to let the women of the house know that a man is coming through.

'Would you like me to recite for you the poem I liked the most from the festival?' Karim asked him, as they walked across the front yard to the *sheikh*'s room.

Sheikh Soluman stopped, amused, and nodded encouragingly.

Give me an excess of love
For you, bewildered
Have mercy on a heart
Scorched by a glance
And if I ask to see you truly
Then allow me, graciously
And let not your answer be,
'Thou shalt not see'

Sheikh Soluman stared at the boy for a moment. 'How old are you?' he asked.

'Come inside, my father is here,' Karim said, before he answered, as they both stepped into the *sheikh*'s room. 'I am eight years old.'

In his room, *Sheikh* Hussein had another guest, their neighbour Ibrahim-Hamada. The two greeted *Sheikh* Soluman warmly. *Sheikh* Hussein gestured to his son to sit down with them. The *sheikh* had heard the conversation that passed between his son and the Sufi *sheikh* outside his door, and it did not surprise him.

'Since the festival,' *Sheikh* Hussein said, 'my son has developed an interest in Sufi poetry.'

'*Mashallah!*' the Sufi *sheikh* could not conceal the look of disbelief that framed his face. '*Mashallah!*' he repeated.

'Karim is no ordinary boy,' Ibrahim-Hamada said. 'He has memorised more poetry than anyone on the face of the earth.'

It was true – Karim had earned a reputation for his exceptional ability to memorise everything he read, saw, heard or experienced, word for word. An ability that had made him stand out in school and amongst the regulars in his father's circle.

Karim loved the praise, but his father always reminded him to be humble and not let his ego get in the way of his learning. So he tried to stay focused on his questions. 'What Sufi path do you follow, *Sheikh* Soluman?' he inquired.

'I follow the path of the Algerian leader Ahmad al-Alawi,' *Sheikh* Soluman answered. 'The man was a hero in the resistance against the French.'

'How? How is it that you follow the path? What do you do?' Karim persisted in his questioning.

'Every week we gather in a prayer circle, *halaqat dhikr*. Your neighbour and personal advocate here, Ibrahim-Hamada, joins us too.'

'Really?' Karim had no idea.

'Yes,' Ibrahim-Hamada laughed. 'It's good for the soul. And we see the miracles of God.'

Karim reflected on the idea of the miracles, but all he could imagine was the festival's tricks that were clearly more performative than they were divine. The miracles of God, as the Sufi *sheikh* put it, did not interest him. But the poetry, oh the poetry, and the melodic chants – they still rang in his ears.

His father considered him, as if reading the thoughts that were running through his mind, before he finally said, 'Karim, would you like to go to the *halaqat dhikr* with *Sheikh* Soluman?'

'I can take him,' Ibrahim-Hamada offered. 'We can walk there and back together.'

Karim was dumbfounded. He couldn't believe his father would offer him this. He looked at *Sheikh* Soluman and Ibrahim-Hamada, both smiling and nodding encouragingly.

Sheikh Hussein spoke again. 'I want to encourage my son to seek diverse sources of knowledge, both academically and spiritually.' He turned to his son, 'Karim, you'll be on the path of Ahmad al-Alawi, the man who began on the *Darqawiyya* path before he established his own order, the Alawiyya, which combines the essence of spirituality and its relationship to resistance to evil.'

'There is another important reason you need to consider,' Ibrahim-Hamada said, as he sipped on his coffee, '*Halaqat dhikr* always end with a feast of *lahmah we maftool*, couscous with lamb!'

'You can be assured you would be getting at least one good meal every week,' laughed the *sheikh*.

Overjoyed by the prospects of food and poetry, Karim clapped his hands and chanted, '*Allah hay!* God is alive!'

20

GLORY

1952

The following summer, Karim returned to Mohamad Khodry for work. The merchant, pleased with the boy's exemplary manners and efficiency the previous year, hired him as the store's errand boy. This job proved to be more demanding of Karim's time, requiring him to be at the store from the moment Khodry unlocked its large, green, iron door in the morning, until late in the evening when the door was locked again – but the pay was far more lucrative. Karim was paid one Egyptian pound every week, almost more than his father's weekly earnings during the school season.

Khodry's store was in Gaza's ancient quarter in the heart of Souk al-Zawya, a colourful indoor–outdoor market that stretched from the entrance of the Great Omari Mosque all the way to the city's main square. Khodry's shop was at the start of the souk, just before the narrow entrance to the arched ancient bazaar known as al-Qaysariyya, where gold and silver jewellery shimmered behind shiny windows. Some customers came to Souk al-Zawya seeking luxurious textiles and fashionable accessories, either locally made, or imported from Egypt and Syria. Others came for the fresh fruit and vegetable market and the sweet stalls, but most came to restock their pantries with aromatic spices, dried fruit, freshly roasted nuts and cardamom-infused coffee. It was the latter group that came to Khodry's store.

At work, Karim was tasked with cleaning the tiled floors, re-stocking the shelves, hosing the ground outside to keep the dust from rising, keeping count of the money received, and fetching beverages for special customers and other merchants who often dropped by. Karim was a fast learner; he quickly memorised all the names and faces of Khodry's customers and their preferred styles of shopping. Some liked to be paid attention, others liked to browse in peace. Some loved to haggle, others had no patience for that, and only wanted to know the bottom line.

Standing behind the counter in Khodry's shop, Karim watched as a vibrant sea of shoppers and merchants passed through. A few faces were familiar, but there were many he did not recognise. Occasionally, he found himself staring at a beautiful girl going by, or a scantily dressed woman; a sight the boy was not accustomed to seeing in his neighbourhood. During such times his boss repri-manded him gently. 'Keep your eyes on the merchandise,' he often repeated, lest Karim forgot.

Across to the left from the shop, Karim watched Borno, the cobbler who stood all day behind his cart mending leather straps, or shining the shoes and the egos of his customers. Next to him was the Shojayah cafe, with its radio blasting a fusion of songs and news bulletins, and where mostly older men sat on uncomfortable wooden chairs across from each other, sipping tea, puffing ciga-rettes, playing backgammon and arguing politics.

On the footpath outside the cafe, Khidiw Abu-Abbas, the street barber, had set up his chair – which he called ambitiously a mobile salon. Abu-Abbas rightly believed that anyone who had time to sit in a cafe, probably had time for a haircut. Karim loved watching Abu-Abbas the most, as he hovered over his customers, shaving, cutting, trimming and dyeing one head after the next, while his mouth constantly moved and his voice projected tirelessly louder than the cafe's radio, carrying songs, stories and crass swearwords across the market.

One hot, summer afternoon in July of 1952, as Karim tended to his duties behind the counter, he sensed a new kind of excitement spread through the old market like wildfire. He stood outside the shop while others hovered near the cafe, all listening to a radio news broadcast: 'Officers from the Egyptian army, who call themselves the Free Officers Movement, have successfully overthrown King Farouk.' At first people looked at each other in disbelief, but soon cheers resounded everywhere.

The first to come to Khodry's shop demanding a celebration was Ibrahim-Hamada, Karim's Sufi companion and next-door neighbour. Soon after, Borno the cobbler, thrilled by the news, packed up his tools, locked his cart, and came to Khodry's shop to celebrate. Delighted, Khodry sent Karim to the cafe to get tea for his guests, but Borno objected. 'This occasion requires something fancier than tea.'

'Of course, it does!' Khodry laughed. 'Karim, get us two bottles of Coca-Cola from the cafe.'

Outside the cafe, Abu-Abbas, the street barber, was yelling to the jubilant customers inside the cafe, 'The king of whores had it coming!'

Khodry shouted at the barber from across the road. 'The cafe is too full, why don't you come here to celebrate with us the fall of the king of whores.'

Karim smiled when he heard his boss cursing the ousted king in public. It was very unusual for Khodry, or any merchant in the market, to engage in political discussions relating to Egypt. Since 1948, Gaza had been under Egyptian rule, and almost all of Gaza's economy depended on Egypt. No one dared to curse the king.

At the cafe the radio ran the news broadcast on a loop, although the sound was drowned by the noisy animated discussions all around. Karim strained his ear to listen: 'Breaking News: The Free Officers Movement led by General Muhammad Naguib and Lieutenant Colonel Gamal Abdel Nasser have orchestrated a coup and succeeded in overthrowing King Farouk.'

Yes, but how? Karim really wanted to know. And what happens now? He wished he could just run home and discuss this important event with his learned father. His thoughts were drowned by the noisy cheers. Every time the announcement was repeated, the crowd at the cafe reacted as if they were hearing the news for the first time.

While waiting for his turn to order the drinks, Karim noticed several younger men, new faces to the market, sneak into a room at the back of the cafe. His curiosity got the better of him. He followed the men into a packed room at the rear of the building. He stood at the back, leaning on the wall in utter shock, as he saw Hafez, his maternal uncle, standing on a chair, delivering a fiery speech. What is going on here? he wondered.

'Comrades. Brothers. *Fedayeen*. Four years have passed since 1948 and we are still stuck here in refugee camps while the Jewish invaders sleep in our beds. We are suffering the cold while they lie warm under roofs we raised. We are surviving on rations while they harvest fruits we planted. We are exiled into the far corner of our historic homeland, and they want us to believe there is no Palestine anymore. We are denied the right to return to our homes. We are denied the right to citizenship. We are denied the right to autonomy and to freedom. But as God is my witness, we will be free – and we will return.'

The crowd roared. Karim was blown away. So, this is where the illusive resistance meets? He had heard rumours of the *fedayeen*, but he had no idea his uncle was one of them, leading them even, it seemed.

'Israel built a state on the ruins of our nation!' Hafez continued. 'The good Egyptian officers who came to fight with us were betrayed by their rulers. The son of dogs King Farouk gave them weapons that backfired. Well, he had only one priority: to serve his English masters. He served them at the expense of his Egyptian subjects, at the expense of Palestinians, and at the expense of all the Arab people!'

The crowd roared again in anger.

'And if that wasn't enough,' continued Hafez, 'when King Farouk's Egypt handed Israel its victory, it declared Gaza as its protectorate. So, we formed the All-Palestine Government in Gaza – our own government – and you know what Egypt did? Well, let me tell you comrades, it wasn't only Israel that exiled us – it was also King Farouk's government, when they ordered the relocation of our autonomous government to Cairo!'

'Shame! Shame!' the crowd shouted.

'A government in exile,' Hafez shouted back. 'Forbidden from returning to Gaza!'

Hafez paused for a moment. His features relaxed. He smiled. 'Today, my comrades, all of this has changed.' His voice softened with promise of hope. 'Today the Egyptian freedom fighters have risen. Today Egypt is reborn. Today we can look forward to building a new resistance. To working together with our Egyptian brothers.'

A hand grabbed Karim by the shirt. 'You shouldn't be here,' Salem pulled him out of the room.

'Stop!' Karim tried to wriggle out of Salem's grip. 'You're here, so why can't I be?'

Karim wasn't entirely surprised to see Salem. He had heard rumours that Salem had joined the *fedayeen* fighters. Although the two boys had grown up together in the same neighbourhood, they were not close friends. Salem was a few years older, and Karim viewed him as an extension of the *sheikh*'s stick, for he was the one who would bring Karim to the *sheikh* whenever Karim did something wrong.

'Your father would want me to keep you away from here. You're too young for this. Now get back to your work!'

Karim was annoyed with Salem's interference and his condescending tone, but he had no choice. His boss was waiting. He picked up the beverages and ran back to Khodry's store.

When he gave Borno, the cobbler, the Coca-Cola bottle, the man's eyes nearly popped out of their sockets.

'How strange,' said Borno, as he stared into the glass bottle. 'How did they manage to squeeze this large piece of frozen ice into the bottle?' This was the first time the cafe had used its new freezer, an electric device not known to many in the old city. The men stared at the frozen piece in the bottle with awe, bewildered by its large size and the narrowness of the bottle neck.

Borno squinted, staring into his glass bottle, and he nodded, like he had a great idea. He declared the cafe owner had cheated him by putting ice inside the bottle, not coke, so he should get a discount.

Abu-Abbas laughed. 'Beside your gift for mending shoes and dyeing leather, you certainly have a God-given gift for finding creative ways to get discounts.'

Khodry laughed. 'Once when Borno travelled with me to Cairo, he haggled the clerk at the hotel so hard that at the end of our stay, the clerk reached into his own pocket and paid him just to get rid of him.'

As the men continued to banter and laugh, Karim was growing restless and bored. He was eager to go home and discuss with his father the revolution in Egypt and the brewing Palestinian resistance he had witnessed in the back room at the cafe. He wanted an intellectual analysis, not the shallow interpretation of merchants and empty talk at the bazaar.

As soon as Karim locked the shop at the end of the day, he walked with Ibrahim-Hamada to the Shuja'iyya station, where the two could take the train back to the Muhatta railway station near their home in Tuffah. They walked along Omar Al-Mukhtar Street, and perused the shop windows, the lively cafes and the beautiful fancy automobiles.

'Look!' Ibrahim-Hamada pointed to the shop window of the only photography studio in Gaza. The studio belonged to an Armenian who was known for his quick changes of portraits in his window in response to the political trends of the day. Since 1949, the Armenian photographer had displayed a large portrait of King Farouk in his shop window. That night, the portrait of the king was gone, and in its place hung a beautifully framed portrait of General Muhammad Naguib, the leader of the Free Officers Movement in Egypt.

'This man gets his news faster than Abu-Abbas, the barber!' Ibrahim-Hamada smiled.

Karim and Ibrahim-Hamada stood silently for a few minutes, staring at the portrait of the young Egyptian officer in uniform. From all around them, through the cafes, and from the balconies and the open windows, they heard one song playing all through the night. It seemed all the radios in Gaza were tuned in to the same station, broadcasting the enchanting voice of Egypt's most celebrated singer, Umm Kulthum, as she sang 'Egypt speaks for itself . . . the people stand up to see . . . how we build our glory . . .'

21

SOUHAILAH

GAZA, PALESTINE, 1954–1956

Some people mark the years by the rise and fall of political powers, revolutions, collective victories, and shared losses. Some mark the years by the state-of-the-art innovations and fashion trends. But there are those who believe that it is in the hidden folds of the spectacular, and within the margins of historic events, inside what we deem as unremarkable, usual, or even mundane, that the most precious memories are made and kept. Souhailah was such a person.

Souhailah paid attention to the details of daily life. She kept her drawers organised and her appearance impeccable. She accepted the way things were without questioning. She accommodated her father's and her older brothers' lack of interest in her life. If they seemed passive and emotionally out of reach, she blamed it on their long hours working at the family's carpentry workshop. She admired her mother's strength, trusted her commands and obeyed them. And she was grateful that Karim was always there to offer her a window into the big world outside.

Souhailah, 1958.

Karim was kind and gentle. He took time to ask about her school, help her with her homework and whenever she was ill, he was the one who had to take her to see the doctor and to follow up to ensure she knew what medicine she needed to take.

Once, during the holy month of Ramadan, while everyone was fasting, Karim caught Souhailah standing under the almond tree, discretely eating an almond. She was so embarrassed. Women were allowed to break their fasting only when they were ill, nursing, or when they had their period. Karim knew it was the latter. Souhailah blushed at the thought of him knowing, and blushed even more when a broad smile stretched across his face.

'There is nothing to be embarrassed about,' he said gently. 'Congratulations! You are a young woman now!'

Karim plucked the almonds off the tree, used a rock to crush their hard shells, and watched her eat with delight, even as he fought his own hunger pains from the fasting.

Souhailah loved seeing the world through his eyes. He brought her books that she devoured, told her about the Egyptian films he had watched at the cinema, sang for her the songs of Abdel Halim Hafez – and always had a poem or two to recite. Mostly the poems were written by others, but once in a while, when he gathered courage to share his own, Souhailah's heart fluttered with every word. At night, as she lay down to sleep, she could almost hear his voice reciting her favourite love poem that she knew he had written just for her:

> You are inconceivable happiness
> Your palms hold eternal bliss
> A fragrant bouquet of lilies and roses
> Your face is tranquil
> Like a new dawn
> Elegant and glorious

Souhailah woke up with a terrible pain in her abdomen. Her mother, Fatima, pregnant and caring for an army of children at home, called on Karim to take her to hospital. At Al-Shifa Hospital, the doctor diagnosed her with a nasty case of worms. She was quickly admitted into the children's ward. For an entire week, the then eleven-year-old girl had no visitors at all, except for Karim. Her mother had her hands full at home and was heavy with her sixth child, and her father and older brothers worked long hours at the family's carpentry workshop. If it weren't for Karim, Souhailah would have cried alone in her hospital bed, all seven days and nights.

On the first two days, the twelve-year-old Karim sat beside Souhailah's bed and read her stories from the Persian fables of *Kalila and Dimna*. On the third day he laid out for her, scene by scene, the details of a film he saw at the cinema called *Maw'ed Gharam*, *Appointment with Love*, starring Faten Hamama, Abdel Halim Hafez and Rushdy Abaza.

On the fourth day Souhailah was permitted to leave the ward, so she walked with Karim to the nearby beach. It took them fifteen minutes to get there, and Karim was quiet almost the entire time. Souhailah could sense something was wrong.

They selected the perfect rock, with a wide, smooth surface, and they sat with their feet dangling over the crushing waves. When Karim still did not speak, Souhailah asked, 'What's new?'

He smiled. 'The Armenian photographer took down the portrait of General Muhammad Naguib and replaced it with a poster of Egypt's new president, Gamal Abdel Nasser.'

'Come on.' Souhailah offered half a smile. 'That's old. Tell me now,' she insisted. 'Why are you upset?'

Karim looked away into the blue horizon. He couldn't bring himself to tell her that despite his best efforts, the money his family made was not enough to pay for the school fees, and that he and his brother Rahim were served with a suspension notice and told not to return to school until they had settled the account.

He inhaled deeply, held his breath for a moment, then exhaled an ocean of sea salt and troubles into the air. He looked into Souhailah's hazel eyes. 'Don't worry,' he assured her. 'It's a small problem I need to take care of.'

Souhailah did not ask any more questions. The two sat together in compatible silence for a while, content to watch the colourful wooden fishing boats dance on the tip of the horizon.

The following day, Karim and Souhailah returned to the same spot on the rock. She could sense from the moment he picked her up from her hospital room that whatever had weighed him down the previous day, had been lifted.

'You seem much happier,' she noted as she gathered her curls into an elastic band.

'Yes,' Karim said, sitting beside her.

'You took care of that problem you had yesterday?'

'I did.' Karim nodded smiling. 'Yesterday, Rahim and I were suspended from school because we couldn't pay the fees.'

'Oh my God!' Souhailah gasped.

'Don't worry – I fought the system with the only weapon I have, and I won!'

'What? What weapon?'

'I stormed into the principal's office, poetry blazing.'

'That's a new one!' Souhailah giggled. 'Blazing poetry? So, that's your weapon?'

'Yes. And it worked,' Karim boasted. 'Would you like to hear it?'

'Sure!' Souhailah tried to pull a serious face.

Karim stood up on the rock and projected his voice, raising it above the crashing waves.

'Banished from school
They slammed the door
Be gone they yelled
You are too poor
No money for fees

Don't bother return
You cannot afford
The price to learn
What have we done?
How could this be?
Who turned education
Into a commodity?
Isn't this the dawn
                of Nasserism?
Equality for all
Not elitism.'

Souhailah stood up and clapped enthusiastically. 'Bravo! Bravo!'

'When I finished the poem, the principal laughed, and said, "Enough, son. You're going to start a revolution. Just go to your class."'

'And so you did, right?' Souhailah laughed.

'No, of course not. I said, "What about my brother?" The principal sighed and told me to tell Rahim he can go back to his classes, too.'

'Did you read this poem to your father?'

'Only after the facts, when it got me back into school.'

'Was he impressed?'

'Not overly.' There was a hint of sadness in Karim's voice. 'My father worries that if I become a poet, I will end up being a mouthpiece for rulers and factions. That's the only poetry that gets famous and is platformed – poetry backed by power. I promised him that I would never let that happen.'

'I don't understand.' Souhailah was puzzled.

'My father believes that professional poets – the ones who depend on writing for a living – inevitably end up selling their souls.

How else would they put food on their table? It's that simple,'
Karim explained.

On the last day of Souhailah's hospital stay, Karim brought her a
basket of peeled cactus pears, and a change of clothes that Fatima
gave him in the morning for Souhailah to wear when she left.

'Oh my God! I love cactus pears, but no one ever wants to peel
their thorny skin for me.'

'I promise you,' Karim said, as he reached for a juicy sweet
cactus pear and held it close to Souhailah's mouth. 'I promise
you, I will be your personal cactus-pear peeler from this day on!'

Souhailah laughed with delight and took a big bite.

The two walked home together, taking slow steps and choosing
the longest roads possible. They spoke of many things along the

Baba on his bicycle, date unknown.

way, but never spoke of love. Why would they? It would have been like saying the sun is bright, and the sky is blue.

As Souhailah and Karim grew into their early teens, their parents placed restrictions on what time they could spend together, and how and where they spent it. Books provided the perfect cover for their meetings. Karim, a legitimate educator in the *sheikh*'s school, took on the task of educating Souhailah on the works of Arab poets and novelist and, whenever possible, sharing with her his own poems and stories. As the two grew older, so did the nature of the material they shared, moving away from adventure books and children's stories, into a world of romantic novels that expanded their imaginations, and ignited their yearnings.

When Karim gave Souhailah the romantic novel *Al-Wisadah Alkhalyah*, meaning the vacant pillow, by Egyptian author Ihsan Abdel Quddous, Souhailah devoured each word with hunger. She imagined herself the protagonist, Sameeha – the beautiful young woman who wins the heart of the hero, Salah. She imagined Salah to be Karim, of course – the starstruck lover who ached for Sameeha, and pursued her relentlessly. Heart pounding with desire, Souhailah must have read a thousand times the part in the book when Sameeha and Salah kiss – she wore out the page where it was written. Souhailah wept when Sameeha's parents objected to Salah's marriage proposal and forced Sameeha to marry another man. How could the power of first love not win in the end? How could the universe allow such a travesty?

Souhailah immersed herself into Salah and Sameeha's story so much so she had become oblivious to her surroundings. Lost in the world of love and heartache, she didn't see her older brother Azmy walk into her room and watch, with shock, what she was reading, until he snatched the book out of her hand. It all happened so fast – one moment she was imagining the meeting of Sameeha and Salah's lips, the next moment Azmy was towering above her, waving the book and shouting at her.

'How dare you read this shameful book!' He was livid. How was it possible his innocent little sister was reading adult fiction? He knew that book. He had read it himself many times, and he enjoyed all the sexual undertones. It was okay for him to read it – in fact, it was natural. He was a young man. But, his sister, he thought she was too young and innocent.

'How dare you!' Azmy stormed outside, holding the book up like dangerous, damning evidence found at a crime scene.

'*Yumma*,' Azmy called out, searching for their mother. '*Yumma*, where are you?'

'At the Champs-Élysées,' Fatima yelled back sarcastically from the garden, where she was hanging the laundry. 'Where else would I be?'

Azmy ignored his mother's sarcastic response, and charged towards her waving the book in his hand. '*Yumma*, your daughter is reading dirty books!'

'I am not!' Souhailah came running after him. '*Yumma!*' she looked at her mother with eyes pleading for rescue.

Fatima took a deep breath and smiled resolutely. 'Okay, let me be the judge. Read to me the dirty parts.'

Azmy immediately found the page with the steamiest scene.

'You knew exactly where to look?' Fatima teased him. 'You must have this book memorised.'

'It opened naturally to this page because your daughter wore it out. Besides,' Azmy huffed defensively, 'I'm a man, and I'm almost sixteen years old. Not a silly little girl.'

'I am not a silly little girl,' Souhailah shouted indignantly.

'Go on,' Fatima refereed. 'Show me.'

'Look,' Azmy pointed to the passage on the page. 'It's right here!'

Fatima leaned over and read out loud: 'They threw themselves into one another's passionate embrace . . . dot dot dot' she smiled as she read the dots out loud.

'You see?' Azmy shouted.

'Really? Dot. Dot. Dot?' his mother shook her head.

'These dots are not innocent,' Azmy insisted. 'We all know what they mean.'

Fatima knew the dots were like blank spaces inviting readers to fill in with their imagination. Fatima also knew that it was Karim who gave Souhailah this book, as he gave her many others – a situation of which she wholeheartedly approved, and had no intention of bringing to an end.

'*Yumma*, this is adult content,' Azmy insisted. 'It will open her eyes.'

'So what?' Fatima's judgement came with a shrug. Azmy's jaws dropped in disbelief.

'So what?' Fatima said again, as she picked up the final shirt from the hamper and clipped it on the clothesline. 'Your sister is not a silly little girl, as you say. She is a young woman now. She needs to open her eyes to the world.'

Karim and Souhailah sat next to each other under the pomegranate tree in their shared garden. That was the only place they were allowed to sit together now. They were not children anymore and could no longer play behind closed doors, or inside dark corridors, or on the rooftop, or anywhere the whole world could not see them. So they sat on the garden bench under the pomegranate tree, between their two family homes, in broad daylight and in full view of anyone who cared to look.

'I made you something!'

Karim, nervous, presented Souhailah with a book made up of a dozen pages folded in the middle and bonded together with a crimson velvet ribbon, nestled inside a hard cover made of white cardboard and decorated with elegant Arabic calligraphy.

Souhailah held the small book, her heart pounding with joy, curiosity and wonder. She examined the art on its front cover. It took her a second or two to realise that she was looking at their names, Souhailah and Karim, scribbled in stunning Arabic calligraphy.

'That wasn't me,' Karim said with impatience. 'Rahim drew the cover. But I did all the writing inside. So, *yallah!* Go on, open it!'

Slowly Souhailah turned the cover and began to read the neatly arranged handwritten pages. Aware of Karim's gaze upon her, she twisted the ends of the velvet ribbon around her finger and tried to manage her breathing as she savoured every word she read slowly, in pleasurable silence. When she reached the end, she closed the book and smiled.

'You wrote our story. You left out nothing.'

'How you were dressed like a bride on the night of my circumcision . . .'

'How we slept next to each other in Khan Yunis during the bombing of 1948 . . .'

'How we always meet on this bench, under the pomegranate tree . . .'

Karim drew closer. 'Let me show you, see on this page here? That's my favourite one. Remember how we hid from Rahim and Azmy near the cactus bush?'

'But still,' Souhailah laughed. 'They managed to find us.'

'True. But your mother covered for us. She told them she had sent us to pick cactus pears.'

'My mother is too smart. She found a way to punish you, and to keep you in her debt forever.'

'Yes,' Karim agreed, smiling. 'From that day, I had to pick the cactus pears off the thorny bushes whenever they were in season.'

'But I have always wondered, why do you go the distance? My mother only asked you to pick the cactus pears. But you go the extra mile – you peel them, too.'

'I pick the cactus pears for your mother. I peel them for you. So you may enjoy the sweet fruit without enduring its thorns.'

Karim and Souhailah's eyes locked momentarily. Desire, like an electric pulse, charged through them. Souhailah, afraid and shy, turned her eyes away.

'Tell me,' she whispered softly. 'What happens in the ending of our story?'

'We get married, and we grow old together.'

22

THE SUEZ CRISIS

GAZA, PALESTINE, 1956

It began like any other autumn night. Darkness descended over the hills and valleys of Palestine and the moon was dispatched high into the sky, its silver rays dancing to a familiar ancient lullaby. The men, women and children yawned and stretched, tossed and turned, on beds, on mattresses, on straw mats, on concrete floors, in the arms of a beloved, in the bosom of a mother, inside a home, inside a refugee camp, inside a hospital, a mosque, a prison cell, on the sand by the beach or out under the stars in the open fields. The still darkness lulled them all to surrender their thoughts, worries, to-do lists and plans, and fall asleep. But the night had deceived them. Warplanes ambushed their dreams, and the moonsong turned to explosions as the warplanes signalled the return of the *majnoon* in the sky.

Gaza's mayor, Munir Al-Rayes, drew a deep sigh and turned away from the window, unable to withstand the pain of what he was witnessing. He had known they were coming. He had been notified of the withdrawal of the Egyptian administrative staff from the municipality before nightfall descended. And as all of Gaza went to sleep, he did not. He stayed awake. He knew they were coming.

As morning light and Israeli tanks rolled into the Gaza Strip, the mayor wore his suit and tie and kissed his wife and children goodbye. His eldest, eighteen-year-old son Nahed, followed him to the iron gate of their beautiful, two-storey home in the affluent suburb of Rimal.

'Let me come with you, Father.'

'No, Son.' The mayor spoke with a heavy heart. 'You must stay and look after our family. I need you here for them.'

The mayor parked his Renault automobile outside Gaza's municipal building and climbed the stairs to his office. He couldn't help but mutter under his breath, '*Hasbi allah we na'am alwakeel*, God will suffice and in him we trust.' The Egyptians, who were responsible for protecting Gaza, who had been administering to the city since 1949, who filled the offices of this building, had all abandoned their positions. They literally left the keys of our city for the invaders to claim, he thought, repeating, '*Hasbi allah we na'am alwakeel.*'

In his office, the mayor waited for the Israelis to arrive. He wanted to be there, at his post, until the last minute. He was an astute, educated man – brave, like the people of his city, and just as stubborn. It wasn't long before he heard the grating sound of tanks, as they rolled in and surrounded the building. He looked out the window and saw the soldiers march inside. He took a deep breath to fill his lungs with air, and his heart with courage.

'*Ya allah*,' he prayed, as he heard the echo of the soldiers' boots bounce off the cement steps and against the narrow walls in the stairway. '*Ya allah!* Strengthen me with courage so I may best serve my people.'

Four young Israeli soldiers stormed into his office. He stood up straight and looked them in the eye. He was not afraid, but he noted the fear in their eyes. They were young, the same age as his son Nahed. The soldiers, antagonised by his courage, quickly pointed their rifles at him.

'Don't be afraid,' the mayor said calmly. 'I'm the only one here. I am not armed. No need for all this bravado with the rifles.'

A soldier stepped forward and took out a letter from his pocket. '*Inta rayes baladyah?*' he asked, addressing the mayor in broken Arabic.

'Yes, I am the mayor.'

'We have a letter for you from the Israeli government.'

The soldier handed the mayor a sealed envelope. The letter inside announced Israel's authority over Gaza. It ordered the mayor to inform the Palestinians in his city that they must cooperate with the Israeli occupation. It assured him that he would be able to continue to act as mayor under Israeli rule, and it ended with an assurance that his obedience and conformity would be rewarded generously.

'No.' The mayor crunched the letter in his fist and threw it into the garbage bin. 'I do not now, nor will I ever recognise the authority or the legitimacy of the Zionist entity you have created on our soil, after you murdered and dispossessed our people. No. I will not cooperate with your criminal state.'

The young soldiers were at first confused, but soon their confusion gave way to fury. 'We have orders to arrest you if you refuse to cooperate,' they threatened.

'Arrest me,' was the mayor's response.

The mayor was dragged by the soldiers out of his office and down the echoey stairs, his voice ringing throughout the municipality building and amplified into every home in Gaza: 'I will never legit-imise your theft of our homeland. I will never legitimise your theft of our homeland.'

The mayor was taken to a military prison and placed under administrative detention, and the army dispatched another unit to bring in his deputy mayor.

Dragged from his home in his pyjamas, the deputy mayor was taken into the mayor's office and ordered to sign.

'Congratulations,' the soldiers said, rifles pointing at him. 'You are now the mayor of this city.'

And so it was, at gunpoint, that the deputy mayor of Gaza signed what history now calls the Gaza surrender agreement of 1956.

News of the mayor's arrest and Gaza's surrender spread fast throughout the city. An army curfew was enforced in all the main streets, and families stayed in their homes in fear and silence. Refugees who had escaped Israel's ruthless massacres and war of 1948 relived the trauma of their flight and dispossession as the Israeli tanks rolled into the streets of the old city for the first time, and towards the refugee camps.

The men walked the narrow alleyways of Tuffah to avoid being seen by the army, and gathered one by one at the *sheikh*'s home, anxious to find out what was going on and how they could protect their families and livelihood under this newly announced Israeli occupation. They listened sombrely to Abu-Awny's radio as it blasted the BBC Arabic news through the speaker in the *sheikh*'s room while Rahim filled their cups with an endless stream of coffee. Karim sat next to his father, old enough now to participate in such important discussions and to offer his opinion.

'They want to break Arab resistance against Western imperial interests.' The *sheikh* spoke in a tired, deflated voice. 'Since President Nasser nationalised the Suez Canal, France and Britain have plotted with Israel to bring him – and, of course, all of us – to our knees.'

'President Nasser had no choice,' Karim interjected, eager to show off his political knowledge to Souhailah's father, Abu-Awny, who sat quietly sipping on his coffee.

'The US broke its promise to fund the construction of the Aswan Dam,' Karim added, but Abu-Awny still did not seem to notice or care about Karim's comments. Karim went on, 'Nationalising the Suez Canal is the only way to cover these funding shortages.' Still Abu-Awny did not offer Karim even a glance. 'Also, what really antagonised France is Nasser's endorsement and support for the Algerian heroic resistance against French imperialism.'

Noting the young man's valiant effort to impress the father of his beloved, Karim's friend and Sufi teacher Ibrahim-Hamada stepped in to help.

'*Mashallah!*' Ibrahim-Hamada mused theatrically, 'May God protect you, Karim, from the evils of envy. What a very know-ledgeable young man you are!' To ensure Abu-Awny was paying attention, Hamada added for good measure, 'Abu-Awny, don't you agree? Karim is one of the smartest and finest young men in Tuffah.'

Abu-Awny glanced with unmistakable disdain at Karim, and returned his gaze back to his coffee cup. He disagreed with his wife, Fatima, over the suitability of Karim as a husband for their daughter. In fact, this was increasingly becoming a source of heated arguments between them. He disapproved of Fatima's role in playing matchmaker between Karim and Souhailah. 'As if Souhailah needs your help to find a suitor!' he had shouted at Fatima the night before. 'Our daughter is a fine young woman – beautiful, educated, from a good family – she deserves someone older and far more financially secure than this Karim you keep pushing her towards.'

Abu-Awny's thoughts were interrupted with Abu-Sa'adah's grating, loud voice. 'At least this time we know we have strong powers on our side,' he shouted, as if leading a protest. 'It's not like in 1948 when the Arab armies stood alone. This time, the Soviet Union supports the Egyptian demands. You'll see! Israel and its chief of staff, Moshe Dayan, the one-eyed dog, will suffer a great defeat.'

Abu-Sa'adah's performance did the trick. It lifted the deflated spirits in the room. They all nodded earnestly. The *sheikh* said nothing. Let them have hope, he thought to himself.

But Abu-Awny seemed to disagree. 'We are all living hand-to-mouth,' he said, clearly trying to restrain the anger in his voice. 'War after war, invasion after invasion, occupation after occupation, one calamity after the other – it seems Israel will not leave us alone. We can't go on like this! I'm trying to run a business, to feed my family, and this cannot be good for any of us!'

The economic impact of another war was terrifying not just for Abu-Awny, but for all the people in Gaza, refugees and Gazans alike. Money was becoming increasingly scarce. The men nodded in silence, each one quietly wondering how to ration their income and their food to keep their families from starvation.

'*Salam alaykom!*' Azmy greeted the sombre crowd. Before they had time to return his greeting, the young man looked at his father

Abu-Awny with tearful eyes. '*Yubba*,' he said. 'I just heard the Israelis have massacred hundreds of people in Khan Yunis.'

At hearing of the Khan Yunis massacre, Khadija ran across the garden to check on Fatima. She knew her friend and neighbour would be terrified for the wellbeing of her family who lived there.

Khadija threw her arms around her friend, and a deep wound gushed open. She thought of her mother, Aziza, who was still missing; she thought of her childhood village, Salama; she thought of her family scattered in refugee camps. The two women wept together for all the losses and sorrows they and others had endured and witnessed since 1947. Suddenly, they heard shouting coming from the street.

'The Jews are coming! They're coming!'

Heart filled with terror, Khadija ran back to her home. She called out the names of her sons, one by one, and gathered them together in the *sheikh*'s room. Moftiya rolled out the prayer mat and prayed like she had never prayed before.

'Please, God! *Ya allah*, protect my son and his family. Don't let them hurt us. Don't let them hurt us.'

The family all echoed '*Amin*.'

Across the garden, Fatima and Abu-Awny had little time to think. They had heard the Israeli army conducting house-to-house searches, ordering all men of fighting age to go outside in the street where they were gathered – and who knew if they planned to shoot them or detain them. Fatima and Abu-Awny didn't want to take a chance. Although Azmy was not of fighting age, he could be mistaken for being older than his years. They also worried for Souhailah, who had blossomed into womanhood, and they had heard of stories of Israeli soldiers sexually assaulting young Palestinian women. Abu-Awny dug a hole in the backyard for Azmy to hide in, and spread palm leaves and tree branches over it. Meanwhile, Fatima made Souhailah wear a peasant dress, a *thawb*, wrapped her chestnut curls under a scarf and looped the scarf to cover her face, only letting her eyes be seen, in hope of making her look older and less attractive.

The Israeli tanks rolled into the Tuffah district. Soldiers were ordered to search for fighters and weapons. They shouted their orders through megaphones, calling on all men of fighting age to leave their homes and stand outside in the open. They threatened that any man found hiding inside would be shot on the spot.

Abu-Awny went outside into the street with the men and prayed his family would be safe inside. The tricks worked – the soldiers ransacked their home, and moved on.

Their next stop was the home of the *sheikh*. Surprised to see a man still sitting, they held their rifles in the *sheikh*'s direction ready to shoot.

'I can't . . .' The *sheikh*'s eyes watered up. 'I can't leave . . .'

The boys, in that moment of terror, acted instinctively. Rahim threw his arms around his grandmother Moftiya, Latif and Muti clung to their mother Khadija, and Razak cried in his father's arms. Karim stood by the door, watching the scene unfold, his mind racing with thoughts of how he would defend his family. He was almost fourteen, but he was the eldest male with working legs in that room. He did not want to cry, but his tears escaped his eyes when he saw his father's tears.

'I can't . . .' the *sheikh* repeated in utter humiliation.

Khadija and Moftiya both yelled at the soldiers, '*Mashlool!* *Mashlool! Mashlool!*'

It was a word they had never uttered before – not in front of the *sheikh*, and certainly never in front of his sons. *Mashlool*, paralysed, handicapped, disabled . . . the *sheikh* was bigger than such words. But at that moment, that is all he was. A helpless *mashlool* who cannot walk and cannot defend his own family.

The *sheikh* picked up his left paralysed arm with his right working one and dropped it. Karim felt deep shame at seeing his father, the great intellect, the *sheikh*, put on display for the enemy soldiers his weakness. The soldiers understood that the man was handicapped. They moved on after they ransacked the home, searching all the rooms, turning mattresses upside down, and emptying drawers, bottles and pots on the floor, looking for weapons. None were found.

A few days later the military curfew was lifted, but the schools and shops remained shut. Mass fear and confusion continued to spread. Another massacre by Israeli forces took place in Rafah where more than a hundred Palestinian refugees were killed. This created more terror and panic, and the UN Relief and Works Agency (UNWRA), the official authority looking after the Palestinian refugees, pulled its officials out of Gaza, leaving behind UN storages full of food rations.

As soon as word got out that UNWRA officials had cleared their posts, refugees and Gazans alike stormed the UN storage warehouses and helped themselves to the rations.

Karim, too, ran with the crowd and elbowed his way through the stampede, ducking elbows and feet, until he secured a sack of flour. He held on tight to the flour and allowed the movement of the maddened crowd to spew him out into the clearing and land him back into the street.

Karim brought the sack of flour home but that was not enough, as the days turned to months and the occupation of Gaza continued. With schools shut, the only work Karim and Rahim could find to feed their family was picking oranges and loading crates in the orchards that surrounded their district. It was hard labour, but they had little other option.

The *Sheikh* completed his prayer and turned to his wife, who prayed behind him. Khadija sat still in deep meditation on the prayer rug. He said nothing and manoeuvred his body back to his mattress. He closed his eyes hoping to catch a few more minutes of sleep before daylight broke.

Khadija lingered on the prayer mat, legs folded beneath her and head rotating from her right to her left shoulder, as she whispered the final *salaam* ritual to the angels. '*Assalum alaykom*, with Allah's mercy and his blessings. *Assalum alaykom*, with Allah's mercy and his blessings!'

Connecting with the divine five times a day often lightened Khadija's load, but not on that morning. She couldn't push away her worries about her two eldest sons, Karim and Rahim. Her heart ached every night when they came home with new blisters and sores, their sunburnt skin stretching over their skeleton-thin bodies. How difficult their lives had become.

Khadija prayed to Allah, God of compassion, to give her sons strength, and to cloak them in his mercy. She then rolled away the

prayer mat and headed out to the garden to fetch the daily breakfast ingredients: chillies, lemons, basil and tomatoes.

Rahim was the first to wake to the daily pounding of the pestle
crushing the chillies into the hardened pottery mortar. His stomach
urged him to rise, but his aching body begged him to remain under
the sheets.

'Rahim,' his mother's voice cut through his mind's delibera-
tions. 'It is time to get up. Go fetch your brother!'

Rahim dragged his sore bones off the mattress, and grumbled a
few words to his parents that sounded like a morning greeting. Sleep-
heavy, bones aching, he went outside the main room where they all
slept and across the yard to the old barn, now Karim's room.

Two years younger than his brother, Rahim was the second in
command and his brother's most trusted companion and advisor.
Karim even relied on him to keep an eye on Souhailah, and to
make sure she had everything she needed, whenever he wasn't
around. The two brothers were very different, not only in appearance – Rahim's fair skin and blue eyes strongly contrasted Karim's
dark skin and dark-brown eyes – but they were also different in
character. Rahim was quiet, a silent doer of things, a gentle spirit,
while Karim's presence filled the spaces around him with articulate
words and a larger-than-life persona.

After breakfast, the two brothers kissed the hands of their father
and their mother and walked out of their home towards the fields
where they would spend the day picking fruit for meagre wages.
On the way to the orchards they took turns in amusing each other,
Rahim singing his heart out and Karim breaking into poetry, to take
their minds off the pain they felt as the blisters burnt their tired feet.

'Fear God!' Fatima's high-pitched voice rang high amid a chorus of croaking frogs and chirping crickets.

'You should fear God!' Abu-Awny shouted back.

This was the couple's nightly performance of the song of rebuke.

Abu-Awny's workshop did not suffer – though he would never admit to it. He preferred to keep his good fortunes to himself. He didn't want people to envy him, or worse, to ask him for loans. But his wife knew that his business flourished in times of economic hardships. His family's food storage clay pots were always full to the brim.

'You're squandering all the food I worked hard to secure,' he yelled at his wife.

But for Fatima, it seemed only natural that they should share their food with those less fortunate – especially the *sheikh*'s family.

On the surface, it appeared Abu-Awny was forever asserting his power over the family wealth. Yet, deep in his heart, all he really wanted was for Fatima to obey him, to respect his views, to love him unconditionally and without question. But Fatima had a mind of her own. So, Abu-Awny rained upon her head a nightly litany of accusations and criticism, which he later always wished had never rolled off his tongue. Yes, Fatima thought she ran everything in the house to perfection, but he felt he needed to show her that she was flawed, that she made mistakes. That she needed his wisdom and his authority.

When Abu-Awny married Fatima, he was fourteen and she was only eleven. She moved into his family home before she had her first period. Abu-Awny was intrigued by her. She was stunning – her eyes always beamed with intelligence far older than her age. He asked her what she wanted as a wedding gift. She said, 'I never had a doll. Do you know how to make one?'

That was how Abu-Awny became Fatima's own, private toymaker. Later, Fatima would tell her friends how she had asked him for toys only to remind him that she was still a child, and to keep him busy making things with his hands to keep them off her – that is, until she got used to him and until she felt she was ready.

Two-and-a-half years later, a dozen dolls later, a couple of doll's houses later, a swing and a seesaw later, and one year after Fatima got her period, she decided it was time to end a beautiful childhood, one that any girl in Tuffah could only have dreamed of. She was ready to move into Abu-Awny's bedroom and consummate their marriage as man and wife.

'Slowly is the best,' Fatima would later tell her friends. 'Always insist on taking it slow.'

They began slowly. Abu-Awny was gentle, and Fatima was assertive, letting him know exactly what she felt comfortable with and saying no to anything she did not desire. She was at the helm of his heart, his pleasure, his love and his world.

Deep down, Abu-Awny knew he was fated to lose every argument. Fatima was too strong-willed, and he loved her too deeply – even to the point of humiliation. He was ashamed of her hold on him, ashamed of her strength that made him feel weak, ashamed of his love and the powerlessness it bestowed upon him. So he hid it all under a coarse layer of shallow resentments that grew deeper with the passing of years. It was as if he felt his love for Fatima was a secret he had hidden carefully for so long, that he himself had forgotten where he had placed it.

The argument ended the same way all their other arguments did. Fatima had the last word.

'Khadija is pregnant!' Fatima told her husband. 'I will share my food with her. She needs to eat well. Now, go to sleep.'

23

NASSER

GAZA, PALESTINE, 1957

The voice of the BBC Arabic reporter blasted from every home:

'This is the BBC.

In today's news, Israel, France and Britain, pressured by the United States and the UN, will cease all hostilities in the Middle East.

After five months of Israeli military presence, Israel will begin withdrawal from territories it occupied, beyond the 1948 armistice line.

A UN peacekeeping force is said to take over the administration of the Gaza Strip.

Gaza's mayor, Munir Al-Rayes, who was detained by the occupation, has been freed and will resume his duties as mayor of the free Gaza Strip.'

Excitement swept through the streets. Old women ululated and men in cafes took to singing nationalist songs for the love of the homeland as they celebrated their victory.

Muti ran back from al-Qaysariyya, where he was dispatched to fetch cardamon coffee from Mohamad Khodry's shop. As usual, he took the opportunity of his absence from home to sneak into the fighters' secret meeting place behind the cafe across the road. He felt he needed to get his fix of the fiery speeches the refugees and fighters delivered in the back room. Although Muti went to these meetings as often as he could, he was never seen or caught. Unlike his older brother Karim, who was escorted out a few times, Muti had a quiet presence and talent for completely disappearing in a crowd.

When Muti arrived with the coffee, the *sheikh*'s guests had already assembled to celebrate Israel's withdrawal. Muti smiled at Rahim, who was sitting gleefully next to Karim in the men's circle. Working hard in the orange orchards for months had won Rahim a new special status in the family. He was no longer the coffee pourer and errand fetcher of things; this was now his younger brother Muti's job. Rahim had ascended to the status of breadwinner and respected member of the *sheikh*'s nightly circle.

'Israel did not want to withdraw,' the *sheikh* told his guests. 'It took the UN two months to reach a withdrawal agreement with the Anglo-French forces, and much longer to get Israel to do so.'

'Their butcher, Prime Minister Ben-Gurion, told his people that the 1949 armistice line has no validity,' Karim said. 'Israel thinks it can decide where its borders begin and end.'

Khadija's brother Hafez lit a cigarette, drew in a long breath, and exhaled a cocktail of smoke and words. 'Sometimes, it is astounding how much agreement we can have with our enemy,' he said. 'The armistice line is what separates us from our homes on the other side. It has no validity for us, either. That country that calls itself Israel has no validity. Nothing it holds has validity.'

The men nodded in agreement, while the *sheikh*'s sons Karim, Rahim and Muti stared adoringly at their uncle Hafez, mesmerised by the refugee fighter's words and his smoke and fire theatrics.

'How much longer must we wait here before we can go back to our homes, our land, our old life?' Ibrahim's voice was laden with sorrow and memories of Salama and a life forever disrupted. He signalled to Muti to pour him more coffee. Muti rose to his feet immediately and reached for the boiling kettle on the fire. Ibrahim and Hafez looked at each other and shared a knowing smile. This made Muti nervous. Did they know he snuck into their meetings? Would they tell his father?

'How old are you?' Hafez asked Muti.

'I'm ten years old.' Muti poured him the coffee.

'You were a baby when Palestine was stolen,' Hafez said.

'Yes,' Muti said, faking a confident smile. 'I am nearly the age of *Al-Nakba*, the catastrophe.'

'Yes, you are – and don't ever forget it.' Hafez smiled.

'I will never forget that. Uncle Hafez, I know we will liberate Palestine. And you and all the refugees will go home.'

The passion of Muti's words brought tears to the eyes of the men in the room. Were they moved by the promise of a new generation of fighters rising? Or were they moved by the promise that they will return to their homes? Or was it knowing that there is hope and that their story will not be forgotten?

Muti paid close attention to what people said in the streets, in the gatherings and especially in the conversations between his older brother Karim and his friends about Israel, the massacres and the refugees. Many nights Muti sat quietly in the background listening to Karim discussing his ideas of non-violent resistance; Karim was taken by the teachings of Gandhi and Martin Luther King.

Muti adored his older brother, and deeply valued his opinion, but when it came to revolutions and resistance, he was beginning to form his own ideas. Non-violent resistance was not one of them.

Ibrahim-Hamada ran into the *sheikh*'s gathering, panting for breath. 'Quick!' he said. 'Turn on the radio. Nasser is speaking.'

Muti ran up to Abu-Awny's house to turn on the radio, and sprinted back across the garden to listen. Egyptian President Gamal Abdel Nasser's confident and playful voice travelled through the cable to the speaker in the *sheikh*'s room and echoed throughout the speakers and radios of the entire Arab world.

'. . . In the past, when *Time* magazine wrote one word, the head of the Egyptian Government would fall. Today, they insult us, but we can insult them too.'

Abdel Nasser was taking long pauses between his words, giving the adoring crowds he was addressing time for laughter.

'Our papers can insult Britain's queen and their prime minister. Didn't you write something to them on the walls here in Port Said?' he asked the crowd, who roared with laughter once more, both through the radio and inside the *sheikh*'s room.

'Should we find the words on the wall and read it to them?' Abdel Nasser asked, and the crowd applauded their victorious leader. 'You wrote your queen is what?' Abdel Nasser asked.

'A bitch!' shouted the crowd. There was more applause and hysteric laughter.

'We can . . . when it comes to insult . . .' laughter . . . 'We feel we are strong,' Abdel Nasser said. 'We feel the world has changed. When the British broadcasting calls Gamal Abdel Nasser a dog, we say you are the sons of sixty dogs . . . we're very good now. In the past *Time* magazine could write something and the head of the Egyptian Government would fall, but today, Port Said made the head of the British Government fall. The world has turned over. The world has changed!'

Karim quietly withdrew from his father's circle. He walked across the garden and inhaled the sweet smell of spring. His chest expanded wide enough to contain the entire universe. This is what hope is made of!

He strolled out into the street and to the nearest streetlamp. There, he sat down with his favourite book, *The American Crisis* and, together with Thomas Paine, he spent hours plotting his people's liberation.

The following morning, he woke to news of the arrival of a new baby brother. The *sheikh* named his sixth-born son after the Egyptian president. Abdel Nasser, worshipper of the God of victory.

'Nasser! Nasser! None but Nasser!' Karim, flanked on the shoulders of protestors, chanted into the megaphone. 'No to UN forces in Gaza!' the crowd repeated after him, as they marched through the streets of Gaza City.

Inspired by the teachings of Thomas Paine, Karim was on the frontline of every non-violent protest in Gaza that called for the return of the Egyptian administration and a rejection of the presence of UN forces.

'Egypt! Egypt! None but Egypt!' The massive crowds moved towards Gaza's municipal building. 'Nasser! Nasser! None but Nasser!' The young skinny dark boy from Tuffah continued to lead the chants.

When the crowds arrived at the Gaza municipal building, one

of the protesters climbed on the pole and brought down the UN flag and replaced it with the Egyptian flag. The crowd roared.

'Nasser! Nasser! None but Nasser!' 'Egypt! Egypt! None but Egypt!'

It was a glorious day, and Karim felt his heart bursting and adrenaline coursing through his body. After the protest, he bid his friends goodbye and walked home. His steps were light, and a song in his heart chanted, 'Souhailah! Souhailah! None but Souhailah!' An immovable smile formed on his face. He hastened his steps home. He knew what he had to do.

In that moment he believed he was invincible. He believed it was time to make his move. Souhailah was growing more beautiful with every passing day. Suitors were starting to visit her family. Karim was worried if he did not propose now, he would lose her forever.

24

LOVE

GAZA, PALESTINE, 1957–1959

'*Yubba*,' Karim put down his teacup and mustered the courage to speak to his father. 'I want to marry Souhailah.'

The *sheikh* considered his son's request carefully.

'Son,' he weighed his words with care. 'You alone, can decide your destiny. You are the eldest, and you lead this family after me. But you are still young. You still have time to grow and to love. Are you absolutely sure you are ready to marry?' The *sheikh* paused for a moment before adding in a grave tone, 'Son, if you ask for Souhailah's hand, you must know that a word is like a bullet: once fired, it cannot be taken back. You must be committed to your word. You cannot change your mind. You cannot walk away. So, again, are you sure beyond any doubt that you want to marry Souhailah, and that you want to ask for her hand now?'

'Yes, Father, I am certain beyond any doubt this is what I want.'

The *sheikh* pondered for a moment, took in a deep breath, and exhaled. 'Then, let us do it. We will stand with you and support you no matter what the consequences may be.'

Karim was too far in love to read between his father's lines. He did not stop to consider what 'consequences' the *sheikh* might be speaking of. He did not think for a moment that anything could possibly go wrong.

Tradition in Palestine dictates that a potential suitor's family would go to the home of the bride to ask for her hand in marriage. But the *sheikh* had reached a stage where he was no longer able to walk at all. So instead, he invited Abu-Awny to visit.

When Abu-Awny arrived and saw the nervous, well-dressed Karim sitting next to his father, he felt as though he had stepped into a trap. Fatima must have known this was going to happen, the horrid voice in his head hissed. Why didn't she warn me? Is she standing outside the room with Khadija and Moftiya, waiting to ululate and to bring in the tray of celebratory juice? Like this is a done deal? Like I have no power? How could they all take me for a fool like this?

Abu-Awny simmered in silence. He gave little consideration to Souhailah or to the marriage. Only one thing dominated his destructive stream of thought: this whole affair was a new battleground between himself and Fatima. This, he thought, will be a decisive battle. For once, he had all the power and she had none. Society gave him the sole authority to say yes or no. And if Fatima expected a 'yes', he would no doubt deliver a 'no'. It was that simple.

His face reddened and hardened as the *sheikh* went through the polite formalities, the obligatory introduction to the topic, the build-up, the description of Karim's good manners and promising future, leading to the grand finale – the request for Souhailah's hand in marriage. Abu-Awny sat quietly but did not hear a word the *sheikh* had uttered. All he could hear was that hissing voice in

his head telling him they had all struck a deal behind his back –
and that he would not be made the fool.

'What do you say?' asked the *sheikh*. 'Should we read the *Fatiha*?'

Abu-Awny looked Karim up and down with disdain. 'Grow up
first,' he said. 'When you grow up and become a man, I promise not
only to find you a suitable wife, but to even pay for your wedding
myself.' Abu-Awny stood up. 'Souhailah is not for you!' he barked.
'She deserves to marry someone more worthy.'

With these humiliating words Abu-Awny left, noting as he
walked out that his wife Fatima was indeed, as he had suspected,
standing outside with Khadija and Moftiya with the juice trays,
ready to celebrate.

🌵

Karim was ordered by his family to never speak to Souhailah
again. If there was not to be a marriage between them, he had to
let her go. Heartbroken and angry, he fell into new and destructive
habits. He stopped reading and paid little attention to his education. He went out with his friends every day and came home late
every night. When his parents reprimanded him, he took it out on
his brothers. He fought with them, and they all fought with each
other. Irritability and tension spread like a disease, and peace was
lost in the *sheikh*'s home.

Peace was also lost next door. Souhailah stayed in her room and
cried for weeks. Fatima, unable to console her, directed her anger at
Abu-Awny. 'You are cruel!' she scolded him. 'You broke our daughter's heart.'

Abu-Awny was unapologetic, and fought back. 'It is you!' he
shouted at Fatima. 'You and your stupid matchmaking! You made

Souhailah think that Karim was a suitable boy. You are to blame for her misery, and for everyone else's!'

When Fatima and Abu-Awny grew tired of yelling at each other, they took their anger out on their boys. The boys fought and yelled at each other. The house was at war with itself.

Weeks passed and the tension grew thicker and more unresolvable. Fatima could not stand the poisoned air they all exhumed. She made the *sheikh*'s family a peace offering: a pot of *foqa'ayah* silverbeets with lamb and chickpeas. To her horror, Khadija refused to accept it.

'We don't accept charity from strangers. You are strangers to us,' Khadija snapped, and the pot was returned untouched.

Abu-Awny stopped attending the *sheikh*'s circles. The *sheikh*, wounded, sent Muti to return the radio speakers to Abu-Awny's house with a handwritten message: *We want nothing from you. We are not 'worthy' of your possessions.*

A month passed, and Fatima tried once again to make peace. She waited until she saw Moftiya out in the garden feeding her chickens. She ran to the old woman and appealed to her.

'You are our beloved elder,' Fatima said in an emotional voice. 'They will listen to you. You must stop this mad war!'

Moftiya clicked her tongue and pointed her one good eye straight at Fatima. 'You dare come here? You did this. You made Karim think that Souhailah was his destiny. Not once did he – or any of us – expect a refusal. You have pushed Souhailah on us since she was a baby. You made the poor boy fall in love with her. And you dare come here and ask me to correct your error? Go away!'

Fatima was at a loss for words. She turned back but only took a few steps before she stopped and yelled at the old woman, whom she had described only a minute ago as a beloved elder. 'You are a spiteful old woman,' she said. 'As the saying goes, when they told the cat your shit is a balm she quickly dug and buried it. You would rather do nothing than anything that could be of benefit to others!'

'Oh, I will do something,' Moftiya threatened under her breath. Insulted by Fatima's insolence, the old matriarch issued a decree forbidding any of Fatima's brood, young and old, from coming into their side of the garden. But children are creatures of habit. They grew up playing in the shared garden and did not know where the boundaries of their property began or ended. The orders were impossible to obey.

Moftiya had no choice but to appoint Rahim, Latif and Muti as border guards. Their job was to mark the borderline between the two gardens clearly and make sure no child of Fatima's ended up on the *sheikh*'s side.

This did not go well. The children shoved and pushed each other over the invisible boundaries. The older boys came to the rescue, and the event ended in a horrible fistfight between Karim's brothers and Souhailah's brothers. Tired, injured, bloodied and bruised, the boys went back to their homes at the end of the day. Life had become intolerable for both families, as they tended to their kids.

'There is no other way. We must build a wall between us,' the *sheikh* told Khadija.

On the other side of the garden Abu-Awny said to Fatima, 'This situation cannot go on like this. They have gone too far. Tomorrow, we must build a wall.'

The following morning, the older boys from both families, under a joint parental decree, came face-to-face once more, and set out to build the wall. They worked together mixing earth and water to make bricks and to pile the bricks on top of each other. At first, they worked in silence. But when Rahim began to sing, they all joined in. By the time the wall was complete, the boys had forgotten why they built it in the first place and they all went out together to play a game of cards on the fruit boxes, away from their homes, under the streetlamp in Mohatta Street.

Karim did not join them. He did not forget. He stared at the ugly wall. He grieved the garden that was split in halves, and yearned for the bench beneath the pomegranate tree that was now on the other side of the fence, out of reach – like his beloved Souhailah. All that was left on Karim's side was the chicken coop, the vegetable garden, the sycamore tree and the cactus bush.

The young Tuffah poet, as Karim had become known, was on his way home after a day on the beach with his friends Raja'a and William. In his mind, he was reconstructing the details of the astonishing figures of the Armenian beauties, who mesmerised him as they skipped the waves in their revealing bathing suits. He smiled when he remembered how they turned their heads slightly and giggled as their delicate fingers pointed in his direction. A delicious, warm, tingly feeling washed over him that he wanted to hold on to, to savour, but it faded away as the sound of urgent footsteps behind him grew louder and a dramatic voice called his name persistently.

'Karim, Karim, Karim!'

He stopped and turned around. It was Barzaq, from the Daraj Quarter in the north-western part of the old city. Karim sighed. He knew Barzaq from the activist gatherings he attended. Barzaq identified himself as a Ba'athist, belonging to the party founded in Syria that espoused the ideology of pan-Arab socialism,

for our flyers or distribute them ourselves. All factions – Marxists, Socialists and others – they have their own printers, publishers, budgets and money pouring in from outside, which would make our lives much easier. It could also make you famous. Your writing will be printed in many languages, and you will be invited to travel the world. Just pick a goddamn faction!'

'No!' Karim was resolute. 'I need to maintain my independence of thought, even if that means missing out on having organisational support. Factions look after their own; they print and publish their own ideas, and their ideas alone. But a real seeker of knowledge cannot be boxed in. I don't want to tour other countries to spread someone else's ideology. I don't want to be boxed or – worse – turn into a mouthpiece. I am a thinker. I cannot be beholden to any faction.'

'Okay,' Barzaq was resigned. 'If you reject the leftist factions, as you do, why don't you just join the Muslim Brotherhood?'

Karim laughed. 'You can't be serious. Did you hear a word I said? Do you even read what I write? The flyers you distribute?'

Barzaq did not answer. He was embarrassed to say he did read the flyers, but he did not understand a word.

'I believe in modernity, progressive thinking and non-violent tactics,' Karim explained. 'I'm happy to court left-leaning factions, such as socialists, Marxists and communists. I do attend their meetings, and I do support their actions. They are closer to my ideals in their way of thinking. More importantly, they know how to enjoy art, poetry, films and music. The Muslim Brotherhood, on the other hand – they don't. But in the end, like I said, I will join no faction. I will remain independent of thought.'

The summer months went by, and Karim spent his time between the cinema, the beach and the nightly revolutionary meetings, writing, reading and dreaming of a big future. But every night, as he began to fall asleep, an image of Souhailah always appeared before him, illuminating his mind's eye and casting its brilliant light upon all thoughts and images; even the alluring figures of the Armenian girls skipping the waves, faded under her bright star.

September came around and Gaza's lifecycle began once more with another school year. Mothers in Tuffah mended and patched hand-me-down uniforms, shoes, schoolbags and books. Fatima finally pushed the last of her army of boys and girls, now eight in total, out the front door and she strolled down to the *sheikh*'s home for her usual morning coffee, which she liked served with a side of treason.

The two families were still officially at war, but Fatima, with her charm and persistence, was eventually able to wear down any feelings of animosity the *sheikh*'s family might have harboured against her. Alone, she revolted against the declaration of separation and won with her daily incursions into the *sheikh*'s territory.

Fatima was a believer in the art of soft diplomacy and in the power of women to shape destiny. She never thought, as her husband did, that he had won the war. He'd only ever won a small battle. She could have intervened to pressure him to accept Karim's proposal, but she had her reasons not to. She wanted Karim to grow up a little bit more and to work harder at earning Souhailah. She believed the harder you work to gain someone's love, the more appreciative you become of them.

Karim was angry at Fatima's lack of intervention. He couldn't understand why she didn't force Abu-Awny's hand. It was no secret;

everyone knew Fatima got her way. So why didn't she try? Karim avoided her for a long time, feeling so betrayed by her. But that morning when he literally collided into her, as he was rushing out the door and she was rushing in, there was no escaping her.

Fatima's face was made more beautiful by her glowing smile when she saw Karim. 'How are you, Karim?' she tenderly asked.

Karim looked at her with explosive anger. 'I am fine, Mrs Fatima,' he said, highlighting the words 'Mrs Fatima' to let her know how formal their relationship had become.

'Mrs Fatima? Whatever happened to Aunty Fatima? Am I no longer an aunty?'

'I have no aunties,' Karim barked, and he took off as fast as he could.

Karim and Raja'a met at the Al-Samer Cinema to watch, for the third time, the Egyptian romantic comedy *Ghazal Al Banat*, starring Leila Mourad and Naguib el-Rihany, a story of impossible love, which stirred Karim's emotions and reminded him of his own tragic love story.

Afterwards, the two young men went to the cafe across the road from the theatre where avid moviegoers often congregated to battle plot twists, character build-ups, dramatic arcs and better endings. Karim ordered a cup of tea with fresh mint leaves and sat quietly listening to the arguments that erupted between those who liked the ending of the movie, who thought love must prevail above all else, and those on the other side, who did not like the finale.

A familiar voice shouted through the crowd: 'What if there was a wall? How does love triumph over a wall?'

Karim recognised the sarcastic tone. It belonged to Azmy, Souhailah's older brother. He braced himself for another fight as he saw Azmy walk towards him. But, in a surprising turn of events, Azmy offered him a bottle of ice-cold Coca-Cola.

'Have this,' he said. 'It is more useful to you in this heat than the tea you're drinking.'

Karim accepted Azmy's peace offering with suspicion. He hadn't talked to Azmy since the day his proposal was rejected. He couldn't shake the question away. 'Why did your father reject me?' he asked bluntly.

Pulling a seat next to Karim, Azmy smiled. 'Because he says you are no good for her. He says you waste your days between beaches and cinemas.'

'Guilty as charged,' Karim nodded. 'But tell me, what else is there to do in Gaza other than go to the beach or to the cinema? It is not a crime. The beach soothes the soul, and the cinema ignites the imagination – it's a form of education, a window into the world. Besides, it's not like I do nothing else. You know how well I'm doing at school, and you know that I tutor after school.' Karim saw that Azmy was listening with friendly interest. He continued, 'Azmy, I'm not idle. I'm a responsible young man who can provide and feed a family. I love your sister. I will take great care of her.'

'Why her?' Azmy's question came almost as a surprise. Why her? Karim had never asked himself that question. It was always her. There was never anyone else but her.

'Some questions cannot be answered,' he said. 'Some feelings cannot be described in words. Souhailah is a part of me. She is a part of who I am. If I lose her, I will live the rest of my life missing a part of myself. Please, you know that no one else in the world will take better care of her or love her the way I do.'

Karim and Azmy at Gaza Beach, 1958.

'Well . . .' Azmy stood up. 'It was nice catching up. Leave it with me.' He patted Karim's back and left.

Hope sprung once more through the cracks of Karim's broken heart.

Word had got out that Souhailah, daughter of the carpenter and scrap-metal collector Abu-Awny and his socialite wife Fatima, was ready to receive marriage proposals. Souhailah was well brought up, she had completed primary school and was halfway through her vocational training in fashion design and sewing. Souhailah had a full, curvy figure, delicate features, high cheekbones, long, light-brown hair and beautiful milk-white skin. Of all her attributes, it was the last, the 'white skin', that brought to her door mothers from all over Gaza wanting lighter-coloured grandchildren.

Although Souhailah enjoyed being at the centre of attention, she systematically refused all the mothers and their sons who came to meet her. When her father insisted on reasons for her dismissal of each caller, she could always find at least one. 'This one is too short, Baba.' 'This one is too tall.' 'Him? He's too fat.' 'No way. He is too skinny.' 'Did you not hear how he speaks? He's too rude.' 'No. Too stingy.' 'No, no, no, too gruff.' 'No' and 'No' and 'No'.

One day a perfect suitor – Adel – came, and her father was beside himself with joy. 'That's the one!' Abu-Awny exclaimed. 'You will not find anything wrong with this one. So, my dear daughter, it is a yes, right?'

Adel was from a very well-known and respected family. He was handsome, of suitable age, educated, employed in the Egyptian civil service, well-spoken and generous in the gifts he brought every time he visited with his mother, whom he treated with tenderness and care.

Souhailah couldn't find anything wrong with him. Nothing.

'Well?' Abu-Awny asked again. 'Is it a yes?'

'Still, no!' Souhailah said, running to her room and slamming the door shut. What reason could she give for her refusal this time? There was none that her father would accept as a reason.

Abu-Awny and Fatima stared at one another for a brief second, long enough for a feeling to pass between them, an acknowledgement that the battle between them, over control of Souhailah's destiny, still rages on.

Fatima enjoyed having suitors come to the house for her eldest daughter, but she enjoyed even more seeing them leave.

'Don't worry,' she said to Abu-Awny. 'There are still many more to consider.'

Abu-Awny was not irritated so much by what Fatima said, but by the blatant joy evident in her voice – the joy of yet another victory. He wasn't about to give up. He desperately wanted to prove to Fatima how right he had been about refusing Karim, and how much better Souhailah could do. He needed to change strategy – befriend his daughter, win her to his side. He went to Souhailah's room and sat on the edge of her bed.

'Daughter,' he spoke softly. 'This man, Adel, he is perfect. He has enough money to get you everything you need, but not too much that he would feel we are beneath him.'

'No,' Souhailah said.

'Daughter,' Abu-Awny tried again. 'Adel has a very good reputation. He will open doors for you into good society.'

'Still no.' Souhailah was unwavering.

'Daughter!' Abu-Awny could no longer play the friendly father game. He stood up and shouted, 'You know that Adel is a million times better than that skinny dark boy you mistook for a man. I, personally, will not refuse him. I will grant him permission to keep coming here, and I will wait. I know he will win you over eventually.'

And so it was, Adel and his mother were welcomed into Abu-Awny's home. They visited, and visited again, and again. Each time they brought chocolates or pastries, but not once did Souhailah come out to sit with them. Souhailah barricaded herself in her room and refused to come out for the length of their visits.

'Abu-Awny,' Adel's mother finally said, 'it is in your power to say yes or no. We don't want to play games. We want this matter resolved. We must have an answer. We can't keep coming to your house like this – for nothing.'

Abu-Awny opened his mouth, but Fatima spoke first. 'The answer is not ours to give. And as you can see, our daughter has not come out of her room. If you push for answers now, you will get a "no". It is up to you if you want to wait. You are welcome to visit as many more times as you like.'

'Well, Mother,' Adel, the once polite, perfect prospective suitor, barked, 'I don't think I want to keep coming here anymore. The only thing this family is interested in are the chocolates and sweets we bring.'

With that, he picked up the box of chocolates they had brought with them and yelled in the voice of a child throwing a tantrum, 'Not this time – you don't deserve these chocolates!' He stormed out of the room and into the front yard, his mother ran behind him, barely keeping her balance on her high heels. But, in the short distance between the house and the front gate that led out into the alleyway, Adel was ambushed by Souhailah's younger brothers Fakhry and Saady. The boys, still not of school age, were extremely active and moved with the agility of monkeys. They were not going to let Adel keep his present! They snatched the chocolate box out of his hands and before he could say anything, disappeared into the house.

Fatima and Abu-Awny witnessed with horror their children's behaviour. But the minute the suitor and his mother were out of view, and the front gate was shut firmly, Abu-Awny and Fatima broke into hysterical laughter – so wonderful and so contagious it brought Souhailah out of her room. A ceasefire was declared. Tension washed away as the family sat together, passing the box of chocolates between them and recalling with laughter Adel's ungracious exit.

In his heart, Abu-Awny was relieved that Adel was gone. Deep down he had dreaded the idea of giving his daughter away to a stranger who lived in another district.

Fatima always knew Adel would also be refused. This was a game Fatima excelled at playing. She knew how to be a driving force for the big events in their lives. She knew Souhailah was going to refuse all the suitors. She knew Abu-Awny would eventually give up. She also knew that when she told Azmy to go to the cafe and make up with Karim, a door would open and Azmy would return, ready to fight in Karim's corner.

'*Yubba*,' Azmy looked at his father across the backgammon board. 'This man, this Adel, he is a stranger to us. I'm glad he's gone. Yes, we did ask about him, but people only tell you what appears on the surface. Can you imagine that if he were to marry Souhailah, we would know nothing about her life.'

'I know, Son.' Abu-Awny tossed the dice. 'I had the same thoughts.' He moved his chips and waited for Azmy to play his turn. 'What are you waiting for?' he prodded him.

'Ahem.' Azmy cleared his throat while he arranged in his mind the perfect sequence of words that could change the course of his sister's life. 'I met with Karim,' he finally said.

Abu-Awny sat back in his chair and fixed his gaze on his son.

'He still loves Souhailah,' Azmy continued. 'And he is willing to do whatever it takes to earn your approval.'

Abu-Awny nodded pensively. Azmy took his father's reaction as a sign to continue with his plea. 'Karim, he's one of us. We know everything about him. You have known him since he was a baby. He is smart, he works hard and he has been earning money since he was eight years old. He is educated, and has great potential. Most importantly, we know how much he loves Souhailah.'

Abu-Awny considered his son's advice. He had reached the same conclusion when Souhailah refused the most perfect suitor he could come up with. Also, Abu-Awny really missed being part of the *sheikh*'s nightly circle.

'If he wants my approval,' Abu-Awny finally responded, 'he must do what other potential suitors have done. He must come to my house and ask me for her hand. This is the honourable way of conducting this kind of business.'

The next day, when the fifteen-year-old Souhailah came home from her fashion design vocational school, her mother greeted her at the door with a big smile. 'Here comes our beautiful bride!' Fatima said, as she threw her arms around her daughter. Souhailah's heart sank and the first thought that came to her mind was that her family had accepted Adel's proposal. The tears welled up in her eyes, she threw her bag on the floor and charged towards her room. Her mother grabbed her arm, shouting 'Congratulations! Karim is coming to ask for your hand!'

Souhailah stopped. Her heart quickened. She turned to look at her mother. 'How? My father —'

'Your father agreed!'

Souhailah threw her arms around her mother, and wept tears of joy!

Karim and Rahim arrived at Abu-Awny's home dressed in their finest white shirts and black pants.

Fatima welcomed them at the door, with a look on her face that could only be described as triumphant.

'Follow me to the guest lounge room,' she said. 'Abu-Awny and Azmy will soon join us.'

'Wow, the guest lounge room!' Karim whispered to his brother.

'They don't receive anyone in the guest lounge room, except on *Eid*.'

'I don't think I've ever seen a guest lounge room in real life,' Rahim whispered back. 'Only in the movies.'

The young men were ushered into a part of Abu-Awny's home they had never had access to before. It was a stuffy room draped in red velvet curtains and matching seat cushions over gold-leaf gilded armchairs made of beechwood and decorated in ornate floral carvings.

'Welcome!' Abu-Awny and Azmy came in and greeted them. 'Welcome! Please sit down.'

Karim and Rahim sat down. Karim shifted with unease on the soft chair. The economic disparity between Abu-Awny's family and his own was so clearly articulated in that room. He had the same feeling he had when he was a young boy riding on the bus with his mother to Salama, and he had realised for the first time that his family was poor.

What am I doing here? he thought to himself. I'm taking her from this house and into a room that was a barn only a few years ago? Karim swallowed a lump that had formed in his throat.

Souhailah walked in with a tray of coffee. Her hands trembled as she lowered the tray for Karim and Rahim. They reached out for the small cups in the floral-patterned saucers, politely accepting the coffee.

'*Shokran*,' Karim smiled his thanks, aware how unnatural his smile was. Everything about this performance is artificial, he thought. Everything is rehearsed, formal, suffocating. How I wish I could take Souhailah by the hand and run away with her now.

Souhailah smiled at him, as if she could hear his thoughts. She took a seat next to her mother and they all sat in silence, waiting for the guests to speak. But the guests did not speak.

'Welcome!' Abu-Awny said once more, impatience reflected on the features of his face.

Rahim, the fifteen-year-old young man who was officially tasked to represent the *sheikh* in all the formalities of this monumental event, was too distracted. His eyes wandered through the room's furnishings – the clock on the wall, the throw cushions on the sofas, the low, wooden coffee table with its matching side tables, and the glass-stained lamps. He had never seen a room like this.

'They sent two boys to do the work of men,' Abu-Awny murmured under his breath. Azmy squeezed his father's hand as if to say be patient. Wait.

Karim sensed the tension rising, he nudged Rahim with his elbow. '*Yallah*, Rahim,' he whispered for him to begin.

Rahim took in a deep breath, sat up straight and coughed a little. 'In the name of God, the compassionate, the merciful!' he began. 'We thank you for your gracious hospitality and for opening your hearts to receiving us. My father sends you his best regards, and he has blessed our participation in this gathering. Although, as you are aware, his condition prevents him from being here, he is here through our presence, and we are but an extension of his will. We have come to appeal to you, and our wish is that you do not deny our request.'

Rahim's introduction was impressive, and in line with what Abu-Awny had hoped for. This is the proper way of doing things, he thought. To honour me and to ask for my daughter's hand in my home. Not like last time, when they trapped me in the *sheikh*'s room. Of course, I had to refuse their request back then.

Rahim continued his much-rehearsed *tolba*, the request for a bride in marriage, highlighting his brother Karim's most positive attributes, buttering up as much as possible Abu-Awny's ego, counting the virtues of Souhailah and her exemplary upbringing, complimenting her entire family – mother, brothers and sisters. When he finally reached the end of his speech, he looked at Abu-Awny and asked the most important question of all.

'What do you say, Uncle Abu-Awny? Will you grant us our request?'

Abu-Awny nodded. '*Tawkalna ala allah*,' he said. 'I accept your proposal. But as you know, my approval is not enough. God has commanded us to ensure the approval of the woman who is entering into the marriage.' He turned to Souhailah, and felt a sudden catch in his throat. This was the real thing. None of the other suitors were going to take his little girl, but this one, he knew, has already won her forever. He took a sip of water and wiped a tear from his eye. 'Souhailah, do you accept this young man in marriage?'

Souhailah's face flushed crimson. She could feel everyone's gaze upon her. They were all waiting for her to speak. She opened her mouth, but her throat felt dry and the words were stuck. She closed her mouth and nodded.

'Not so fast,' Fatima cut in. 'I have one condition. My daughter does not know how to cook or clean. She is not to be made a servant in your home, not to you and not to your family.'

Karim, totally smitten, gave a swift and entirely untraditional response. 'I love Souhailah so much; I am prepared to wear an apron and to be her servant forever.'

'Easy there,' Rahim quickly jumped in. 'You know if *Sitty* Moftiya hears what you just said, she will be mortified. So, how much will you give me to keep this deal a secret?'

Everyone laughed.

The sound of *zaghareet* echoed in both houses and spread

throughout their neighbourhood, announcing the marriage approval.

During the months that followed, Karim and Souhailah's relationship evolved into a game of cat and mouse. Karim became bold with his expressions of love and Souhailah, aware of her mother's firm instructions to guard her reputation, and of her mother's eagle eyes that saw and knew everything, always managed to find creative ways to keep Karim's passions at bay.

When they were together, Karim sat so close she could feel his hot breath on her bare neck. When he looked at her, he stared too long – she didn't know where to rest her eyes away from the fire in his. And there were a few times when he tried to catch her alone and steal a touch, a glance, a kiss. She did not surrender to his passion. She waited, and insisted he wait – even for a touch of her hand – he must wait, until the wedding night.

The wall came down. The shared garden was returned to its former glory as preparations for Karim and Souhailah's wedding began.

Fatima insisted that Souhailah's dresses must rival that of the most sophisticated in Gaza society. She spent weeks designing and sewing all seven bridal garments, each with its own distinct choice of fabric, style and colour, each to be worn on a different night of the week leading up to the night when Souhailah, in her white dress, would be ushered in a ceremony of song and dance, across the garden, and into her new life with Karim and his family.

Souhailah totally surrendered to her mother's wishes. She was like a doll being dressed up and moved around in accordance with the various ceremonies. Salwa, the beautician of Tuffah, became a full-time lodger of Abu-Awny's home. She prepared pastes to keep Souhailah's skin smooth, sticky sugar to remove unwanted hair, facial masks so the bride may glow and all the while, throughout the week leading to the wedding night, she continuously fussed with Fatima over Souhailah's hair and make-up. Music and singing did not stop throughout the seven days; nor did the guests stop coming.

Across the garden, at the *sheikh*'s home, the atmosphere was much more subdued. Karim was struggling to make ends meet. The sixteen-year-old groom's income, and that of his father's combined, could barely keep up with the cost of hosting the seven days and nights of wedding celebrations. There was no money left to spend on buying new clothes for anyone in his family, not even for the groom himself.

'So, what are you going to do?' Khadija asked Karim, as the family sat on the floor to eat their dinner.

Before Karim could answer, Rahim yelled his displeasure when seeing what was on offer for dinner.

'Again, *Yumma*? You cooked zucchini stew again? You know when we die and they bury us in the soil, a zucchini garden is going to grow over our graves.'

'*Yeslamo edeeki, Yumma*,' Muti, ever the diplomat, interjected when he saw the hurt on his mother's face. 'Rahim, what's wrong with zucchini every day? Don't you know how blessed are the hands that can cook something from nothing?'

'You should all say *Alhamdulillah*,' the *sheikh* grunted. 'Praise be to God we still have food after three days of Fatima's guests coming and going, coming and going, coming and —'

'They're our guests too!' Tears had formed in Khadija's eyes. 'And he is our eldest son!' The tears streamed down her face. 'And this is his wedding. Our celebration.' More tears. 'And we can't even spare money to get him a suit!'

'*Yumma*, I will manage.' Karim threw his arms around his mother. 'I can borrow a suit from someone.' He kissed her hands. 'Don't you remember how good I am at borrowing clothes?'

Khadija smiled, remembering the night Karim borrowed an entire outfit for her so she could attend the neighbour's wedding. 'That didn't end well!' Khadija laughed at the memory of her ungracious fall into the mud.

'No,' Karim said. 'Only because you didn't know how to walk in high heels.'

'Enough nonsense!' Moftiya's voice was decisive. 'I will pay for Karim's suit.'

There was silence in the room. No one believed their ears. The old matriarch never parted with her meagre earnings.

'What?' Moftiya was indignant. 'Khadija, do you think Karim is your son alone?'

'No,' Khadija laughed through her tears. And for the first time since Karim was born, she was ready and willing to share him with her mother-in-law.

'Who's wedding is this?' asked the old tailor on Omar Al-Mukhtar Street, when Karim walked into his shop and gave him the money to make a suit on the same day.

'Mine. I'm the groom,' said Karim, with immense pride.

'You?' The tailor looked Karim up and down and let out a

sarcastic laugh. 'You're so young. Do you even know how to do what a groom is supposed to do? You're still in school, aren't you?'

Stung by these words, Karim stormed out. How dare this man belittle him? How dare he not recognise that he is a rising poet, a tutor of many and the son of the *sheikh* of Tuffah. How dare he? But the tailor ran after him and pulled him back into the shop. 'Wait,' he said. 'I was just kidding. Of course, I'll make you the best suit there is – the best within your modest budget.'

Karim let the man take his measurements and said he would return a few hours later to collect the suit. He was irritable and exhausted. The days and nights of celebrations were wearing him down. He only met with Souhailah briefly during this time to sit through the various ceremonies, him in his sandals and casual clothes and her looking like a movie star.

On the final day, the couple travelled to the Armenian photographer's studio in Omar Al-Mukhtar Street to have their wedding photos taken. They could only afford two photos. Karim wore his suit in both. Souhailah wore her black dress in the first and her white dress in the second.

On the final night, Karim's friends chipped in to pay for the *janaki* dancers. At first, the *sheikh* was apprehensive about the idea, but decided to turn a blind eye, despite his wife and his mother's objections.

'This is a respectable home,' his mother reproached him. 'These women perform for the gaze of lusting men.'

The *sheikh* smiled. 'Let the guests have fun,' he told her. 'It's a wedding!'

When Moftiya found out the dancers were paid for by Karim's friends, she was more susceptible to the idea. Khadija, on the other hand, remained unhappy. She didn't want the *sheikh*'s eyes to

Karim and Souhailah on the day of their wedding, 1959 – one of two official
photographs, Souhailah in her black wedding dress. (Kegham studio, 1959)

wander. The *janakis* often wore less than modest clothes as they
sang and danced provocatively at wedding parties, with the overt
purpose of arousing the bride and the groom.

In preparation for the *dokhla*, the night when Souhailah and
Karim would become husband and wife, Fatima cooked a big
meal for her daughter. 'Eat!' she coaxed her. 'You need to eat well.
Tonight is a big night for you, and Karim plans to devour you!'

The women giggled and exchanged stories of ravishment on
their wedding night. Souhailah listened with excitement and fear
as she allowed the women to wash her, dress her and constantly
feed her. Someone always fixed her hair, carried her dress, refreshed
her make-up, while all the while she was being told not to
exhaust herself and to save her energy for the night to come.

Across the garden, Karim had the opposite experience. He was running around receiving guests. He had no time to eat, and there was no food on offer. Only more zucchini stew, which he could no longer stomach.

The wedding ended with a joyful procession of song and dance, and Souhailah and Karim were finally led into their room. Karim wanted to take Souhailah into his arms, to kiss her, to melt into her, but he was too tired and very hungry and irritable. The body simply could not do what the heart desired.

Defeated, Karim collapsed onto the bed and pulled Souhailah to him. The two lay down on their sides, facing one another, and – still fully dressed in their wedding clothes, still wearing shoes, still holding hands, still madly in love – they both drifted into sleep.

Fatima and Khadija lingered outside Karim and Souhailah's room for hours, waiting to get the news that the marriage was completed. Khadija wanted to celebrate her son's sexual vitality, while

Baba next to the *Sheikh*. This was during my parents' wedding celebrations.

Fatima wanted to make sure her daughter was well treated and that there were no issues that couldn't be resolved.

Fatima had already given Souhailah the talk about the importance of enjoying sex, even framing it within the Islamic teachings. 'Desire must be mutual. He must care that you are satisfied. Our *deen* gives women a licence to divorce their husbands if they weren't satisfied,' she told her. 'Never allow him to hurt you, or to do anything to you that you do not want or desire.'

Fatima and Khadija began to worry when hours passed, and the couple had not resurfaced to give their mothers the news that all was well. Too much was riding on this. Khadija put her ear to the bedroom door and listened. 'Silence,' she whispered. 'All I hear is silence.' She lifted her ear away from the door, unable to hide the panic in her eyes. 'I'm sure they enjoyed themselves and tired themselves out. Of course, they're sleeping.' She let out a nervous laugh.

The next morning, Fatima went to check on her daughter. Souhailah opened the door still dressed in her white wedding gown with sleep in her eyes. Shocked, Fatima stuck her neck in and saw Karim sleeping in his suit on the bed. She grabbed her daughter's hand and pulled her away from the room.

'What happened?' she said, trying to hide the outrage in her voice. 'He didn't even touch you! What is wrong with him? Is he no good?'

'Mama, please lower your voice,' Souhailah begged. 'He's good. I know he's good. But last night we were both so tired.' Souhailah looked around her to make sure her in-laws were not in earshot. 'Mama, can you believe his mother didn't make him any real food. They've been eating zucchini stew for a week.'

Fatima didn't want to hear any more. 'Okay. Get back in there, take off these clothes, shower, put on the red, spaghetti-strap dress.

Make sure you don't wake him until you've changed and until I have returned.'

Fatima ran up to her house, rolled up her sleeves and began her magic. Within an hour she had prepared a tray of fried pigeons stuffed with rice, and carried it over to the couple's room. When Karim woke up starving, Souhailah greeted him in her red dress and hand-fed him the delicious stuffed birds. As they ate to their heart's content, the couple laughed and reminisced over the events of the previous night. Laughter turned to flirtations, and flirtations led to kisses. They were relaxed, at ease with one another and, most importantly, they felt the weight of the pressure to perform was lifted.

Souhailah and Karim let go of all inhibitions and surrendered to one another's desires.

When Karim stepped out of the room smiling and Souhailah asked shyly for her mother, Khadija let go of all her worries. She stood triumphant and let out a *zaghroota* for the world to know that Karim and Souhailah had consummated their marriage.

25

BELONGING

GAZA, PALESTINE, 1959–1963

Karim ran into his classroom, panting for breath. His classmates greeted him with the usual clapping and whistling, and the teacher, with a familiar smile, ordered the class to give him a standing ovation. Late students were often reprimanded and punished, but not Karim. He was different. He wasn't just a student – he was a married man, with a child on the way. Even the principal of his high school, Mahmoud Shehab, a man known for his strict disciplinary measures, even he often turned a blind eye to Karim's almost regular late arrivals. He told himself the young man was married, and sometimes newlyweds can get distracted – especially in the morning. 'Karim is gifted linguistically and romantically,' the principal would often muse whenever Karim's name came up.

Karim's linguistic talent had reached new heights. He was a rising star in the world of poetry. He participated in every poetry contest in Gaza, and always won first place. He was awarded the highest poetry prize in Palestine, at a ceremony that included some important guests, officials such as the administrative officer to the Governor General, Said Abu-Shark, as well as poets from Egypt and other parts of the Arab world. The prize was handed to him by the beloved mayor of Gaza himself, Munir Al-Rayes, who was freed when Israel withdrew from Gaza in 1957. It was events like these that opened Karim's world to new horizons and opportunities.

This was the case when one day, Karim skipped French class and went to the cinema instead. He was a fan of the Egyptian actress Soad Hosny, and eager to see her in all her glory on the silver screen in the movie *Eshaet Hob, A Rumor of Love*. Karim left the cinema daydreaming, clouds under his feet and song in his heart, when he walked straight into his neighbour Abu-Sa'adah.

'Are you blind?' Abu-Sa'adah shouted, his facial expression changing from anger to curiosity when he recognised it was Karim who had run into him. 'What in God's name are you doing here?' he inquired with a hint of concern in his voice. 'Shouldn't you be in school?'

Karim receiving a poetry prize from Munir Al-Rayes, mayor of Gaza,
September 1959.

'Yes, uncle,' Karim answered. 'In fact, I was in school this morning. I am only skipping the French class.'

'Why?' Abu-Sa'adah asked, and almost immediately regretted asking. He was clearly in a hurry and by asking, he was now forced to wait for an answer. He hoped Karim would not be in too much of a mood for a long chat.

'Uncle, skipping French class is a matter of duty and principle. It is a form of civil disobedience,' Karim began. Abu-Sa'adah shifted on his feet, but knew he had to stay until Karim finished. 'By refusing to learn the language of the country that has colonised and brutalised our beloved Algeria and its steadfast people, I am making a conscientious stand.'

'*Tayeb tayeb*, that's fine.' Abu-Sa'adah couldn't care less about France, or French classes – he needed to run. 'I must go, I don't want to miss the land lottery.' He waved goodbye and walked away with fast steps across the road.

'The land lottery?' Karim's mind began to churn. He had heard about the way the Egyptian Government had divided up some large, publicly owned properties in Gaza and was selling them for a nominal fee through a lottery system. Even I could be a landowner, he thought. This could be the opportunity of a lifetime! Karim took off in his neighbour's trail.

Karim made his way through a much older crowd of men who had gathered in hope of winning the lottery and owning the land. At the centre of the crowd, a few Egyptian clerks sat behind a big table and instructed people to register their names on small pieces of paper and to place their names into the box for the draw. Karim followed the instructions, wrote his name on a piece of paper, folded it, and slipped it into the box.

'So, what is up for sale next?' he asked the clerk behind the desk.

Karim on Omar Al-Mukhtar Street, 1959.

'Mashrou Amer,' the clerk said. 'Twenty *dunams* up in the north by the seaside.'

Abu-Sa'adah was irritated when he spotted Karim chatting with the clerk. 'Why did you come here?' he yelled. 'You're too young, and you don't have enough money – not even a minimal amount. Go home, son!'

Karim ignored his neighbour, and the glares of all the other men around him, as he took his place in the circle of men waiting for the lottery draw to begin.

The Egyptian clerk stood up and coughed to clear his throat. The crowd grew silent. '*Bismillah alrahman alraheem*, in the name of God the merciful, the compassionate!' The air was thick with anticipation. 'Up for lottery now is Mashrou Amer. This lot is made up of twenty beach-side *dunams* in the north Gaza district. It can be purchased for as little as 500 Egyptian pounds by the lucky winner. A deposit of fifty pounds is required upon signing the contract.'

There was some movement in the crowd. A few men left after hearing the price, which, although truly a token amount given the value of the land, was not something they could ever dream of affording. Abu-Sa'adah looked at Karim, waiting for him to leave, but Karim had made up his mind to stay the course and try his luck.

The Egyptian clerk stretched his hands forward and into the box and pulled out a piece of paper. He looked up at the crowd with dramatic flair and called out the name of the winner. 'The lot goes to Abdul Karim Sabawi!'

'That's my name!' Karim's joy was immeasurable! 'That's my name!' he shouted over the sea of men. 'That's me!' he shouted, as he made his way to the clerk. He didn't stop to think of the deposit money – there was no room for hesitation.

'He doesn't have the money!' Abu-Sa'adah called out from the crowd. 'We need to try again. A redraw please! He's just a boy!'

'A redraw!' other men shouted.

Karim looked at Abu-Sa'adah and realised that his good neighbour was anxious for him. 'It's okay,' Karim shouted at Abu-Sa'adah through the roar of the crowd. 'It's okay. Don't worry – I can manage to get the money. Trust me.'

Sitting behind the table to oversee the signing of the deeds was the acting administrator for Gaza, Said Abu-Shark. Karim recognised him immediately as the man who had sat next to the mayor the night Karim received the poetry prize.

'So, the winning poet wants to own land?' Abu-Shark smiled, as he extended his right hand to Karim.

'Yes, sir!' Karim shook Abu-Shark's hand with confidence. 'I will sign the purchase contract now, but can I ask you for a favour?'

Abu-Shark nodded.

'May I pay the deposit in a few days?'

Abu-Shark thought for a minute. 'I was impressed not just with your poetry, but also with your confidence. You are a man of your word. Of course, I will give you as much time as you need.'

Karim signed the deed and walked back to Tuffah with Abu-Sa'adah. The older man looked Karim in the eye and asked, 'Do you really have fifty Egyptian pounds?'

'To be honest, Uncle,' Karim smiled, 'I don't even have five coins to buy shaving cream.'

'I thought as much!' Abu-Sa'adah laughed.

It took Karim a few weeks to borrow the money needed for the deposit from his rich relatives, promising them free tuition for their children in return. It then took him years to pay off the price of the land through small monthly instalments. But he did it! He pulled it off. That was how the poor boy from Tuffah, the young man with not enough money to buy shaving cream, became a landowner.

Content. Souhailah felt utterly content. What more could she ask for? The small bedroom she shared with Karim was an entire universe. The bed, a world of passion, discovery and adventure, where her days began and her nights ended. Her neatly organised drawers and cupboards brimmed with stylish clothes, lingerie, romance novels and sewing projects to keep her busy in the long stretches between waking and sleep.

Souhailah's presence softened the hard edges of the masculine landscape that had characterised the *sheikh*'s household for decades. Her youthful femininity stood in contrast with the coarse skin and dreary wardrobes of Moftiya and Khadija. The two matriarchs who had never raised a daughter competed for Souhailah's attention and allegiance, and exempted her from their daily squabbles.

In the evenings when the family gathered around the *sheikh*'s mattress, Karim and Souhailah next to each other, the *sheikh* whispered prayers of gratitude. '*Alhamdulillah*, praise be to God.'

'Do you know what your name means?' the *sheikh* once asked Souhailah.

'Yes, it is derived from the word Suhail, a bright star in the Southern Constellations,' she answered.

'Well done!' The *sheikh* was pleased. 'And did you know that you are the brightest star in our constellation?'

Souhailah smiled; her cheeks reddened, and her heart flooded with love.

When Souhailah got pregnant, Karim became brazen with his expressions of love. He tore through all traditions with recklessness never seen before in all of Palestine. He cooked whatever food she craved, he cleaned their room while she watched and laughed that a man was doing housework, and once a week he rolled up his shirt sleeves and his trouser pants and squatted in the garden with Souhailah by his side, as they both worked their way through piles of laundry soaked in soapy lather. In between rubbing garments and squeezing them, they blew bubbles at one another or splashed each other with water, giggles and kisses. Moftiya and Khadija watched this from afar, twisting their mouths and clicking their tongues in bewilderment.

In the spring of 1960, seventeen-year-old Souhailah and eighteen-year-old Karim were blessed with a baby girl. They named her Khulud.

With an infant who cried through the night, classes in the morning, students to tutor in the afternoon and homework to complete in the evenings, it was a miracle that Karim not only graduated high school, but did well enough to be accepted into the Bachelor of Law at Cairo University.

Karim received the news with trepidations, unsure of how he should react. He folded the acceptance letter, placed it in his pocket and began his walk home from the education liaison office. He took slow steps towards Tuffah. He did not understand why his heart felt so heavy. He had been looking forward to this moment yet, now that it was upon him, he felt no joy. What does it mean to go to Cairo? How could he extract himself from his life in Gaza and from all his responsibilities to his family?

On his way home, Karim walked past the fruit sellers under the gigantic tamarix along Mohatta Street. The sight of the fresh fruit and the shouts of the fruiterers lifted his spirits. He thought of Souhailah, now in her second pregnancy and craving apples. He pushed his way through the meandering crowd, who seemed to be doing more looking than buying, and called out to the seller, 'I'll take one apple, please.'

The gruff-looking old man behind the beautiful shiny display of red apples looked Karim up and down with disdain. 'Finally,

I get a real customer – but he only wants one apple,' he murmured. 'What great misfortunes have cast me into this penniless neigh-bourhood?' he grunted through his teeth.

Karim pretended not to hear the man's rude comment. He took the apple, gave the man a coin, and walked away.

The seller is right, he thought to himself. The man needs to feed his family – but who has the money to buy fruits these days?

He imagined how happy his brothers would be if he was to come home with a bag full of apples. Alas, he thought. This cannot be. I need to hide this one apple for Souhailah. She's pregnant and if she doesn't eat what she's craving, the child will be born with an apple birth mark on its skin.

Thoughts of Souhailah's pregnancy, their small family and his bigger family, weighed him down. His mind was telling him to seize the opportunity, to accept the offer at Cairo University, and to let the chips fall where they may. But his heart sang a dif-ferent tune. His heart belonged to Souhailah and was anchored in Gaza, and in his responsibilities as husband, father and eldest son. How could he possibly leave? And how would they make ends meet? The *sheikh*'s income had almost completely stopped. Most students in Gaza were now registered in government day schools. The old home school, the *kottab*, was a thing of the past.

At home, Karim walked into the *sheikh*'s room where the family gathered each night. He kissed his father's hand, his mother's and his grandmother's, and he smiled at Souhailah, who sat next to the *sheikh* working on her embroidery, baby Khulud sleeping in a basket next to her.

Moftiya was the first to notice the sweet scent of apples rising from Karim's pocket. She closed her one eye and inhaled deeply, filling her lungs, before she slowly exhaled. Years had passed since the old matriarch tasted an apple. The fruit was not grown locally, and the ones sold in the market stalls were too expensive for the *sheikh*'s family to afford. Moftiya fixed her one eye onto Karim's and he froze, nervous, expecting her to lecture him on the evils of squandering one's money, but she said nothing. She nodded and smiled.

It didn't take long before others got a whiff of the delicious scent. Rahim asked, 'What is this I smell?' and Karim's brothers laughed, and began to sniff Karim's jacket. The *sheikh* decided to intervene and to release Karim and Souhailah from the obligatory gathering.

'Karim,' he said. 'Your wife looks tired. Take her inside to lie down.'

'Thank you.' Karim was relieved.

Khadija and the *sheikh* exchanged warm smiles as Karim grabbed Souhailah's hand and the two disappeared into their bedroom, leaving the sleeping baby behind.

Souhailah savoured every bite of the apple while she listened intently to Karim as he read his letter of acceptance into the Bachelor of Law at Cairo University. She had a calmness that puzzled him.

'Well?' he asked.

'Well, what?'

'What do you think?'

'Congratulations. I think this is wonderful!' she said.

'If I accept the offer,' Karim explained, 'you would be here without me.'

'No,' she smiled, with a confidence that disarmed him. 'We will always be together! You will always find a way to keep us together. Won't you?'

Karim felt even more burdened as he truly struggled to find a way. But he said nothing. He kissed Souhailah and went back to the *sheikh*'s room, hoping his father's wisdom could help him make the right choice.

The *sheikh* listened to Karim as he read the letter. His face was beaming, his chest expanding to make room for all the pride in the world that settled into his heart. Khadija and Moftiya were also happy – they could now brag to their neighbours that their boy was going to university. But soon enough, they both realised what the word 'going' would mean, and their joy was overshadowed with floods of tears.

'Don't worry,' the *sheikh* comforted them. 'He will not be gone for long. And he will return a scholar.'

'But Father,' Karim asked. 'Who will bring in money for the family?'

'I have other sons, too.' The *sheikh* already thought this through. 'Your brother Rahim will take your place with the chores and tutoring. Latif and Muti can also work now – they are good, strong boys.'

'And Souhailah?' Karim's voice trembled. This was becoming too real.

'She is our daughter. We can together take care of her and your children. We will all be fine. Now go and get your papers in order.'

Heart comforted by his father's words, Karim managed to push the thought of his pregnant wife and daughter out of his mind.

Of course, they would be looked after. He was only eighteen and wanted to study abroad – he wanted to travel, and to get the highest education possible. He was infatuated with Egypt: *Om El Donya*, mother of the world, the cradle of post-colonial resistance and the forefront of Arab nationalism. He believed in its revolutionary, anti-colonialist president, Gamal Abdel Nasser, who mocked and defeated England, France and Israel, and he loved Egyptian music, culture and literature. Souhailah and the children could wait.

Karim expected Egypt to throw her arms around him and take him in like he was one of her own, if not even better than her own. After all, Egypt's President Nasser had ordered Egyptian universities to exempt Palestinian students from many of the entry requirements. When asked why Palestinians were given exemptions for which Egyptians didn't qualify, Nasser said 'Palestinians were dispossessed and disarmed. I want to arm them with education.' This was the Egypt that Karim loved!

Karim handed his birth certificate and the university offer to the Egyptian officer at the embassy. 'What papers do I need to fill out?' he inquired. 'I want to go to Cairo.'

'Another Palestinian brings me his birth certificate,' the officer mocked. 'Do you people not understand the concept of a passport? You need to bring me a passport.'

'Why?' Karim was genuinely puzzled. 'Egypt is the government in charge of Gaza. We are literally under Egyptian rule.'

'Passport,' the officer repeated impatiently. 'Palestinians in Gaza are not allowed to travel into Egypt without a passport.'

'But President Nasser . . . he believes in Arab nationalism. How could Nasser's government require Palestinians crossing into Egypt to have a passport?'

'No passport, no visa,' the officer shouted. 'Next!'

'No, wait,' Karim begged him. 'Please. I'm a Palestinian. I don't have a passport. I don't have a country.'

The officer wiped the pearls of sweat streaming down his face, and tilted his head slightly to see a growing line of young men – all students – waiting for their turn. He was annoyed at the thought of having to repeat the same words over and over again, to each and every student. He raised his voice so everyone could hear him. 'We cannot process your visa application if you don't have a passport. Those without passports must first apply for a refugee travel document. Only then you can apply for a visa to enter Egypt.'

'A refugee travel document?' the crowd murmured. Karim didn't move from his place at the window. 'Sir,' he said loud enough for everyone to hear. 'There is a mistake. I'm not a refugee. I am from Gaza. I live in the same home my father was born into, and his father before him. We are not refugees. We are on our land. In our homeland.'

'Son,' the officer said, exasperated, 'no country, no government, no passport, no visa. May God help you, just register yourself as a refugee and get a damn travel document. Next please!'

It took a few weeks of running through Egyptian and United Nations bureaucratic red tape, but Karim finally obtained a refugee travel document. He returned to the Egyptian embassy, filled out the appropriate forms and was told to come back the following day. He did.

'Not approved.' The same Egyptian officer handed Karim back his travel document. 'Your name has come up on the Muslim

Brotherhood list, and as you know, the Muslim Brotherhood is banned in Egypt.'

'What?' Karim was bewildered. 'The Muslim Brotherhood? I don't belong to any factions and certainly not to the Muslim Brotherhood. I believe in President Nasser's Arab nationalism. Please, there must be a mistake.'

The officer smiled, and nodded sympathetically. 'It's out of my hands,' he said, flashing his uneven yellow teeth and fixing his gaze into Karim's as if trying to say something without actually saying it. Karim didn't understand. He took a few steps back, confused.

'Son,' the man standing behind Karim waiting for his turn whispered. 'Son, he's looking for a little bribe. You must give him something if you want your application to go smoothly.'

Karim looked back at the officer, who smiled in anticipation, and he finally understood the rules of the game. 'I see,' he said to the man. 'Well, if this is Egypt, I want nothing to do with it.'

Karim left the embassy feeling relieved, like a load that sat on his shoulders for weeks had been lifted. No more worries about leaving Souhailah and the children and the family, and leaving Gaza. This is where he wanted to be. When he returned home, he sat down with his father and shared the story of the officer who wanted a bribe.

'For all Nasser's idealism as a leader,' Karim concluded his story, 'he has not changed the rotten and corrupt culture of the lower ranks.'

'Nasser, and all leaders in general, should not be confused with gods,' the *sheikh* commented. 'Even the best of them could only go so far to change the culture of those they rule, and those who surround them.'

'When I left the embassy, I did not feel anger or disappointment,' Karim confided in his father. 'Instead, I felt a deep sense of relief. I'm not sure if, deep inside, I was just waiting to find a reason to stay. I'm not sure if it was the dehumanising process of assuming a status of refugee in my own homeland that made me not want to leave, or my disgust at the corruption of the officer at the embassy.'

'Son, I know you well enough to tell you the reason,' the *sheikh* said, smiling. 'What it was that made you want to stay is your deep sense of duty to us, to your wife and children. No matter what, you were not destined to go. Souhailah will be happy.'

'I hope so.' Karim smiled. 'Can you believe she never once told me to stay?'

'I can,' the *sheikh* laughed. 'Souhailah's faith in you is only matched by her sense of pride. She is too proud to ask you to stay.'

Karim's heart brimmed with love for his wife. He looked for her and found her outside in the garden watching their daughter, Khulud, play under the trees. 'Get ready, wife,' he grinned. 'We are going to the beach!'

With that, Karim scooped up Khulud with one arm and then ran into the house to grab towels with the other. Souhailah waddled behind, feeling her heart sinking. He seems happy, she thought. He must have gotten the visa. He must be leaving soon.

The man behind the wheels of the black Mercedes taxi asked, 'Where to?'

'Mashrou Amer. North of Gaza Beach,' Karim answered.

The man clicked his tongue. 'I heard that lot was sold in the lottery to a penniless boy.'

Karim was in too good of a mood to take offence. 'You heard right,' he laughed.

Karim ran his finger around the perfectly built sandcastle to create a deep, circular track, and poured water into it.

'Voila!' he declared. 'I give you a grand castle with a moat!'

'I'm sorry,' Souhailah laughed, 'but the little princess you've built the castle for has abandoned you long ago for a game of chase and run with the waves.'

'I don't blame her,' Karim said. 'This is not my greatest work. But one day I will build right here, on this land, something much more impressive than this sandcastle!'

'A house with big windows, facing the sea?'

'Maybe. Or maybe something much bigger than that. A place where poets, artists and intellectuals can gather. Perhaps a club with a pool and a theatre.'

'*Inshallah!*' Souhailah smiled, placing her hand gently on his shoulder. 'I still can't believe we own land!'

Karim tugged at her hand. 'Come here! Sit with the "penniless boy".' He opened his arms wide. 'Don't worry, I'll make you comfortable!'

Souhailah rubbed her large belly. 'Believe me, nothing can make me comfortable these days. Besides, if I sit down, you will need to hire a forklift to get me back on my feet again.'

Khulud seized the opportunity of her father's open arms and ran into his embrace. He was beside himself with joy! 'My beautiful little girl!' He kissed her hand. 'Sing for Baba!' He held her tightly, and she sang to the beat of the rolling waves, '*Thahaba al-laylo Tala'a al-fagroo*, the night is gone, and dawn is rising!'

Souhailah's eyes welled up with tears. She could no longer hold

My father and sister Khulud in Mashrou Amer, c. 1964,
standing on the land my father bought in the lottery.

back the dreaded question she had on her mind all day. 'What happened at the Egyptian embassy?' she finally asked. 'Did they say your visa will be approved?'

Karim smiled. 'I thought you'd never ask,' he teased her, but seeing her teary eyes he felt terrible for his insensitivity. 'I decided to stay, and to accept the full-time teaching position I was offered at Saladin Primary School. Does that make you happy?'

Souhailah breathed a sigh of relief. Beneath her calm and confident exterior she had agonised over the possibility of Karim leaving, but she never wanted to give him the satisfaction of knowing that she needed him even more than she needed the air she breathed.

'Are you happy?' Karim asked again.

She did not answer. Of course, she was happy, but Fatima had taught her well. 'Never let your husband know how much you love him. Men like to chase, so make sure your man is constantly chasing you!'

Yet as much as Karim loved the chase, he knew it was just a game. He understood Souhailah so well, he could read her like an open book. He knew how happy she was that he had decided to stay.

The wind picked up and a strong breeze pushed Souhailah's dress against her body, tracing her full breasts, her round, pregnant belly, her full thighs. Karim's eyes filled with desire. 'You only grow more beautiful every day!' he said.

'You're half right,' Souhailah laughed, and pointed at her belly. 'I only grow!'

At night, Khulud slept in Karim's arms while Souhailah lay down on her side next to him, her belly moving in waves as the baby tossed and turned inside her womb. Karim was in heaven. His life made perfect sense. He was where he wanted to be.

26

PALESTINE NEWS NEWSPAPER

GAZA, PALESTINE, 1963

Karim, the twenty-one-year-old poet, teacher and father of two, stood behind the podium of the new Arab Cultural Center, hand holding the microphone and eyes scanning the audience. Seated in the middle of the front row, across from him, were Yusuf Al-Ajrudi, the Egyptian governor general of the Gaza Strip, and Gaza's mayor, Munir Al-Rayes. The seats on both sides of the two men and in the rows directly behind them were filled with highly distinguished guests and top-brass Egyptian army generals. Behind them, the rest of the audience consisted of Palestinian and Egyptian politicians, journalists and intellectuals.

The humidity in the room was unbearable. Karim pulled a handkerchief out of his pocket, wiped the sweat beads that trickled down his cheek, took a deep breath and began to recite the poem he had composed especially for this momentous occasion – the opening ceremony of the Arab Cultural Center in Gaza.

The ceremony was one of the most important of that year. The establishment of the Arab Cultural Center in Gaza came upon direct orders from President Gamal Abdel Nasser himself, a leader known to champion the cultural progress and education of the Palestinian people. And so, for the days leading up to this moment, Karim had laboured over composing a fine poem in classical Arabic, using perfect metrical patterns, in praise of Nasser, the revolutionary president and the Arab nationalist – the man who was going to liberate Palestine. His delivery of the final few lines brought a standing ovation:

'Listen
Carefully
This thunder
This explosion
Is Nasser the Arab
Victorious in the battlefields
Spreading revolutions across the land
Turning us all into revolutionaries.'

The audience roared and cheered. They responded to the poem with enthusiastic applause, whistles and calls for encore.

After the ceremony, the speeches, poetry and formalities, the crowd was led into the reception hall and invited to mingle over small bites and big ideas. Karim navigated such environments with a sense of disbelief and wonder, always the youngest in such settings. His gift for poetry had opened doors for him into the world of Palestinian and Egyptian cultural and political elites, and there, Karim had to hit the ground running. He was a quick learner; his exceptional memory enabled him to socialise with ease. He remembered everything about everyone he ever met, even if only once and in passing. He remembered who they were, where they worked, what jokes they told and whether or not they were poets. And he had the extraordinary ability to remember word for word the poetry they recited, when and where.

'Ostath Karim,' a voice called out to him. Karim turned around and saw a short stubby man in thick glasses, wearing a formal blue suit, gesturing for him to come over. Earlier, when Karim scanned the audience, he registered the face of the gentleman as someone who sat in the second row, close to the centres of power.

'Sa'ad AlDein Al-Welely,' the man introduced himself, extending his hand to Karim who quickly grabbed it. 'I work for —'

'Egypt's national newspaper *Akhbar el-Yom*.' Karim finished the sentence, warmly shaking his hand. 'Of course I know who you are, sir.'

'I'm sure you do,' Al-Welely nodded. 'You are a great poet, Ostath Karim.' Al-Welely considered the young poet before him, checking him from head to toe. 'Where do you work?'

'I teach at Saladin Primary School,' Karim answered, not sure why Al-Welely was asking this mundane question. Al-Welely followed up with a barrage of other questions that seemed strange to Karim. 'How old are you?'; 'What was the highest level of education you've attained?'; 'Do you belong to any faction?'; 'What are your thoughts on religion?'; 'What is your political ideology?'; 'Where do you live?'; 'Are you married?'; 'Which poetry do you like to read?'; 'Who is your favourite columnist?'; 'Who is your favourite author?'

Was this an interrogation? Karim could feel his shirt become heavy with his own sweat. His heart raced as he tried to answer each question as quickly as it came at him. Did I say something offensive about Egypt? he thought to himself – or, worse, did I say something bad about Nasser?

Karim wiped the sweat on his brow with his handkerchief, and continued to answer the questions. Despite having developed many reservations about the men who served under Nasser – especially the handful of corrupt officers who regularly squeezed the people of Gaza for bribes – Karim still believed in Egypt the nation, and in Nasser the leader. He had not said or done anything but praise them. So why, he wondered, was he being interrogated? Maybe Al-Welely was working for the Egyptian *Mokhabarat*, the internal intelligence police – why else would someone so important take up so much of his precious time with me? Karim concluded in his mind, while he continued to answer the questions thrown at him.

'I'm twenty-one years old,' he said. 'I'm married and have two daughters. I don't belong to any faction. My political ideology is progressive and humanist . . .' and so on, and on he answered.

Al-Welely nodded his head as he listened to Karim's answers. Finally, the questions came to an end, and Al-Welely smiled broadly.

'We're going into partnership with a newly formed Palestinian newspaper,' he said, handing Karim his business card. 'It is called *Akhbar Felesteen*, Palestine News.' Al-Welely spoke in a matter-of-fact way. 'The newspaper will be based in the Gaza Strip. We're looking to build a competent editorial team. I think you will make a perfect editor. The newspaper's work is mostly done in the afternoon, so it should fit in with your day job.'

Karim's heart nearly stopped. This was a job interview? Not an interrogation? He couldn't believe his luck. An editor in a newspaper, his brain repeated on a loop.

'Thank you!' He grabbed Al-Welely's hand, shook it enthusiastically. 'Thank you! Thank you! Thank you for the opportunity!'

Akhbar Felesteen, 1963. From left to right: Abdul Karim Sabawi, Darweesh Al-Waheed, Zuhair Al-Rayyes, Zaki Al-Radwan, Mahfouz Al-Rayyes.

'Hold on,' Al-Welely withdrew his hand politely. 'First, you must meet with Zuhair Al-Rayyes,' he said, as he turned his back and began to walk away. 'He can confirm your appointment to the editorial board. Try to impress him as much as you have impressed me!'

Within a week, Karim met with Zuhair Al-Rayyes and was offered a job as editor in Gaza's new and one and only newspaper, *Akhbar Felesteen.*

Quietly, Karim rolled out of bed. Now a father of two, he put on his best shirt and pants and swept up his daughters, Khulud in one arm and Abir in the other, leaving Souhailah to catch up on another night of lost sleep. The six-month-old Abir was still feeding through the night, leaving Souhailah constantly hungry and tired.

Karim stepped out into the yard and walked across to the *sheikh*'s room. '*Yumma!*' he called out to Khadija. 'I brought you two gifts!'

Karim put Khulud down and handed Abir to Khadija, who curled her nose and complained that she only seemed to receive 'gifts' with poop in their nappies. Karim laughed, while Khulud made a straight line to the *sheikh*.

'*Sido!*' She threw herself into her grandfather's arms. 'Would you like me to recite the alphabets?' Before the *sheikh* had a chance to accept or decline, Khulud began: '*Alef, ba, ta . . .*' When she finally reached the last letter '*ya*', the *sheikh* clapped.

'You are my favourite student!' he said. 'Now, be a good girl and get me some tomatoes and chillies from the garden so I can make breakfast.' Turning to Karim, the *sheikh* asked, 'Will Souhailah join us this morning?'

'Souhailah will need to eat more than just tomatoes and chillies,' Karim answered, as he dramatically produced two eggs from his sleeves. 'I'm making eggs for my wife!'

Moftiya, who was brooming off the dust outside the *sheikh*'s room, heard the word 'eggs' and her mind began to spin. She ran inside, broom in hand, yelling, 'Where did you get these eggs?' Moftiya did not heed to the *sheikh* and Khadija's laughter; she had grown used to their amusement at her expense. 'Show me the eggs!' she persisted, as she continued to wave her broom at her grandson.

Karim lifted his hands in the air, one egg in each, trying hard not to laugh. '*Sitty*, these are not your eggs. I bought these yesterday from the chicken farm down the road.'

Moftiya was not convinced, but there was nothing she could do or say. She guarded her brood of hens closely, and was the first to wake daily at dawn to collect their eggs. 'One must keep both their fortune and their misery to oneself!' she often repeated. But her chickens were not at all consistent. Sometimes they laid four eggs, sometimes two, sometimes six – there was no way to tell if anyone was to pinch one or two. If Karim was stealing her eggs in the dead of night to feed his wife, who was always either pregnant or nursing, she couldn't be sure. Then there was that voice in her head: poor Karim, his salary is hardly enough to feed his five growing brothers, his parents, and his wife and daughters. She ignored that voice as often as she could, and used her own. 'You spoil your wife too much!' she shouted at Karim. 'All of this you do for her, and she has only given you two daughters? What will you do if she gives you a son?'

Without missing a beat, Karim shot back, 'I might have to cook your chickens to feed her. Eggs alone will not be enough!' Karim smiled and kissed Moftiya on her cheek. Her defences came crashing down. She pushed him away and hid her face behind her veil to hide her own smile. How she loved being teased by him, and how his smile always managed to break through her iron exterior.

'*Sitty,*' Karim reached out to his grandmother, pulling her into his arms. She pushed him away only enough to make him pull harder. He reached for her bristly hand and kissed it. 'I need your blessings – today is my first day working as an editor in a newspaper.'

'*Allah yerddha aleek!* May Allah grant you all that your heart desires!' Moftiya mumbled. She picked up the broom and slowly walked away, feeling a tiny piece of her heart secretly melting beneath her bony rib cage.

At the first sound of the end-of-school bell, Karim threw himself into the tsunami of primary-school students who made their way, pushing and shoving, out of the school building, and ran all the way to Omar Al-Mukhtar Street. He didn't want to be late for the first editorial meeting, headed on the Palestinian side by Zuhair Al-Rayyes, editor in chief, and Zaki Al-Radwan, editorial manager, of the soon-to-be-established newspaper, *Akhbar Felesteen*. The two men were notable iconic figures in Gaza's cultural circles. How they managed to convince a giant like the Egyptian newspaper *Akhbar el-Yom* to form a partnership with them was a testament to their visionary outlook and resourcefulness. The entire team of editors was in attendance, as requested by the Egyptian editorial team, who were led by one of the prominent Amin brothers, the founders of Egypt's modern Western-style press.

Amin began the meeting by acknowledging the efforts of Zuhair Al-Rayyes and Zaki Al-Radwan in the creation of the partnership, and in the birthing of this new and much-needed newspaper for Palestine. Amin also welcomed Elias Azzam, the nominated editorial secretary, and the newly nominated editorial board. Karim's heart exploded with pride when his name was included in the names of the members of the editorial board.

'You should all be excited to be part of this historic moment,' Amin went on to say. 'Together, we will launch the largest newspaper to be published in print and in distribution in Gaza and in all Palestine, since the 1948 *Al-Nakba*. We, at Egypt's *Akhbar el-Yom*, will supply you with modern, state-of-the-art printers, we will train you on how to use them and we will mentor your journalists and your editorial board. In fact, two of our finest journalists, Ahmad Zein and Maryam Robin, will make themselves available to guide you through this process. And now over to you, Ahmad!'

Ahmad Zein coughed a little to clear his throat. 'To run a successful newspaper,' he began, 'you must ensure its financial sustainability. Therefore, when it comes to allocating space within the paper, your priority should be advertisements. To attract advertisers you need to have readers, and to build your readership you must find engaging stories such as unthinkable crimes or big scandals. For example, a headline that reads "Dog Bites Man" is not engaging, but "Man Bites Dog" is a good news story! That's what sells. You must also have a comprehensive sports page. Men everywhere read the sports page.'

The Palestinians in the room started shifting uncomfortably in their seats. 'What about political analysis?' asked Zaki Al-Radwan.

Ahmad Zein didn't appreciate the interruption. 'Political analysis and literary pieces are for whatever spaces remain,' he said. 'Religion belongs to the mosque – leave it there. Education belongs to the schools and the universities; it is not the business of the media. Art is the domain of literary journals and cultural centres. But, make no mistake about it, journalism requires profit to pay the salaries. Listen,' he said, in a more sympathetic voice, 'you have no country to subsidise your press. You want your paper to be free from factional and political influences, right? What other choice do you have than to rely on sensational stories and advertising? That's how the free press generates salaries!'

Ahmad Zein's words were sobering. Inside Karim's head, there was one simmering question: what about Palestine? The question was so persistent, it forced itself out. They all looked at him. 'What about the cause?'

Zuhair Al-Rayyes mumbled an old proverb in classical Arabic, 'Beware the wrath of those who don't share your predicament!'

Ahmad Zein snapped, 'Can you speak in Arabic, so we can understand you!'

The Palestinians exchanged glances. It was strange to them that a newspaper man did not have a good command of classical Arabic, that he wouldn't understand it.

Zuhair switched to Egyptian dialect. 'It was nothing,' he said. 'Don't worry about it!'

When the meeting ended and the Egyptian delegation left, Zuhair Al-Rayyes asked the Palestinians remaining to follow him into his office.

Sitting behind Zuhair's desk was a handsome young man editing an article to be published in the first edition of *Akhbar Felesteen*. The young man greeted the incoming editorial board warmly and handed the chair behind the desk back to Zuhair, who asked everyone to sit down and listen.

'So, that's it!' Zuhair shook his head. 'Sensationalist journalism! We're supposed to write stories to tantalise and excite, not educate and resist! So why do we even call it Palestine News, *Akhbar Felesteen*, if it is a tabloid for entertainment news and advertisements? What do you think, Musa?'

Musa Saba was nominated to oversee public relations. He was a well-spoken, well-mannered young man, a leader of the Christian Youth Club and a friend to many of the factions in the area.

'The Amin brothers,' Musa said pensively, 'Ali and Mustafa, are trying to score political points with President Nasser by pretending to care about Palestine. They're using us. But we must be mindful of the fact that our readers will be mostly refugees. So what advertisements can we run? You really think the refugees have anything to advertise or sell? Or money to buy with? Do you think we will run ads selling UN rations of flour and sugar?'

'Just forget everything these new orientalists told you in that room.' Zuhair waved his hand dismissively, his voice was decisive. 'We will make this newspaper a home for nationalism, hope and resistance.'

'What about our salaries?' Al-Radwan asked with a nervous smile.

Zuhair responded with dramatic flair. 'We will be paid in glory, my dear resistance fighters.'

Everyone laughed.

'My apologies,' Zuhair remembered. 'I haven't introduced my cousin, Nahed Al-Rayes. He has just completed a law degree at Cairo University, and has been appointed District Attorney in Gaza.'

Karim had heard about Nahed Al-Rayes, the mayor's son, and he was curious to meet him.

'He is a great poet, like you,' Zuhair said to Karim, as if he read his mind. 'He volunteered to edit our art and literature columns!'

After the meeting, Karim invited Nahed to a drink of Seven Up. The two sat on the wall of the newspaper building, their legs dangling over the edge, overlooking Omar Al-Mukhtar Street. Watching the cars underneath speeding in both directions, Nahed took one sip from the chilled bottle. 'Poets are always desperate for a good listener!' he said to Karim, teasing. 'I accept your refreshing cold bribe. Go on! I surrender. Recite your poetry – I'm listening.'

Karim laughed. 'The bribe was not for you to listen to my poetry. The bribe was so I could listen to yours,' he said. 'You've just returned from Cairo, the beating heart of Arab culture and nationalism. I'm curious to hear from you.'

Nahed didn't hesitate. 'I will recite a poem I wrote for Ahmed Ben Bella and all the freedom fighters from the National Liberation Front of Algeria who were kidnapped and imprisoned by France:

'Do you yearn for the sea breeze
          at a café by the port?
And for the taste of Moroccan Green tea?
My sweet Gaza, do you not have a sea?
Do you not have passionate followers of Ben Bella
Send him some of your gentle breeze
          in his exile
Send him messages from Haifa,
          where an old fisherman is listening to the radio
          and raising his palms in prayer toward Algeria:
Give me a ray of freedom
          to light my path
          because the rays of the sun here can no longer suffice
The sun here rises equally over Israel and those it has dispossessed
But you do not give of yourself to those who are not worthy.'

Karim was moved to tears. He hadn't heard poetry like this before, nor met anyone close to his age who had this depth of intellect, and generosity of spirit.

The two young men stayed up all night perched on the wall trading poetry and watching the cars below, until there were no more cars left in the street.

27

THE LOST CITY

GAZA, PALESTINE, 1964

Moftiya gasped. She wished her eyes had never witnessed such horror. There he was, her eldest grandson – next patriarch in line, primary breadwinner of the household, published writer, esteemed editor, respected teacher and beloved poet – there he was, squatting on the floor like a woman, plastic tub between his legs, plucking a freshly slaughtered chicken.

'What is he doing?' Moftiya shrieked to Khadija, who stood nearby.

'You wanted to know what he would do if his wife gave him a son?' Khadija laughed. 'Well, now you know!'

When Souhailah became pregnant with their third child, Karim prepared ahead. He wanted to ensure this time that there was a nutritious plan in place to sustain his wife post-pregnancy. He went to the market and bought a box of tiny live chicks. Moftiya had assumed that he was raising them for their eggs – a sound plan, in her opinion, and the only business plan she ever knew. But that was not the case. Karim was fattening the chicks so he could feed his wife chicken after the birth. How frivolous he seemed to his grandmother, to waste his chickens in that way. Worst of all, how degrading for him, a man, to be plucking the chickens himself.

There was nothing unusual about Souhailah's third pregnancy. The same midwife who assisted her in her previous two home births had predicted that this would be a quick delivery. But the delivery was anything but quick. It lasted for twelve hours, and when the midwife finally announced 'It's a boy! A big, fat, white boy!' her voice was trembling. Only a second after the umbilical cord was cut, the midwife was shouting in panic, 'She needs to get to a hospital – now.'

Souhailah was haemorrhaging, and lost consciousness. Karim stood frozen, sick with worry and feeling faint. Rahim acted quickly, lifting Souhailah and rushing her into a neighbour's car while Latif slung his arm around Karim, giving him of his own strength and calm, and assisting him into the car.

Souhailah was kept in the hospital for two days, and Karim never left her side. She required a blood transfusion and luckily, Karim, had the right blood type to give. The two days passed like two years. When the doctor finally released Souhailah, he told Karim that she needed to eat well. Fortunately Karim's meal plan, which he had prepared ahead of time, was ready. The chicks had grown into big, fat chickens.

When they returned home, they were greeted with *zaghareet* and heartfelt congratulations. Souhailah was drained, and went straight to her room. Khadija, who had been looking after the newborn, brought her the baby, and she got to hold him for the first time. He was named Hussein, in honour of his grandfather.

'He's beautiful!' she cried, curling his little finger around hers. She put him against her breast, and he immediately latched on.

'I was scared he would reject me,' she said, tears of joy streaming down her cheeks. 'I was worried the bottle had ruined him.'

'What, with all that milk in your breasts?' Khadija laughed. 'Your son Hussein is a smart boy; he takes after his grandfather, the *sheikh*, not only in name but in intelligence!'

Khulud and Abir stood by the door, curious and shy. Souhailah didn't call them to her. She was too tired and too focused on the newborn. Their uncles, Nasser and Razak, still themselves children, called out to them to play in the garden.

Karim wasted no time following the doctor's orders. His wife needed good nutrition and he was a man on a mission to provide it. As he plucked the feathers over the hot tub of boiling water, he could see Moftiya rushing in his direction. He knew that no man in all of Palestine had undertaken such a lowly task as plucking chickens for their wife, a task reserved for only women. At least, he knew that was what Moftiya was thinking.

'Don't you have something better to do?' Moftiya reproached him. 'I can do this for you. Leave it!' she ordered him.

'*Sitty*,' Karim said in a tired voice that hadn't known sleep in two days, 'if only you knew all the things I could be doing right now, but this, here, is what I want to do the most.'

It was true. When it came to things to do, Karim was spoiled for choice. Gaza in 1964 was a vibrant hub for politicians, diplomatic delegations, arts festivals, revolutionary intellectuals and frontline resistance fighters. Being on the editorial board of the newspaper afforded Karim the opportunity to meet and exchange ideas and poetry with some of the greatest Palestinian and Arab minds of the time, like Yousef Al-Khatib, Ghassan Kanafani, Elias Sahab, Khairy Hammad and Abdel Kareem Alkaramy (abu Salma), to mention but a few.

His editor and boss, Zuhair Al-Rayyes, gave Karim special attention – he was a patient teacher, and a great mentor. Karim listened intently to his every word, in the same way he did to the words of his own father.

Karim rubbed the plucked chicken with flour, rinsed it in cold water, chopped it into pieces, threw it into a large pot with onions, mastic drops and cinnamon sticks, and left it to simmer on the stove. He checked on Souhailah; she was sleeping with baby Hussein in her arms. He checked on his daughters; they were playing in the garden with his youngest brothers Nasser and Razak. This was the perfect time for Karim to sit down with his father and relax until the food was ready. He fixed two cups of tea, and headed to the *sheikh*'s room.

The *sheikh*'s face beamed when he saw Karim. 'Abu Hussein, father of Hussein!' he exclaimed. Congratulations, son! Thank God your wife has come home.'

The *sheikh* loved those increasingly rare moments of quiet conversation with his eldest son. Karim kissed his father's hand, and passed him the teacup.

'What are you reading these days?' asked the *sheikh*, while he watched Karim drop fresh mint leaves into the teacups.

'An Arabic translation of *The Road to Beersheba*, a novel Zuhair Al-Rayyes gave me by the British author Ethel Mannin. It's the first English-language novel to document our story of dispossession, the *Al-Nakba*.'

The *sheikh* did not seem interested in hearing more about that novel. He had grown suspicious of the Western gaze on the Arab and Palestinian plight. 'What else are you reading?' he asked.

'I'm also reading the work of Islamic scholar Ibn Rushd.'

This sparked the *sheikh*'s interest. 'Ibn Rushd is one of the most influential Muslim philosophers of all time!' he exclaimed approvingly. 'But before you read his work, you have to read the theological writings of his predecessors, Al-Ghazali and Avicenna Ibn Sina.'

'I have.' Karim smiled, though it never surprised him that his father was always a few steps ahead of him intellectually. 'It's a shame he was the last of his kind,' Karim said. 'We need more scholars like him to challenge the small-mindedness of the current Sunni teachings.'

'This is precisely why they made sure he was the last of his kind.' The *sheikh* spoke gravely. 'Authoritarian powers can only exist through the people's blind obedience. So, they hand us pre-packaged religious beliefs and make us so busy performing the shallow rituals that we forget how to think for ourselves, and how to ask questions. 'Tell me,' the *sheikh* fixed his eyes into Karim's, 'what have you learned so far?'

Karim felt he was still a student in his father's *kottab* school.

'I will tell you,' he said, laughing. 'But you must promise you will not use your stick if I don't give you the answer you want.'

The *sheikh* laughed wholeheartedly.

'I have learned that religion cannot be detached from philosophy,' Karim said. 'On the contrary, philosophy must be an integral part of religion. Philosophical theology, like that of Ibn Rushd, was a spark in the enlightenment of European minds. His translated work played a crucial part in the lead-up to the industrial revolution in Europe, and in building its democratic institutions. I have learned how tragic it is that his work was ignored within an Islamic world that continues to spiral into ignorance and corruption.'

The *sheikh* listened to Karim, and wondered if his son would soon be sailing ahead of him in the sea of knowledge. That thought made him exuberant with pride. He was grateful to know that although his son had missed out on higher university education, his love for reading, his extraordinary ability to memorise and analyse what he read had turned him into a scholar to be reckoned with.

The *sheikh* took a deep breath, and the aroma of Karim's chicken stew fuelled his appetite. He smiled, and said, 'Not only are you a good scholar, my son, but it appears you are also a most competent chef!'

The night's breeze was warm and the sea's waves gently embraced the shoreline, flickering silver foam under the rays of the full moon. On the beach a group of young men gathered in a circle listening to poetry, clapping and cheering after each poem. At the centre, Karim and Nahed were locked in a fierce poetic duel that lasted for hours, and would have continued into the next morning had it not been for their friend Musa Saba's intervention.

'Clearly, there will be no winners tonight,' Musa Saba declared. 'You are both brilliant poets and you both hold in your hearts millions of poetic verses. But us mortals, we get tired and sleepy – and we have wives to go home to.'

The men laughed and agreed that if they stayed any longer, their wives might not let them into their beds. One by one, they said their goodbyes and left. Musa, Nahed and Karim walked together, slowly, towards the main street.

'Dr Haidar Abdel-Shafi returned from Jerusalem,' Musa said. 'I heard he is very excited about being part of the first

Palestinian-only conference. He seems positive about the establishment of a Palestinian organisation to represent us at both the diplomatic and the resistance fronts.'

'That's right,' Nahed said. 'He visited my father when he came back. He said the organisation will be named the Palestine Liberation Organization, and it will open itself to membership from all political Palestinian factions everywhere.'

'Dr Abdel-Shafi is a man to be trusted,' Karim commented thoughtfully. 'But I have an issue with Palestinians trying to do two opposite things at the same time. We are building the Palestinian Liberation Organization in order to lead the resistance against Israel, while at the same time, we are advocating for the idea of pan-Arabism and Nasserism, which at least in theory means that the liberation of Palestine is the responsibility of the entire Arab World, not just us alone.'

'It is possible to do both,' Nahed said, in a hushed voice. 'We are in no position to provoke the insecurities of the Arab leaders, so we can't oppose Nasser and his pan-Arab rhetoric, but we must also look after ourselves. History has shown us that no one in the Arab world will come to save us.'

'Speaking of doing both, have you been following events in Beirut?' Musa weighed in. 'Constantin Zureiq at the American University of Beirut has mobilised Palestinian refugees who are students there. Even groups led by George Habash have joined him. His movement is calling for a pan-Arab revolution, and now they have chapters in many Arab countries. They call themselves the Arab Nationalist Movement.'

'Did they align themselves with Nasser?' Karim asked.

'Not all of them,' Musa responded. 'George Habash and Nayef Hawatmeh are already antagonising Nasser with their Marxist rhetoric, while the rest within the movement are trying to gain his favour. It is creating a deep fracture.'

Karim thought for a moment. 'To follow up on what Nahed said, I think for as long as we are organising resistance from the outside we will be subjected to division. Arab governments will tolerate Palestinian refugee movements, like the Arab Nationalist Movement, as long as they adopt the local political agenda. When a movement has so many chapters, in different Arab countries, who all have opposing agendas, progress will be a huge challenge – to say the least.'

'Zureiq is dedicated to attracting the attention of the intellectual elites,' Nahed explained. 'He believes the learned intellectuals will be the vanguards of a revolution of Arab consciousness calling for Arab unity and progressive modernity.'

'Arab elites are not ready for his socialist secularist values.' Karim realised how much he was beginning to sound like his father, but he pushed on. 'How does Zureiq propose to convince our people to let go of their fundamental religious identity?'

'He shouldn't have to do that,' Musa answered. 'Religion is in the heart. Our liberation cannot be exclusively aligned to one religion or another. I am Christian. You are Muslims. Others are Marxist atheists. It doesn't matter. Israel's divide-and-conquer strategy along religious lines must never be a factor in our struggle or in our liberation movement.'

The three friends arrived at a fork in the road. 'Well, this is where I bid you goodnight!' Musa hugged his friends, and walked towards the Christian sector.

Karim extended his arms out to Nahed. 'And this is where we part!'

'Not yet,' Nahed smiled cryptically. 'I'm still going in the same direction as you.'

Karim was puzzled. He was going towards the old city and the fields behind it. His friend Nahed lived in the new part of the posh modern villas of Rimal.

'You're not going home?' Karim asked.

His friend only answered with a smile. Karim understood.

As well as being a gentleman, a poet and an intellectual, his friend Nahed was also a fierce resistance fighter and the leader of an underground *fedayeen* militia that adopted guerrilla tactics to operate against Israeli soldiers. The fighters held their secret meetings in the Sha'af farmlands that belonged to the Al-Rayes family. The land bordered the Tuffah district.

Karim thought of the immense personal sacrifice Nahed was making. He could be going home to his beautiful wife, Siham, and his newborn son, Monir; instead, Nahed chose to abandon the comfort of his bed and the benefits of his status as son of one of the most prominent and wealthy families in Gaza to live and fight in the trenches, risking his life and freedom for the liberation of Palestine.

The lobby of the newly opened Al-Amal Hotel in Gaza was buzzing with excitement as poets from all over the Arab world arrived and greeted one another. It was the eve of the seventh annual Arab Poetry Festival, initially meant to be held in Cairo, but under President Nasser's authority and in accordance with his wishes, the festival was moved to Gaza City as a gesture of solidarity with Palestine and its people.

Karim stood in the lobby, in his best white shirt and casual black pants, impatiently waiting for his friend Musa to arrive.

'Of course, you're already here!' Musa shouted, as he picked up his pace in Karim's direction.

'You're lucky I waited for you,' Karim said impatiently. 'Zuhair is already here, with the most important guests. Let's join them before the night is over!'

The two young men raced up the five flights of stairs to the hotel's rooftop, and eagerly pulled two chairs into the large circle that had formed near the wall, overlooking the white sandy beach.

'You've arrived just in time!' Zuhair said, before he introduced them to others in the circle. 'Mr Musa Saba is the head of our public relations at the newspaper, and Abdul Karim Sabawi is our editor of international news. He also happens to be one of our most gifted poets.'

'Will you be presenting your poetry at this festival?'

Karim tried to maintain his calm as his mind danced in circles and his heart exploded with fireworks. The question came to him from Salah Abdel Sabour, one of the greatest poets in the Arab World! Abdel Sabour's first poetry collection, *an-Nas fi Biladi*, *People in My Land*, had signified the beginnings of the free verse movement in Egyptian poetry. Karim did not want to seem starstruck by the magnitude of the company. He wanted to answer in a measured tone and say something sophisticated, as if he talked to people like Salah Abdel Sabour every day. But all that came out of his mouth was one word delivered with unbridled enthusiasm: 'Yes.' He breathed in, and out, and tried to regulate his rapidly beating heart.

The conversation quickly moved with the rhythm of free verses and poetic articulation, reflecting the wit, diversity and intellect of those present. Amongst them were Yemen's leading poet Ibrahim Bin Ahmed al-Hadhrani and celebrated Egyptian poets

Ali Ahmad Bakathir, romantic poet Saleh Jawdat, and contemporary poet Ahmed Abdel Muti Hijazi; Egyptian academic Doctor Abdel-Azzis Al-Ahawany; and Egyptian poet Malak Abd al-Aziz, the only woman in the circle.

Karim knew all the poets and, because of his superb memory, he could actually recite all of their poetry by heart. But he did not. He sat listening and observing. He found himself gravitating towards Malak. She was a petite, attractive woman in her early forties, with short, black hair and piercing eyes. She was dressed in an elegant, short-sleeved black dress that reached just above her knees, and she had a profound sense of melancholy about her. When she excused herself to leave, Karim quickly gathered his courage and invited her on a sightseeing tour of Gaza's farmlands.

'Don't worry,' he assured her. 'We will not be alone. I will ask my friend Nahed Al-Rayes to join us.'

Malak accepted the invitation, picked up her handbag and walked out with astonishing grace.

'She hasn't been the same since her husband passed away,' Saleh Jawdat whispered to the men as they watched her leave.

With the only woman in the circle gone, the conversation quickly descended into uncensored territories as the men shared wild stories of romantic adventures and traded improper jokes.

Waving his glass in the air, al-Hadhrani demanded their attention. 'Listen,' he said in a Yemeni accent, 'I met a woman in Cairo who told me she was a poet. We went out for coffee, she listened to my poetry and I listened to hers. Afterwards, I took her to my room and we slept together. In the morning, I gave her ten Egyptian pounds.'

Saleh Jawdat was not one to miss an opportunity to score. He pointed at Ahmed Abdel Muti Hijazi and Salah Abdel Sabour.

'She must have been one of your contemporary poets,' he joked. 'Our poets in the classical genre would not have accepted less than 500 pounds.'

Malak, Karim and Nahed sat on white picnic chairs under the shade of a large almond tree in Nahed's family orchard. The two young poets sparred for her attention. She smiled politely, as they took turns showcasing their finest poetic skills and their most refined sense of humour.

Still in mourning over her husband's death, Malak wore a black buttoned shirt and medium-length black skirt, which she made sure to tug and pull whenever she moved in her chair, to ensure her knees were well covered.

At first Malak seemed reserved, although she did listen intently and commented politely. But after a while of listening to the two men's poems, and upon their insistence that she join in, Malak offered the younger poets her own verses and even contributed to the humour with her own sharp comedic comebacks.

Karim had never met a woman like her. Almost twice his age, she was closer to his mother's generation than his own – but she was nothing like his mother, or any of the women he had known. Malak moved with the grace of a gazelle. Her beauty was simple but unwavering. Her short, black hair, though playful, commanded respect. Her piercing, black eyes were shy and captivating all at once. Her voice sprung from a deep well of sadness and yearnings. Her poetry was sorrowful, nostalgic and human in a way that was new to Karim, a poet known for his nationalist poems.

'Thank you for bringing me here!' Malak told them, as she

feasted on the raw almonds that the two young men extracted from hard shells for her. 'But I'm curious, why did you invite me?' she asked.

'You seemed very sad,' Karim blurted out. 'I wanted to lift your mood!'

'Oh! So it's pity, then?' Malak smiled. 'I'll take it. I haven't laughed this way in a long time!'

Karim's answer lacked a degree of honesty. Deep down, he was intrigued by the idea of a woman poet, a female intellectual, someone from the opposite sex whom he could be drawn to in an intellectual realm – not to be frowned upon by his conservative society or his adoring wife. To him, Malak was an experience he had yearned for and wished he could prolong.

Delegates from the 1964 Arab Poetry Festival in Gaza, representing some of the greatest writers in the Arab world. From left to right: Anis Mansour, Abdul Karim Sabawi, Zuhair Al-Rayyes, Mahmoud Hasan Ismail, Malak Abd al-Aziz, Musa Isa Saba, unknown, Salah Abdel Sabour, Abdel Kareem Alkaramy (abu Salma).

'Please forgive us if we transgressed any boundaries,' Nahed offered his apology. 'We are young and inexperienced, and we were eager to practise our charm.'

Malak smiled lightheartedly, 'Young, yes. Inexperienced, maybe him,' she pointed at Karim. 'Certainly not you, Mr Attorney General!'

Laughing, the three began making their way back to the poetry festival.

'Is your poem ready?' Nahed asked Karim as they got into the car.

'Yes,' Karim grinned. 'And it is not what you or anyone expect it to be.'

Based on Karim's history of praising President Nasser, everyone expected his poem at the festival to be more of the same. But Karim had grown and evolved, more in the year of 1964 than he did in any other year before it. Maybe it was his work at the newspaper that had opened him to a bigger world and bigger ideas. His poem was a surprise to everyone present, including the Egyptian poets and authority figures in the room. Titled *The Lost City*, the poem ended with a clear rebuke for the Arab countries that had denied Palestinians the right to forge their own resistance – and that rebuke, of course, was especially aimed at Egypt and Nasser, who had a policy of disarming Palestinian resistance fighters in Gaza.

'I search for you in you
In your eyes for your eyes
In your hands for your hands
Where are you?
Didn't you once fill our hearts with fire?
Didn't you make us think you're a fortress

With the strength of a thousand men?
But you've chained our hand
You've taken our guns
You've disarmed us
And blocked our path.
To the lost city.'

The audience stood up and there was loud applause in the room. It was clear Karim was not the only one who was starting to lose faith in President Gamal Abdel Nasser and in Arab nationalism.

28

RESISTANCE LITERATURE

GAZA, PALESTINE, 1965–1966

The chief editor of *Akhbar Felesteen*, Zuhair Al-Rayyes, returned from a trip to Moscow where he was part of a delegation representing the Lawyers' Arab Union. Jetlagged and unable to stop working, he ordered a meeting for the editorial team in his office along with a large pot of coffee.

'How was your trip?' Musa Saba was the first to ask as the entire team gathered, eager to learn of their boss's impressions of the Soviet Union.

'Communism is a scam,' Zuhair grunted, as he fell back on his black, leather office chair. 'There is no "enlightened left" ready to "lead us to a just and fair world". There is only a tsar. Moscow is pouring money into everything military while ignoring and degrading civil society. Their entire focus is the arms industry, not the people. I was reminded of the wise adage, the democratic industrial countries, the First World, give you freedom and take away your bread. The Eastern Bloc communist-socialist states, the Second World, give you bread and take away your freedom.

As for us, the remaining majority of this world's population, here in the Third World, they take away both our bread and our freedom.'

Zuhair looked around at the disappointed faces. 'Not what you wanted to hear, I know,' he said, shuffling the papers on his desk. 'But we need to have a clear understanding of how our world functions. Our focus must be on building our resistance on strong foundations with awareness and education. And on this note, here are your assignments for this week, gentlemen.'

Zuhair handed the instructions to each one of his team members as they headed out the door, except for Zaki Al-Radwan and Karim, whom he had asked to stay behind.

When everyone left, Zuhair handed Zaki Al-Radwan and Karim their paperwork and grinned as he watched their reaction.

Zaki's face beamed. 'Muin Bseiso? He has been released? This is wonderful news! And this is a great assignment!'

Karim was equally delighted by his assignment. He looked at Zaki and laughed. 'Zaki *Bek*, you might have gotten Muin Bseiso, but I got assigned Ghassan Kanafani!'

'Now, Karim,' Zuhair intervened. 'We are in a progressive establishment. No need to descend into using titles like *Bek* that belong to the Ottoman era.' The men laughed. 'We can all agree it's a great time to be in Gaza,' Zuhair continued. 'So, let's get down to business.' He pulled out his cigarette box from his shirt pocket, took out a cigarette, and passed the box on to Karim and Zaki, who each took one. 'Do any of you have a lighter?' he asked. 'The Russian minister of information kept admiring my Winston lighter; in the end I had no choice but to give it to him.' Zuhair accepted Zaki's lighter, lit up his cigarette and, blowing out the smoke, he said, 'It could have been worse. Manar, a member of our delegation, poor woman, she was forced to surrender her Max Factor lipstick to the Russian minister's wife.'

Laughter and smoke filled the room.

'Now we can talk!' Zuhair sat back in his chair. 'First, Muin Bseiso. He is one of our greatest poets and activists. And, as you know, he was jailed twice by the Egyptian authority for his communist views and for questioning their policies in Gaza – especially their role in keeping the Palestinians disarmed.'

'Yes, we will not die . . . but we will uproot death from our land!' Karim recited the last verse of Bseiso's famous poem, which had become popular amongst Palestinian prisoners.

'You'll have to be careful with this,' Zuhair said to Zaki. 'You want the story to get out, and to bring Muin into our team, here at the newspaper, but you need to do it without antagonising the Egyptians to the point of shutting us down. Also, I've been told that he is a little depressed and feels that during his time in jail other poets have risen to take his place like Nizar Qabbani and Abd al-Wahhab Al-Bayati.'

'Don't worry,' Zaki assured Zuhair. 'I don't need to mention other poets to him.'

'As for you,' Zuhair turned to Karim, 'Ghassan Kanafani is a powerhouse. I need you to take a delegation from the newspaper and attend the elections of the first Union of Palestinian Writers, as that's his primary reason for being here. I want you to cover as many of the conference highlights as possible. By the way,' Zuhair added, 'I saw Ghassan Kanafani this morning; he tells me he will be spending considerable time in Gaza, not only for the Union of Palestinian Writers' election, but also for a book project he is working on. So, be a good host. Show him around, if you can.'

Karim and Souhailah sat every night in the garden catching the cool evening breeze, and watching over their children playing, while they swapped stories about the day's events. But of late Karim had become more distant, and on this evening he seemed miles away.

'What are you thinking about?' Souhailah prodded, reluctantly. She knew that at times Karim's silence indicated a process of either constructing or memorising a poem. Being pulled away from that process made him extremely irritable. But this time Karim didn't seem to mind her question.

'I'm trying to figure out where I go from here. I need to do more,' he said, as his eyes filled with tears watching Khulud running around the pomegranate tree, where he used to wait for Souhailah when they were children.

Although Souhailah had seen Karim fall into this mood before, she could never understand his deep desire for what he described as 'more'.

'More of what?' she whispered, almost hoping he would not hear her question. It was not an honest question. It was more of a statement from a woman who had never wanted more, and was afraid of all that 'more' could mean.

'Never mind,' Karim said dismissively, recognising the fear in her tone. 'Did I tell you I'll be meeting with Ghassan Kanafani tomorrow?'

'Who is Ghassan Kanafani?' she asked for the sake of a conversation, rather than from a deep desire to know.

He knew that, but still he answered, 'Ghassan Kanafani wrote the novel *Men in the Sun*. Oh, by the way, I think I might have left the book on our bed, so make sure Hussein doesn't rip it into pieces. It would be good, if you find you have some time, it would be good for you to read it.'

Karim missed the days when he used to give Souhailah books to read, and she would devour them with interest and excitement. Those days, he knew, were long gone.

'What's the story about?' Souhailah asked, half-heartedly. She knew she wasn't going to find the time to read the book. When would she find the time? It took all her morning hours to wash and hang the dirty laundry and the endless amount of cloth diapers, all her afternoons to make food and feed the children and all her evenings to bathe them and get them ready for bed while collecting, folding and ironing the day's load. She never slept at night, with Hussein nursing and Abir still bedwetting, and Khulud's endless nightmares. When would she find the time to read? She could barely hold a conversation. Nonetheless, she tried. She humoured him. 'Well?' she said again. 'What's the story about?'

'Us,' Karim sighed, and looked into the distance. 'The story is about us. It's about three Palestinian refugees who pay a smuggler to drive them across the borders into Kuwait. The smuggler hides them inside an empty water tank attached to his lorry. At the final checkpoint, the smuggler gets distracted by an argument he has with one of the checkpoint guards. The argument lasts too long, meanwhile the men in the tank are getting cooked by the heat. The men, although suffocating, decide to stay quiet for fear of being discovered. They suffocate and die in silence.'

'How is this us?' Souhailah asked, deeply disturbed.

'Kanafani wanted us to look in the mirror. To see a reflection of our lives and the poor choices we are given.' Karim paused for a moment. 'Souhailah,' he said with determination, 'I would rather die making noise in the back of the water tank, than suffocate in silence.'

Warriors of the Pen gathered at the al-Nasr Cinema Hall in Gaza City for the first conference and elections of the Union of Palestinian Writers. Karim sat in the front row with his colleagues from the newspaper. He didn't pay much attention to the early speeches and the discussions regarding the mechanisms and results of the elections. He was only there to meet with and listen to the great Palestinian novelist Ghassan Kanafani.

When Kanafani finally stepped up to the podium, an instant curious silence hovered. Everyone held their breath, ready to listen to his every word.

The handsome, young writer spoke with words made of fire. He was a seasoned fighter, activist, political organiser and poet, all rolled into one. He highlighted the need for Palestinian resistance to be anchored in progressive values, and to be part of the wider global struggles for justice and freedom. He spoke about the writer's role in transcending borders. He raised questions about the Arab governments' boycott of Palestinian writers who had remained on their land, inside the 1948 borders, on what became Israel. He gave an example of how a new talented Palestinian poet, Mahmoud Darwish, had found himself subject to this senseless Arab boycott. 'Why should we censor the words of Darwish,' he asked the crowd, 'just because he finds himself living under the entity of a country that was founded upon the ruins of his homeland?'

After the speech, Karim introduced himself to Ghassan Kanafani and invited him to a meal at the Sha'af farmlands to meet Nahed and his group of resistance fighters. Ghassan welcomed the idea. 'I would love to see Nahed,' he said instantly. 'He is one of our finest men. He has been growing fierce —' Ghassan intended to say resistance but, aware of the Egyptian officers nearby, Karim quickly cut him off '. . . fierce oranges. He has been growing fierce oranges in his Sha'af orchard!'

The men cheered when Nahed and his fellow fighter Abu-Talal emerged, carrying a huge tray of *mansaf*; tender lamb pieces, served on a bed of rice soaked in yoghurt and topped with roasted nuts. The men placed the tray on the table and invited everyone to take a spoon and dive in.

'Comrades,' Nahed announced, 'we cannot resist on an empty stomach!'

Ghassan elbowed Karim. 'Your friend is not growing fierce oranges, he is growing fierce bellies.'

The men laughed, complimenting their generous host while competing over the most tender pieces of lamb.

After the meal, the intellectual sparring and drinking began. Karim was feeling increasingly out of place – more and more every day, even amongst his closest friends. They all subscribed to a Marxist socialist ideology, they called one another 'comrades' and they swapped stories about commando units and operational guerrilla tactics. Karim had nothing to contribute to such conversation. He wished he had more.

'I make the men in my commando unit read this before training.' Nahed pulled out an Arabic translation of *Guerrilla Warfare*, the military handbook written by the Marxist revolutionary Che Guevara.

Ghassan was delighted when he saw Nahed's name on the cover. 'You actually translated it!' He flicked through the pages of the book. 'Astonishing! Well done.' Ghassan handed the book to Karim, who sat next to him. 'What about you?' he asked. 'Do you have any field experience?'

Karim gave an awkward smile. 'I prefer to commit myself to *adab al-muqawama*, the resistance literature,' he said. It was a good save. Ghassan laughed, recognising that Karim was in fact quoting him. Resistance literature was a phrase he had coined.

Karim took a sip from his drink and decided to steer the conversation into more familiar territory. 'The Arab League will set up a unified military command called the United Arab Command, headed by Egyptian lieutenant general Ali Amer.'

'To do what, exactly?' Nahed snapped. 'We have units, we have been training in guerrilla warfare. We've been launching successful operations against the enemy, undetected by the enemy and Egypt.'

'That's exactly why,' Ghassan said. 'It is because of your increasingly successful operations that Egypt is feeling the heat,' he explained. 'And with that, it feels the need to co-opt you into its armed forces under the banner of the so-called United Arab Command. Think about it! Nasser discouraged Syrian and Palestinian guerrillas from provoking the Israelis, telling us again and again that he has no plans for war with Israel. But he knows that war is inevitable. Two thirds of our people are living in subhuman conditions in refugee camps outside the borders of their own country, while Jewish immigrants from Europe are living in their homes, sleeping in their beds, eating their food and bathing in their water. The refugees are mobilising. Palestinians are demanding the right to armed resistance. This is the reality that Nasser needs to deal with, and this is his way of doing that.'

'Well, whatever happens, we have no choice but to work with him.' Nahed spoke more calmly, considering his words with great care. 'Nasser has put Ahmad al-Shukeiri in charge of our armed units.

Fatah and other Palestinian factions have either joined, or are close to joining al-Shukeiri's army. So, pragmatically speaking, if Nasser approves the idea of arming the Palestine Liberation Organization, and if al-Shukeiri is able to pull together an army of Palestinian fighters —'

'I would be the first to join.' Karim didn't process the words before they escaped from his mouth. But now that they were fired, there was no taking them back. History was being made, and Karim could no longer sit on the sidelines and watch.

29

BROTHERS IN ARMS

GAZA, PALESTINE, 1965

Patriotic songs blasted the streets of Tuffah and reverberated throughout Palestine and its neighbouring countries. 'Akhi, Ja waz althalemoon al mada, Brother, the oppressors have gone too far!' Mohamad Abdel Wahab's popular ballad articulated the mood of the nation. The call to arms through music and popular culture carried the promise of freedom from Israel's tyranny and liberation of the homeland.

The hearts of the young and the old were pumping to the joyful rhythm of hope, as neighbours and friends gathered around meals and coffee circles to bid farewell to their young men who had enlisted in the al-Shukeiri army.

The *sheikh* sat proudly next to his sons Karim and Rahim as guests from near and far poured into his home to say goodbye. The two brothers were departing on two very different but connected missions.

Karim, much to his wife's dismay, had suspended his work both at the school and at the newspaper and volunteered to join the al-Shukeiri army. He wanted to take a more active involvement in the resistance, and he was going to act upon his desire.

'I don't want to be another mouthpiece writing from the sidelines,' he had told his wife, as she wept the previous night. 'I want to be part of the glorious resistance!'

In order for Karim to seek the glory of resistance, Rahim, his second-in-command, his younger brother, had to step up to support the family. Rahim's gaze was cast outside the boundaries of Tuffah, and to where so many other young men had gone before him, seeking fortunes in the new cities that were rising from the desert sand of Arabia. The oil kingdom had a hungry appetite for young, skilled workers, and had deep pockets to make their desert exile worth their while. Rahim immediately landed a lucrative administrative position at a hospital in Kober in Saudi Arabia and was ready to set sail into the dunes where he could make enough money to support his family in Gaza, while Karim joined the army.

Spirits were running high and the men in the *sheikh*'s circle spoke of the looming victory that Gamal Abdel Nasser had promised in his passionate speeches. They believed that a Palestinian army under Egyptian command would be well trained and well equipped to fight alongside the Egyptians, and to finally lead the refugees back to their homes. They were certain that Palestine was just the last of a persistent wave of decolonisation that had swept the world. Repeated over and over again, in almost every conversation, was the belief that just as Algeria had defeated the French and gained its independence, so too would Palestine defeat Israel and gain its freedom.

But this optimism was confined to the men's circles. Elsewhere, wherever women gathered, the mood was sober. There was no talk of a looming victory – only comforting words and prayers between hearts who knew how to love and nurture, and who feared the violence of war.

In the *sheikh*'s home Khadija and Souhailah went about their chores, avoiding looking into one another's eyes – afraid that if they did, the floodgate of tears would overwhelm them both and reduce them into puddles of sorrow. As for Moftiya – God forbid that anyone should see the old matriarch exhibit signs of weakness – she spent so much time in her room in order to cry in private, and pray and beg God to look after Karim and Rahim on their journeys. She thought about confronting her grandsons. She thought about telling them how her heart was breaking. But what use would her words be, and what could be gained from an old woman's tears?

When the last guest finally left the *sheikh*'s home and the evening came to an end, Khadija lay down next to her husband and sobbed. 'My sons are being ripped out of my heart,' she wept. 'Karim joined the army, Muti the *fedayeen*, and Rahim is going to Saudi Arabia.'

Holding back his own tears, the *sheikh* placed his hand on hers gently. 'What good would it be to try to keep our boys at home in times like these?' he whispered. 'The enemy has already stolen two thirds of our homeland, and now he stands at the gate coveting what remains. Our homes. Gaza. What kind of people would we be if we kept our sons at home, while our own brothers and sisters – your family Khadija, your brothers – while they all linger in the cold in refugee camps, still denied their right to return to their homes?'

Across the garden, in Karim and Souhailah's room, Karim was going through the nightly routine of forging space for his tired body on a bed full of children. First, he carried Khulud to her mattress, then Abir, but when he came back for Hussein, Souhailah stopped him.

'Leave him,' she said. 'He needs to sleep in our bed tonight. He's a bit warm.'

Karim collapsed on the edge of the bed and kicked off his shoes. 'So, it's going to be like this now?' he mumbled.

In the unspoken language between husband and wife, keeping the child in bed was code for 'stay away, and don't you dare think of touching me!'

'Souhailah, my love,' Karim spoke softly, 'this is my last night. Don't you want to say goodbye?'

Souhailah kept her silence as Karim tossed and turned in bed for a few more minutes. Finally, he spoke not softly, but with anger and sadness combined. 'Come on! I know this is hard for you, but —'

'You didn't have to volunteer.' Souhailah cut him off.

Karim sat up. He reached for her across the sleeping baby. 'I thought you, of all people, understood me. Souhailah, I need to be part of this. I can't be a writer and hide from history. Maybe I will write something important and be the Thomas Paine of the Palestinian Liberation Army, inspiring change and boosting the morale of the fighters on the frontline. Or maybe I won't amount to anything. Who knows? No matter what, I need to try.'

Souhailah did not understand Karim, but when he said, 'I need to try.' There was so much sadness in his voice, so much torment, she reached out to him, wanting to hold him, to hug him, but the baby was in the way.

'Okay, Hussein's fever seems to have subsided,' she said. 'You can move him if you want.'

Souhailah chose to surrender. She needed to surrender. She needed to be in Karim's arms, and he needed to be in hers. They held on to one another through the night, only letting go when the rooster began to crow.

After two months of army training, Karim was allowed to return home to see his family. He walked with heavy, tired steps down Mohatta Street. His skin had grown darker, his eyes hollowed and his cheeks sunken. This was his first visit back since he had been deployed. It didn't take long before he was surrounded by well-wishers from his neighbourhood who formed a circle around him, that grew larger and larger until it resembled a celebratory march, accompanying him from the top of Mohatta Street, right down to the *sheikh*'s doorstep.

Moftiya and Khadija ululated as they hugged him, kissed him, and filled their lungs with his scent. The *sheikh* embraced the big man in uniform who was once a fragile, small miracle. 'Praise be to God for your return!' he repeated, as his heart soared to the seventh sky.

The initial greetings and pleasantries soon turned to questions about the army's training, its capacity and strength. Karim's brothers Muti and Latif took turns pouring coffee for the guests. The *sheikh* noticed how overwhelmed Karim seemed to be by the questions and the reception, and how Souhailah had not come out of her room to greet him. So, when Latif offered Karim a cup of coffee, the *sheikh* intervened. 'Don't drink coffee now,' he winked at Karim. 'First, you go to your room and get some rest.' Turning to his guests, the *sheikh* added, 'Please excuse my son.'

Karim kissed his father's hand, grateful for the rescue. In the bedroom he stood still, savouring the sight of Souhailah's beauty. In the few moments she'd had since she'd heard he was spotted walking along Mohatta Street, Souhailah quickly washed, perfumed, put on make-up and wore Karim's favourite yellow, strapless dress. It would have been perfect if baby Hussein hadn't vomited on her shoulders just as she handed him over to Khadija moments before Karim walked in. But none of that really mattered. This had been the first time they had been apart since they were married five years ago. No matter how Souhailah may have looked, or what she may have worn, she would still have been a glorious sight for Karim's sore eyes.

Later in the evening, Karim and Souhailah finally joined the family over a feast of ripe pomegranates freshly picked from the tree in their garden.

'Any news of Rahim?' Karim asked.

'Yes,' the *sheikh* responded. 'I received a letter from him. He is settling well in Khobar. He sends everyone his love.'

'Brother,' Muti jumped in, clearly agitated. 'Brother,' he said again to get Karim's full attention. 'Tell us about your experience. As you know, I have been training with the Fatah guerrillas, and I hear them speak. They don't seem to hold much hope for what the al-Shukeiri army is undertaking.'

Karim smiled. Of course, he thought to himself. It makes perfect sense for Muti to have joined Nahed's guerrilla-style resistance. Muti was sixteen, and the Fatah movement was growing like wildfire in Gaza, throughout the West Bank and in all the refugee camps.

'Sadly,' Karim nodded, 'they are right. Our Egyptian-led militia is entirely outdated. It functions as if it exists in the past, in the era of Mohamed Ali and Suleiman Pasha.' Karim sliced a pomegranate into halves and began to remove the sweet red seeds into a glass bowl. 'It's not just reflected in the way they think and train, it's also in the outdated Ottoman titles they insist on using – the army general is *büyük* general, a major is *binbaâÿi*, and so on.'

The *sheikh* shook his head sorrowfully. 'So this is the army that is supposed to liberate Palestine?'

Karim offered the bowl of pomegranate seeds he had prepared to Souhailah. She accepted it. 'Thank you!' she smiled. 'Now tell me, how did you pass the time while there?'

'By walking in my father's shoes.'

The *sheikh* pointed to his feet, laughing. 'I don't remember the last time I wore shoes, Karim. I'm glad you found them and walked in them.'

'I meant to say that I did what my father used to do. I remember when I was a young boy, he used to summarise the news items for the men in the neighbourhood and then offer commentary on the events. So, to keep myself and others informed, every evening, after reading the newspapers, I summarised the daily news for my fellow officers and tried to trigger intellectual discussions with them.'

'Do you have a rifle?' Young Nasser was keen to talk about what was most interesting to him.

'No. Most of our training focused on learning drill commands: forward march, attention, squad, salute and so on. But,' Karim added, laughing, 'we almost got ourselves a marching band.'

This sounded exciting to Khadija. 'A real marching band!' she exclaimed.

The *sheikh* glared at her. 'I don't think a marching band in this context is a good thing, Khadija.' Turning to Karim, he said, 'So, two months of training and you still haven't even held a rifle?'

'No,' Karim said, his voice carrying grave disappointment.

'Tell me the marching band is some strategic plan meant to trick the enemy, like the Trojan horse?' Muti asked, sarcastically.

'No,' Karim said.

'So, why did you almost get a marching band?' The *sheikh* now felt he had to know.

'At a large meeting in Al-Areesh,' Karim began to explain, 'the Egyptian army general Abdul Mohsen Mortaja asked the various battalions and smaller militias to submit a list of their requirements. So, we all prepared an ambitious list that included hand grenades, V2 rockets and even anti-aircraft guns. Our Egyptian commanding officer collected the list, folded it and placed it in his pocket. When he finally spoke on our behalf, he didn't even take out the list. He told the general, "Sir, we know the importance of lifting the morale of our fighters, and so we request the formation of a music marching band." The general was not impressed. He turned to the governor of Sinai, who stood next to him, and said, "Mr Governor. Why don't you just send them your marching band?" And that was the end of the story. We got no weapons and no marching band.' Karim's smile was bitter as he ended the story.

'So, you have never actually fired a weapon?' His brother Razak seemed thoroughly disappointed. Razak and Nasser had already been telling tall tales to their friends and neighbours about their heroic big brother in the army who had a rifle and was out killing the enemies and liberating Palestine. Karim couldn't stand to see the disappointment in their eyes.

'I've been assigned an administrative position in Rafah, handling all the filing and paperwork for our unit.' Wanting to sprinkle some excitement on the boring placement, he added, 'Now I get to ride on the train for free.' Razak and Nasser's eyes widened. For them, the train was a big slender beast they could only dream about riding one day. Their brother's army service was starting to look good again.

Karim made a few more home visits during his army service, mostly surprising Souhailah in the deep of the night and leaving her asleep before the break of dawn. If it weren't for her sudden feelings of morning sickness and the gradual swelling of her belly, Souhailah might have believed that Karim's visits were only fragments of her sweet dreams.

But these night visits came to a stop when, in the spring of 1967, Karim was pulled away from his office posting and thrust, along with countless others, into the Sinai Desert. An irreversible chain of events had been triggered when Soviet intelligence informed Egypt that Israeli forces were building near the Syrian borders. In an effort to deter Israel from invading Syria, Gamal Abdel Nasser ordered 130,000 troops into Sinai. Karim, and thousands of others in the al-Shukeiri army, many of whom had no training, were handed rifles and given quick basic training in marksmanship. The drums of war were beating louder, and soon the *majnoon* would return to the sky. This time, Karim was hoping he would have the strength to confront and defeat him.

30

AL-NAKSA, THE RELAPSE

GAZA, PALESTINE, 1967

The bare feet of hundreds of men, in white singlets and drab, rolled-up olive pants, splashed into the cool waters of the Mediterranean. Blistered feet that ran in the heat looking for a war they could not find. Feet with soles burning from the scorching desert sand. Feet that were once in boots ready to march and fight for Palestine. Lost feet. Defeated feet. They ran. They splashed. They fell to their knees and cursed.

'How the hell did we get here?' Karim shouted in frustration, an Israeli plane hovering low above them, tormenting them, laughing at their helplessness.

'Hey,' a man lifted his head up, shouting to the plane above, 'did you happen to see the Egyptian second line of defence?'

Karim looked at the men despairingly. 'Why do they follow us in the sky? We are an army of white singlets and bare feet,' he said.

A man at the front shouted across the waves, 'Fuck Lyndon Johnson!' Other men joined, 'Fuck Lyndon Johnson!'

In the days before the war started, US president Lyndon Johnson warned both the Egyptian-led Arab forces and Israel not to be the first to strike. The Arabs stood down and expected Israel would do the same. Instead, a heavily equipped Israeli army launched a surprise pre-emptive strike, using 200 Israeli jets to bomb eighteen Egyptian airfields, destroying more than 80 per cent of Egypt's air force before noon of the first day of what became known as the Six-Day War.

This ambush ensured Israeli dominance in the sky, as Israeli ground troops pushed through with their tanks and artillery, expanding the borders of the Jewish state well beyond the boundaries of the 1949 Armistice Demarcation Line.

Initially, Egypt kept news of its losses out of the public domain and announced victories on the front pages of its newspapers to encourage its allied soldiers to put up a good fight. It was then that the al-Shukeiri militias, where Karim served, were ordered to join the second Egyptian line of defence. So they marched in the June heat into the Sinai Desert looking desperately for the Egyptian second line of defence, but all they could find were army boots scattered here, army helmets piled there, and endless stretches of desert sand.

Still hoping to find the second line of defence, they walked for days, until they arrived at a small Egyptian city east of the Suez Canal. There, they asked the locals if anyone had seen the Egyptian second line of defence. The locals laughed. It was not jovial laughter – it was laughter loaded with the sorrow and bitterness of defeat.

There was no second Egyptian line of defence.

Tearful, the locals told them the war was over. They told them it was a horrible defeat. They told them there were rumours that

Israeli troops took no prisoners, and that they slaughtered hundreds of captured Egyptian soldiers and buried their bodies in unmarked mass graves. Karim and the rest of the men finally understood why they had seen so many scattered boots and helmets along the way. They finally understood they had been walking through a war crime scene.

The locals also told the soldiers that Gamal Abdel Nasser had handed in his resignation, and that not only was the rest of historic Palestine, Gaza, the West Bank and Jerusalem under Israeli control, but so were parts of Syria and Egypt, the Syrian Golan Heights and the Sinai Peninsula.

The men in the army of liberation began to weep as they realised that even the Egyptian land beneath their feet had fallen under Israeli control.

The loss was devastating. The heat was stifling. They began their walk home. Heads hung in shame, they stripped down to their singlets, took off their boots, and began to walk along the coast back to Palestine.

'Fuck Lyndon Johnson!' they shouted at the Israeli war planes that followed them.

Drunk on victory, the Israeli pilots taunted them, swooping down so low that Karim could feel the sting from the heat of the engines burn the hair on the back of his neck. Heads bowed down, the men dragged their feet, while the *majnoon* danced in the sky above.

At nightfall, the men veered inland to escape the taunting of the Israeli war planes. They were hungry, thirsty, and convinced it was just a matter of time before the Israelis tired of humiliating them, killed them and buried them in unmarked graves like their Egyptian brothers. So they decided to only walk at night and stay out of sight during the day, finding sustenance in date trees and water wells along the way.

When they arrived close to the Gaza Strip, they said their goodbyes to one another and took different routes to avoid attracting attention.

Karim walked alone through the date palm plantations on the outskirts of Khan Yunis. 'Karim!' He heard a familiar voice call out his name, 'Karim!' He stared through the veil of darkness; he could make out the features of the man calling him. It was Abu-Talal, the fierce Bedouin fighter who often trained in the Sha'af fields with Nahed.

'What are you doing here?' Karim opened his arms to Abu-Talal's warm embrace.

'I am on duty, patrolling the area and looking out for returning fighters, like you!'

'We lost all of Palestine.' Karim handed Abu-Talal his rifle. 'I didn't fire one shot. We lost all of Palestine and even more. Now Egypt is finished. Now we are finished.'

'Utter nonsense!' Abu-Talal quickly patted Karim on the back with a strong arm. 'This is the beginning, my friend! We are just warming up!' He threw his arm around him. 'Let me take you somewhere safe so I can show you our renowned Bedouin hospitality!'

Karim followed Abu-Talal to a nearby home where he was given generous amounts of food and a warm bed. The next morning, Abu-Talal handed him civilian clothes. 'Put these on, so you can go back to being a poet,' he laughed. 'Leave the armed resistance to us. I promise we will do our best.'

'Have you heard from Nahed?' Karim asked before leaving.

At the mention of Nahed's name, Abu-Talal's smile stretched his rugged face from ear to ear. 'Nahed is doing fine,' he said.

'He is in Sinai setting up a new resistance front. Believe me,' he said to Karim, 'he does not think we're finished – and neither do I.'

Relieved, Karim thanked Abu-Talal and began walking in civilian clothes in broad daylight – just a poet eager to go home.

Karim and Latif paced up and down the corridor at Nasser Hospital's maternity ward, pausing momentarily every time they passed by the window to check if the Israeli jeeps were still parked outside.

'The dogs,' Karim snapped. 'They have been stationed here since we arrived.'

The Israeli occupation forces were detaining anyone suspected of serving with the al-Shukeiri army and coercing them into exile. Hundreds of thousands of Palestinians were forced to flee their homes in Gaza and the West Bank, and to seek safety in the new UN refugee camps that were set up in neighbouring countries.

'Come on, Souhailah!' Karim's nervous voice echoed in the sterile hospital corridor.

'Shhh.' Latif pointed outside. 'Keep it down, or they'll come for you!'

'Push, Souhailah, push!' Karim whispered. 'Push this baby out before they take me away.'

'Actually, I doubt that they're here for you,' Latif said. 'If they were, they would have arrested you hours ago.'

'I think you might be right,' Karim sighed. 'Maybe this is to do with Muti. They are hoping he'll come here to see the baby. They're just using us as bait.'

'Well, you have to admit our brother has really antagonised them.'

Latif smiled. 'I mean, how he gathered all the rifles and ammunitions that were left over from the al-Shukeiri army, and single-handedly transported it all to the *fedayeen* fighters doing two trips a day for weeks, passing right under the Israeli soldiers' noses. I saw him a few times and didn't recognise him – he looked like a poor vegetable seller, transporting *molokhya* leaves in vegetable crates!'

Karim laughed. 'I heard he played Abdel Halim Hafez songs to drown the sound of rifles rattling beneath the *molokhya* leaves!'

While Karim and Latif continued to pace the corridors of the hospital, their younger brother Muti was meeting with the man who would soon become the face of the Palestine Liberation Organization. Yasser Arafat, the founder of the Fatah movement, handpicked the men he trusted to work with. Muti was high up on his list. The two had travelled through Israeli security checks with fake identity documents to meet in a public cafe in Jerusalem, one that was frequented by Israeli soldiers.

Muti had learned in his guerrilla training that placing himself where he was least expected gave him a cloak of invisibility. When Yasser Arafat asked to meet him in this cafe, Muti understood why. Arafat wanted to test his ability to infiltrate into enemy territory.

The two fighters sat casually sipping on their mint tea and watching the well-armed Israeli soldiers stroll the streets of the old city.

'What's the point of victory, if you're going to spend your life hiding behind a bullet-proof vest?' Muti wondered out loud.

'That's why I wanted us to meet here,' Yasser laughed. 'I wanted you to see this. Look,' he said, pointing at a souvenir shop across from the cafe. 'You see the man over there selling the olive-wood crosses? His family has been selling these crosses since Christ was crucified, and they will still be selling olive crosses for centuries to come. Does he look afraid?'

Muti looked at the man. 'No. He does not.'

'Now compare him to these young, well-armed Israeli soldiers who think they have won the war.'

Muti examined the faces of the soldiers.

'They are nervous. Their fingers are on the trigger. They are scared. Do you know why?'

Muti thought for a moment, then said, 'It's because they know that the real war has only just begun.'

Uncle Muti, in uniform.

The doctor stepped out of the labour room to make a short announcement. 'Congratulations! It's a girl.'

'Another girl!' Latif laughed, '*Sitty* Moftiya is not going to be impressed.'

Karim glared at his brother, before he rushed into the labour room.

Karim welcomed the arrival of his fourth child and third daughter, a tiny dark bundle that rested in his wife's white arms.

'My love,' Karim kissed Souhailah. '*Alhamdulillah*, thank God! Finally, you have given me a child that has my colour.'

Karim picked up the baby in his arms and whispered into her ears, 'Baby girl! What a time for you to be born!'

'What are we going to name her?' Souhailah's exhausted voice carried more than the question she asked. It carried deep anxieties about the future. She knew it was a matter of time before Karim had to run. She had been preparing herself for his departure. 'Give her a name, before you . . .' she couldn't finish the sentence.

Karim pressed his lips gently on the baby's soft cheeks. He thought of a popular song he had heard playing on the radio that morning. The song was titled 'Samah', meaning forgiveness. He sang as he rocked his baby gently, '*Asl al samah taba almilah ya bakht meen samah* – the essence of forgiveness is the virtue of good people, lucky are those who can forgive.'

Karim smiled, having found the perfect name. 'We will call her Samah!'

Panic spread throughout Palestine as Israel began conducting house-to-house searches in the lands it occupied, issuing anyone suspected of being part of the resistance an ultimatum: Leave now and you will be spared, or stay and you'll be jailed indefinitely.

'Almost every man in Gaza is part of the resistance,' Karim despaired, as he sat next to his father, sipping tea and contemplating the next steps.

'Yes,' the *sheikh* conceded, 'and they would love for all of us to leave. How else can they get the majority they need for their Jewish state? What do you plan to do, son?'

'For now, stay in hiding . . .'

'Until they find you and throw you in prison? What good will that do – for you, and for us?'

'I can go with Muti, or join Nahed – and this time, maybe this time, I will actually learn how to fire a rifle.'

A faint smile appeared and disappeared quickly from the *sheikh*'s lips. 'Son,' he implored, 'you have far too many responsibilities to choose that option. I have given one son to the resistance already, but you are different. You are a poet. You don't have the heart to kill, and that is what fighters must do. They kill. You have a wife, and four children. You have no choice. You must leave Palestine.'

'The Israelis are facing international pressure to withdraw,' Karim said, desperate to find reasons to stay.

'So maybe it will not be long before you can come back,' his father said. 'But right now, you must go.'

Karim sighed.

'Karim!' they heard Khadija's earth-shattering cry. 'Karim!' she cried again, as she stormed into the room, '*Habibi yabny*, my beloved son, they're at the top of Mohatta Street. They're coming for you. You have to run! Go! Leave now!' she cried.

Karim's eyes searched her face; he wanted to memorise forever the strength she embodied in that horrific moment as she stood on the edge of eternal loss, and he, on the edge of eternal exile.

'Go, now!' She lifted him up with the strength of a thousand mothers. Karim was suddenly a young boy in the first grade, drowning in the flood currents, when his mother lifted him from the engulfing water and carried him all the way home.

'Leave. They're almost here. *Yallah!*' She literally carried him and threw him outside into the garden. Where did Khadija find the strength to lift her grown son and push him out? Did she spend the rest of her life wondering whether she would have done that, had she known he would be gone forever?

Souhailah ran into the garden, surrounded by the children, but neither Souhailah nor Karim can remember if they said goodbye. All that Souhailah remembered was the feeling of having a rib torn out of her chest and a sudden emptiness where her heart was once beating.

The soldiers entered the *sheikh*'s home just as Karim jumped over the cactus hedge at the back of the garden, and into his exile.

31

ERASURE

AMMAN, JORDAN, 1967

Karim's eyes adjusted to the darkness around him. Did he call out for Souhailah in his sleep? Maybe. He could still hear the echo of his cry as he sat up and slowly took in the familiar faces cramped into the unfamiliar surroundings. He knew them all. Laying side by side, stacked like sardines on the floor were his neighbours, colleagues, friends – all of them now, exiles.

Almost one quarter of a million Palestinians were exiled from land Israel occupied in 1967. His was just one story. This was just one room full of broken hearts.

He heard a baby cry followed by the shuffling and quiet cooing of the mother. No doubt she was guiding the baby's mouth to her nipple. He knew these sounds so well. Oh, Souhailah. How he ached for her.

When he had crossed the Allenby Bridge the day before, the Israeli soldiers had ordered him, at gunpoint, to sign a declaration forsaking his right to return. That document probably wouldn't stand in any court of international law, he knew that. But he also knew that it was intended to make clear Israel's intentions of colonising his land. Israel was not planning to withdraw.

He wiped away his tears and stood up as quietly as possible, grabbed his jacket, and carefully navigated the small spaces between the bodies on the floor. Slowly he opened the creaking door, and headed towards the nearest streetlamp. He knew what he needed to do. He had to write a letter to Souhailah, tell her the bad news – tell her he would not be coming home. He needed to be pragmatic. He had to find work and a place to stay. And, she would have to bring the children and join him. Hard as that letter was to pen, it was easy compared to the second letter he needed to write. One addressed to his family, ink on paper that would rip his family apart. Three dreaded words: I can't return. He needed this to be done. They probably already knew, but he had to write it. To admit it. To say it. But how does one extract flesh from flesh, blood from blood and soul from soul?

He sat on the footpath, under the silver light of the streetlamp. He looked across into the distance, where the dispossessed masses had huddled for the night. They were all sharing rooms that they had rented from the previous cohort of refugees. The irony of this world is so poignant. The 1967 refugees rented rooms from the 1948 refugees. Living on the margins of an uncompassionate world.

Karim stared down at the page. The letters can wait, he thought, and began to write his first poem in exile instead:

> When you were parched
> We quenched your thirst with our blood
> Now . . . we carry your burden
> Disgraced, we cry in shame when asked
> Where do you come from?

Dishonoured we die
If only the stray bullets
From the occupier's guns
Were merciful
If only they pierced through our legs
Tore through our knees
If only we sunk in your soil
Deep to our necks
If only we became the salt of your earth
The nutrients in your fertile fields
If only we didn't leave.
The gates of our hearts
Are wide open to misery
Don't ask us where this wind is blowing
Don't ask about a house
Or windows
Or trees
The Bulldozers were here
The Bulldozers were here
And the houses in our city
Were devoured by the monstrous teeth.
They haven't colonised Mars yet
And the moon is barren
Uninhabitable
So carry your children
Your memories
And follow me
We can live in the books of history
They'll write about us;
'The wicked Bedouins landed in Baghdad

They landed in Jaffa
They landed in Grenada
Then they moved on
They packed their belongings
And rode on their camels
They left no print on the red clay
And all their artifacts
Faded with the passing years.'
Does anyone in the world care?
Does anyone care?
What is it worth
To be an Arab . . .
A Native American . . .
Or a dinosaur.

My father Abdul Karim Sabawi on his beloved Gaza Beach, 1960.

EPILOGUE

THE STORIES WE CHOOSE TO WRITE

We sit across from one another at the cafe. Baba sips on his cappuccino and writes a new poem. I tap away on my laptop. I write and I delete, and I write again. Time passes between us in a flick of a second. Time stretches between us into eternity. Two writers locked in the weight of the stories we choose to tell and the poems we choose to compose.

I stop at the year 1967. Because to write what happens to my parents as they begin a lifetime in exile is no longer just writing their stories, but writing the stories of their seven children, their twenty-three grandchildren and their nine great-grandchildren, and still growing. We have become a colony of survivors, victims of colonisation, settlers on this colonised land.

Did I write my father's story to reverse the clock? Maybe.

My grandparents in Gaza often joked that I took my parents away from them. The year of my birth was the year of our exile. How can a baby bring such misfortune? Is this book my atonement?

In chasing the threads to write this book, I took my father home to Palestine. Together we traversed the tracks of his memory, and with these written words I reconstructed his beloved Gaza in all its brilliance and glory before the occupation; the streets of Tuffah, Bab al-Roum, the Mosque of Sayed al-Hashim on *Eid*, the holy fire on the eve of Easter at the Church of Saint Porphyrius, the Sufi Festival of Miracles, the old bazaar, the cobbler, the barber, the *sheikh*'s school, the shrine of Abualazzem, the *sidra* tree, Gaza Beach, the Al-Samer Cinema, Omar Al-Mukhtar Street, *Akhbar Felesteen* newspaper, the farm fields and the aroma of a thousand and one pots cooking in Mohatta Street.

In writing my father's story, I have taken him back to a time when Gaza was a cultural and commercial hub. For the last three years, I have taken my father home. Am I forgiven?

'*Yallah*,' his voice, tender, cuts through my thoughts and the penetrating rays of the Australian sun. 'Fetch my steed!' he says, pointing at the shopping trolley. 'It's time to ride to battle,' he jokes, as I help him up on his feet and wait until he fully leans on the trolley. Slowly, we make our way towards the fruit stalls.

'Souhailah will be very happy!' he smiles, his entire face lighting up.

'Why is that?' I ask.

'Sweet cactus pears are in season, and tonight I will personally peel with my own hands the sweetest cactus pears for my beloved.'

I stop, and I smile too. Yes, I was born in the year of relapse and defeat. Yes, I was born between a lost war and exile. Yes, I was born in the year of lost hopes and dreams. But I was born into love. I was born of love. How bad can this be?

My first and last photo taken in Gaza before we followed my father into exile.
I am only a few weeks old, in my mother Souhailah's arms. My siblings Abir,
Khulud and Hussein stand beside her. This photograph was taken to form an
official identification required to cross the border.

AUTHOR'S NOTE

This book has taken four years of research, two years of editing, countless references, sixty hours of taped interviews, a trip to Gaza and a PhD. While writing it, Gaza has endured three major wars, the third still raging on.

There are at least two stories warring here: the story that I wanted to write, and the story my father wanted to tell; the personal story of a family, and the collective story of a nation.

The creative process was an exhausting, emotional rollercoaster. Together, my father and I resurrected the details of a world that had become out of our reach and recreated the past. The experience was bittersweet. Delving into the warm memories of family, love and homeland, and the horrific trauma of dispossession and loss.

In writing the book I ensured my father's stories were as real to his experience as possible, referring to my interviews as well as drawing from my own knowledge of our family history. But in writing the stories of others around him, including his extended family, I've inserted shades of fiction. This was an important device. Fictional characters gave me the freedom to veer away from my father's personal stories in order to tell the collective story of Palestine, in all its dimensions and geographic landscape. Including the larger context enhances our understanding of the personal experience and the ongoing dance between the story of the individual and that of the nation. For example, my father's real-life grandmother Aziza was part of the population that was ethnically cleansed from Salama. She lived the rest of her life as a refugee. But in this book, Aziza refuses to leave her home and is shot dead by the Zionist militias. Her fictionalised death was necessary to tell the story of hundreds of Palestinians who were massacred in 1948, as part of a systematic policy to depopulate Palestinian villages and towns to establish Israel as a Jewish state with a Jewish majority.

In exile, Palestinians have always managed to find their way to one another – to connect through the forced fragmentation and distance. This was how I found my way to Monir, the eldest son of my father's best friend Nahed, and grandson of Gaza's beloved mayor of the 1950s and 1960s. We met in Cairo in 1989, fell in love and became married. We now have three children – a daughter, Siham, two sons, Nahed and Faris, and three grandchildren, Emad, Jude and Salem.

In July of 2023 I returned to Gaza with Monir and our son Nahed. We visited our grandparents' homes in Rimal and Tuffah, and reconnected with our families who had, until then, remained there. We visited archaeological digs, ancient sites and beaches and saw a beautiful, vibrant city – still under Israeli occupation, but thriving despite decades of siege and war.

We walked along Nahed Al-Rayes Street, a street named after my father-in-law, in honour of his long service to Palestine in politics, resistance and literature. We visited a monument named after my uncle Abdul Muti Sabawi, a known resistance fighter who was martyred in a bomb explosion in the year 2000. I also spoke to university students who were writing doctorates on my father's distinguished literary works. It seemed that everywhere we turned, we had a connection to the land, its history and its stories.

We visited every part and every site I've written about in this book – we even paid tribute to the *sidra* tree that still stood defiant of age and war. We were at home, we belonged, as if our history and our destiny were forever stuck in circular motion, always propelling us back to that city.

I returned to Australia full of inspiration and hope, and began to put the final touches on this manuscript to send to the publisher. But as I reached the last chapter, another war in Gaza was breaking. A war unlike any other the city has experienced.

As I write this, our families' homes in Gaza have been completely destroyed. Most members of our families have been forced to leave Gaza, leaving behind the corpses of their loved ones. The few who remain are facing starvation, while still searching for a safe place where there is none. Rimal, Tuffah, the old city and the new – in fact, most of Gaza has been erased, the city's landscape turned to scorched earth. No longer there.

Will Gaza rise again? History tells us it will. I want to believe that.

SOURCES

Epigraph: *Alsayyed* – from the poetry book *Mata Torek Alqata*, Dar alNawras, Gaza, Palestine 1996, translated by Samah Sabawi

Page 44–45: *The Holy Quran*, chapter 17, Sūrah Al-Isra, verse 8:92, corpus.quran.com

Page 100: 'With Joy' song translated from old Arabic folklore by Samah Sabawi

Page 100: 'Henna' song translated from old Arabic folklore by Samah Sabawi

Page 103: 'Why is the sea laughing' song from Egyptian folklore, translated by Samah Sabawi

Pages 123–124: Poem by Imru' al-Qais, *The Hanged Poems*, translated by F. E. Johnson with revisions by Sheikh Faiz-ullah-bhai *from The Sacred Books and Early Literature of the East, vol. V. Ancient Arabia*, ed. Charles F. Horne, Parke, Austin and Lipscomb, New York and London, 1917

Pages 128–129: *The Holy Quran*, chapter 2, Sūrah Al-Baqarah, verse 2:555, translation by Yusuf Ali, corpus.quran.com

Page 135: *The Holy Quran*, chapter 11, Sūrah Hūd, verse 11:44, translation by Mohsin Khan, corpus.quran.com

Page 142: 'No I'm not one to cry' ('La mish ana illy abky') song by Abdel Wahab, translated by Samah Sabawi

Page 165: 'Give me an excess of love' by Ibn Al-Farid, translated by Sulayman Ibn Qiddees, Beauty in Words, Others' and Mine, blogs.harvard.edu/sulaymanibnqiddees/tag/arabic-sufi-poetry/

Page 175: 'Egypt speaks for itself' sung by Umm Kulthum, lyrics by Hafez Ibrahim, translated by Samah Sabawi

Page 201: BBC report as imagined by author, based on various archival BBC news clips

Pages 204–205: 'In the past' speech by Gamal Abdel Nasser, translated by Samah Sabawi, Egyptian Presidential YouTube, youtube.com/watch?v=mpfuYTSFlVo

Note: Some of Karim's poems as well as the poem of Nahed Al-Rayes 'Do you yearn for the sea' are not published, but are kept in the family library and translated by Samah Sabawi

READING LIST

Amit, G. (2011) 'Salvage or plunder? Israel's "collection" of private Palestinian libraries in West Jerusalem', *Journal of Palestine Studies*, 40(4), 6–23

Khalidi, W. (1992) *All That Remains: The Palestinian Villages Occupied and Depopulated by Israel in 1948*, Beirut: Institute for Palestine Studies

Masalha, N. (2012) *The Palestine Nakba: Decolonising History, Narrating the Subaltern, Reclaiming Memory*, London: Zed Books

Pappé, I. (2015) *The Ethnic Cleansing of Palestine*, Oxford: Oneworld Publications

ACKNOWLEDGEMENTS

This book is a labour of love and a testimony of how incredibly lucky I am to have so many brilliant people in my life who have nurtured, encouraged and guided me.

During the research and first draft phase, my PhD supervisors, Professor Michele Grossman and Dr Rose Lucas, both believed in the importance of this project, and in my ability to write it. They provided me with resources, time and endless encouragement. I can't thank them enough for being truly the best supervisors any PhD student can dream of.

After concluding the PhD, and as I began to shape the work into a memoir, I received an email from Penguin Random House Australia's awesome publisher, Meredith Curnow. It was Meredith's interest in the story and her faith in me as an author, that soon opened the doors for me into the wonderful publishing world of PRH, introducing me to the brilliant and tireless Executive Editor Rachel Scully, whose meticulous and professional edits have made the book into what it is. My deepest gratitude to both Rachel and Meredith and to the team at PRH!

Of course, the entire book would not have been possible if not for my parents. I am so grateful to Baba for the endless hours of interviews, for his insight and intellect, and to Mama for her love, patience and quiet wisdom that gets me through life.

Last but never least, I want to acknowledge Monir, my beloved husband, my life partner and my best friend. Thank you *habibi* for always being mindful of my need to have a space to write, for giving me the courage to explore and push boundaries, and for nurturing me with the kind of love that allows me to grow, fuels my ambition and ignites my imagination. I love you.

Powered by Penguin

Looking for more great reads, exclusive content and book giveaways?
Subscribe to our weekly newsletter.

Scan the QR code or visit penguin.com.au/signup